The Meaning of Marxism

The Meaning of Marxism

Paul D'Amato

AAKAR

THE MEANING OF MARXISM
Paul D'Amato

First Published in India 2015

ISBN 978-93-5002-299-3

Published in agreement with Haymarket Books, Chicago, Illinois, USA for publication and sale only in the Indian Subcontinent (India, Pakistan, Bangladesh, Nepal, Maldives, Bhutan and Sri Lanka)

Published by
AAKAR BOOKS
28 E Pocket IV, Mayur Vihar Phase I, Delhi 110 091
Phone : 011 2279 5505 Telefax : 011 2279 5641
aakarbooks@gmail.com; www.aakarbooks.com

Printed at
Sapra Brothers, Delhi 110 092

Contents

Introduction

The Relevance of Marxism

Every so often—usually after a period of economic instability and crisis that has given way to stabilization and growth—some talking head comes along and declares that Marxism is dead and capitalism is the final form of human fulfillment. As the late socialist author Daniel Singer aptly put it, "The purpose of our pundits and preachers is to doom as impossible a radical, fundamental transformation of existing society."[1]

The most common theme is that socialism has failed to make inroads, especially in the United States, due to the prosperity and social mobility that even the lowliest members of society can experience. "On the reefs of roast beef and apple pie," wrote the German writer Werner Sombart in his famous 1906 book, *Why Is There No Socialism in the United States?*, "socialistic Utopias of every sort are sent to their doom."[2] The Depression years of the 1930s made these ideas harder to swallow, but variations on the argument were dusted off and refurbished during the economic boom after the second World War. Daniel Bell's *The End of Ideology* told us that postwar Western prosperity and the rise of Stalinism signaled "the exhaustion of the nineteenth century ideologies, particularly Marxism, as intellectual systems that could claim *truth* for their views of the world."[3]

Writers on the left, too, like German radical philosopher Herbert Marcuse, could ask, "Why should the overthrow of the existing order be of vital necessity for people who own, or can hope to own, good clothes, a well-stocked larder, a TV set, a car, a house and so on, all within the existing order?"[4] For Marcuse, whose ideas were typical of a whole generation of post–Second World War left-wing thinkers, working-class struggle was no longer the connecting link between our society and a future socialist society. Workers were either bought off or simply so enmeshed in capitalism, and unable to see beyond it, that they were now part of the problem rather than the solution.[5]

The mass general strike of 10 million French workers in May 1968 offered strong evidence to the contrary, as did a whole period of working-class and student rebellion that spanned the globe in the late 1960s and early 1970s (Poland's Solidarnosc in 1980 and the major role played by Black workers in the downfall of apartheid South Africa are two other examples). But those movements receded and capitalism found its footing again, utilizing a period of economic crisis to begin an assault on working-class living standards that has continued unrelentingly to this day. Ideologists once again sprang forward to justify capitalism in its most naked, brutal, "free market" form.

Then came the collapse of the bureaucratic regimes in Russia and Eastern Europe in 1989–1993. We were told then that the "free market" and liberal democracy had triumphed over "totalitarian" systems like fascism and communism. Historian Francis Fukuyama came forward and argued that society had indeed evolved, as Marx argued, from lower to higher forms of human social organization. However, instead of that evolutionary process leading to socialism, Fukuyama argued, liberal free market capitalism constituted the "end point of mankind's ideological evolution," and the "final form of human government"; as such, it constituted the "end of history."[6]

In a flush of exuberance, Western pundits waxed lyrically about a new era of endless peace and prosperity. But if this was the end of history, it didn't seem things were ending all that well.

Instead, we entered a world of incessant war, where the United States, as the world's sole superpower, felt free to throw its military weight around, and did; a world of growing disparities between rich and poor (even in the midst of the economic growth of the 1990s); and a world—as we moved into the twenty-first century—of economic and social instability. It was a world in which the much-touted benefits of free trade and "globalization" dramatically enriched a very few but left tens of millions in ever-worsening conditions. In short, it seemed like we had returned to the days of the robber barons and sweated labor of the late nineteenth century, only on a more colossally destructive, global scale.

The obscenity of capitalism today is expressed in a few simple facts:

- The assets of the world's top three billionaires are greater than those of the poorest 600 million people on the planet.[7]
- Globally, there are seventy thousand people who possess more than $30 million in financial assets—enough to fill a large sports stadium. Half of the world's 587 billionaires (enough to fill a large disco) are Americans, whose wealth increased collectively by $500 billion in 2003 alone. They possess the same amount of wealth as the combined gross domestic product of the world's poorest 170 countries combined.[8]
- More than a third of the world's people—2.8 billion—live on less than two dollars a day.
- 1.2 billion people live on less than one dollar a day.[9]

The statistics for the United States reveal a society that is certainly rich—but only for a minority:

- The average compensation in 2004 for the CEOs of the top 367 U.S. companies was $11.8 million, up from $8.1 million in 2003. On average, CEOs in 2004 made 431 times what a production worker made, up from a 107:1 ratio in 1990 and a 42:1 ratio in 1982.[10]
- CEO pay has increased by 300 percent over the last fifteen years, whereas wages have increased in the same period by only 5 percent (and minimum wage workers have seen their pay fall 6 percent). If wages had kept up with the percentage increase in CEO pay, in 2004 the average pay for production workers would have been $110,136, instead of $27,460.[11]
- The top 20 percent of American households control 83 percent of the nation's wealth, while the bottom 80 percent of Americans control only about 17 percent of the nation's wealth.[12]
- A total of 34.6 million Americans in 2002—12.1 percent of the population—lived below the official poverty line (which is set absurdly low), and 8.5 million of them had jobs. Overall, Black poverty is double that of whites.[13]

Poverty is always horrible. It only becomes an obscenity when the material means exist to eliminate it, yet it persists. But the priorities of world capitalism are such that the two things—unimaginable wealth and great misery—exist side by side. The priorities of capitalism are starkly revealed by the fact that the per capita income in sub-Saharan Africa is $490, whereas the per capita subsidy for European cows is $913.[14]

These obscenities make the case, if not for Marx and Marxism, then at the very least for *some* project to change the world.

That is why, try as the pundits may to bury him—Marx keeps resurfacing. His ideas are alive because his indictment of capitalism—though first penned in the 1840s—is still confirmed on a daily basis. As the misery worsens, the glaring class divisions give rise to what Marx had argued was the motor of historical change—the class struggle. Everywhere around the world, the working class (called the "proletariat" in Marx's day)—those whose labor produces society's abundant wealth in exchange for a pittance—continues to organize, demonstrate, strike, and resist in various ways.

Marx not only exposed the ills of society—many had done so before him—but he revealed how capitalism developed, how it went into crisis, and how it would meet its end. At Marx's grave site in 1883, Marx's friend and lifelong collaborator, Frederick Engels, said that Marx "discovered the special law of motion governing the present-day capitalist mode of production." Even Marx's critics sometimes acknowledge that he had brilliant insights into the nature of capitalism. But, Engels continued,

> Marx was before all else a revolutionist. His real mission in life was to contribute, in one way or another, to the overthrow of capitalist society and of the state institutions which it had brought into being, to contribute to the liberation of the modern proletariat, which he was the first to make conscious of its own position and its needs, conscious of the conditions of its emancipation.[15]

Of course, much has changed since Marx's day. But the essence of capitalism—the exploitation of the many by the few for profit—remains, and wreaks its damage on an ever-expanding scale. The insane anarchy of a world market that can produce enough food to feed everyone, but fails to feed the 6 million children who die every year from malnutrition,[16] remains with us. The unplanned character of capitalist production, with its incessant drive for profit, has created an environmental crisis that threatens the earth's inhabitants like a runaway train threatens its passengers. Indeed, many of the trends described by Marx and Engels—the creation of an increasingly interdependent world market; the system's tendency toward periodic economic crises; increasing productivity and wealth on one side and poverty on the other; the concentration and centralization of capital and the growth of monopolies—give their writings an almost prophetic air.

The task today, set out so long ago by Marx and Engels, also remains the same—to replace competition with association, to build a society in which all wealth is produced and held by its producers in common, and distributed according to human need rather than profit. "In place of the old bourgeois society, with its classes and class antagonisms," wrote Marx and Engels in the *Communist Manifesto,* "we shall have an association in which the free development of each is the condition for the free development of all."[17] Only in such a society can humankind develop its full creative capacities, using our scientific knowledge to enhance lives rather than destroy them.

Moreover, those who loudly applauded the fall of Stalinism left out one important factor: The death of what passed for communism in the East—but what was in reality bureaucratic, state capitalism—paved the way for people to rediscover the real Marxist tradition hidden behind years of distortion in both the East and the West during the Cold War era. It is the tradition of working-class self-emancipation.

Far from being dead, therefore, Marxism is experiencing a rebirth.

The following book began as a series of articles written for a biweekly column in *Socialist Worker* newspaper, called "The Meaning of Marxism." It aims to provide a basic introduction to Marxist ideas, and to show how these ideas remain crucial to our understanding of the world today and the task of changing it.

There is, of course, no substitute for reading Marx and Engels, or the great revolutionary socialists who followed them, such as Rosa Luxemburg, Vladimir Lenin, and Leon Trotsky. I've read and reread works such as Marx's *Civil War in France,* Engels' *Socialism: Utopian and Scientific*, Rosa Luxemburg's *Reform or Revolution*, Trotsky's *Lessons of October,* and Lenin's *State and Revolution*, among many others, and each time I reread them I learn something new in light of fresh experiences.[18]

But as Lenin said in a postscript to *State and Revolution*, "It is more pleasant and useful to go through the 'experience of revolution' than to write about it."[19] Marx and Engels, like Lenin, were not armchair thinkers. First and foremost, they were revolutionaries who fought for a world free of oppression and exploitation. But they understood that to change the world, it is necessary to understand how that world works, and to learn from past struggles the effective levers for its transformation.

Chapter One

From Millenarianism to Marx

The dream of a new society

The idea of socialism is as old as class society itself. So long as there were high priests, kings, lords, nobles, emperors, magistrates, and generals, there were also people who envisioned, and sometimes fought for, a world in which the minority who enriched themselves at the expense of the majority would fall, and the world's wealth would be held in common and shared by all.

Often radical ideas were couched in religious form, but their content was nonetheless unmistakable. "Grace was among them, because none suffered lack.... For they did not give one part and retain another part for themselves.... They abolished inequality and lived in great abundance,"[1] wrote the patriarch of Constantinople, St. John Chrysostom, in the late fourth century of Christ's apostles.

The fourteenth-century English radical preacher, John Ball, a leader in the great agrarian rebellion of 1381, sermonized,

> If we are all descended from one father and one mother, Adam and Eve, how can the lords say or prove that they are more lords than we are—save they make us dig and till the ground so that they can squander what we produce.
>
> They are clad in velvet and satin, set off with squirrel fur, while we are dressed in poor cloth.... They have beautiful residences and manors, while we have the trouble and the work, always in the fields under rain and snow. But it is from us and our labor that everything comes and with which they maintain their pomp.[2]

He concluded from this that, "things cannot go well in England nor ever shall until all things are in common and there is neither villein [serf] nor noble, but all of us are of one condition."[3]

Seeing that the French Revolution of 1789 ended feudal tyranny but not economic inequality between rich and poor, nor the rule of the wealthy, Gracchus Babeuf organized a "conspiracy of equals" and called for a new revolution to establish a society in which all goods would be held in common storehouses and distributed according to need. "Everything will be blended together," he wrote, "and on the footing of a perfect equality."[4]

The United States had its share of radical thinkers, utopians, and socialists before Marx. For example, Thomas Skidmore, author of *The Rights of Man to Property!,* wrote in the 1820s, "Inasmuch as great wealth is an instrument which is uniformly used to extort from others their property, it ought to be taken away from its possessors on the same principle that a sword or pistol may be wrested from a robber." Skidmore believed that new inventions like the steam engine, though "likely to greatly impoverish or destroy the poor," could be beneficial to them on the condition that they "lay hold of it and make it their own."[5]

Emerging industrial capitalism had its insightful critics before Marx. The Swiss economist Jean Charles Léonard Simonde de Sismondi wrote in the 1830s: "Exertion today is separated from its recompense; it is not the same man that first works, and then reposes; but it is because the one works that the other rests."[6] Sismondi grasped the essence of all class societies. It is not simply that some are wealthy and others are not. It is the labor of the many that accounts for the wealth of the few.

In the years following the great French Revolution, a group of socialists emerged who came to be known as utopians. The utopian socialists were known for concocting plans and schemes for a rationally organized society. Brilliant critics of the iniquities of industrial capitalism, which they argued worked against the better part of human nature, the utopians sought to create islands of social or communal living that would set an example for the rest of the world to follow. Their aim was to convince everyone—including the wealthy—of the superiority of their system. Human reason—the sheer logic of their position—would convince the well-born in society to adopt their plans. Indeed, the French utopian Charles Fourier was actually opposed to revolutionary change from below. For the utopians, the working class was only a "suffering class," not a class capable of transforming society by its own actions. Engels put it this way:

> The solution of the social problems, which as yet lay hidden in undeveloped economic conditions, the Utopians attempted to evolve out of the human brain. Society presented nothing but wrongs; to remove these was the task of reason. It was necessary, then, to discover a new and more perfect system of social order and to impose this upon society from without by propaganda, and, wherever it was possible, by the example of model experiments. These new social systems were foredoomed as Utopian; the more completely they were worked out in detail, the more they could not avoid drifting off into pure fantasies.[7]

Virtually all of these utopian experiments—many of which were established in the United States in the 1800s—failed. Rather than changing the wider world, the social and economic priorities of the capitalist world changed them. These experiments, though they sometimes offered a glimpse of alternative ways of organizing society, succumbed to the surrounding hostile capitalist environment. Workers' cooperatives, by the way, have always faced the same problem—that you can't build little islands of socialism in a sea of market capitalism. As Rosa Luxemburg noted, a worker-owned business must, if it is to survive in the market, impose on itself the same exploitative conditions that exist in other capitalist-owned enterprises, or, "if the workers' interests continue to predominate, end by dissolving."[8] Various strands of utopianism remain influential today, often justified on the grounds that such experiments "prefigure" a better world. The idea that you can create autonomous islands of liberation fails on two counts—first, because the "real" world finds a way to impinge, and therefore undermine, the relations that the autonomists try to establish; and second, because they pose no challenge to the capitalist system as a whole by their existence.

What made Marx and Engels' socialism different from the utopians? It was that their socialist ideas were rooted in real, rather than ideal, conditions. Marx and Engels showed that the desire for and vision of another world wasn't enough. The utopians, in criticizing existing social relations and proposing elaborate social plans for a better society, simply counterposed what is with what ought to be. But there had to be something that connected the future with the present. The seeds of a future society had to already exist in the soil of the present for it to spring forth. The material conditions, and social actors, had to exist to make that change both possible and necessary for society to move forward.

"Communism is for us," wrote Marx and Engels, "not … an *ideal* to which reality [will] have to adjust itself." It is "the *real* movement which abolishes the present state of things."[9] The starting point for Marx and Engels, therefore, was not "what men say, imagined, conceived, in order to arrive at men in the flesh." Instead, they wrote, "We set out from real, active men, and on the basis of their real-life process we demonstrate the development of the ideological reflexes and echoes of this life-process."[10]

The point was not that it was impossible to have ideas about freedom before the conditions for their realization existed, or that there was a mechanical one-to-one relationship between people's ideas and their material conditions of life. However, "one cannot be liberated," if one is "unable to obtain food and drink, housing and clothing in adequate quality and quantity." "Liberation," Marx and Engels argued, "is a historical and not a mental act."[11] Socialism, in short, must be more than a good idea. There must be material and social forces, created in the womb of capitalism itself, which have the potential to make it a reality. Put crudely, if there isn't enough food to go around, equality simply means slow death for everyone—an equality of suffering. Sharing on a sustained basis implies that food is plentiful.

Marx and Engels were able to move beyond the utopians for a number of connected reasons. Like other socialists, Marx and Engels saw the tremendous increase in wealth that sprouted up during the rise of industrial capitalism that promised, but did not deliver, a world free of want. But they also witnessed something else: workers' strikes and demonstrations in Germany, Britain, and France. The working class ceased for them to be only a "suffering class" and became before their eyes the active agent of its own liberation—the class whose own emancipation could act as the basis for the liberation of all.

This is the central component of Marxism, so we'll come back to this. But for now a couple of points need to be made. The discovery of the working class was an important breakthrough, because it identified a social force capable, through its own actions, of transforming society. Before this point, there had been, roughly speaking, two views about radical social change, and both saw in the mass of the exploited, at best, a passive element that might aid more enlightened minorities to transform society.[12]

The radical French eighteenth-century materialists, like the utopians, argued that the mass of the people, as products of their social and material conditions, were incapable of getting beyond it. For how can someone molded by his or her environment step outside that environment to change it? What was required, therefore, was an exceptional man, or a group of enlightened men, standing above or outside society—the fact that these philosophers thought enlightened *men* would change the world was, ironically, proof that they, too, were products of the prevailing circumstances—or even an enlightened despot, who would make change from above. Even radicals such as the French revolutionary August Blanqui saw workers as part of a more or less unconscious mass that could provide muscle, but not leadership, to the revolution, which would be made by a group of conscious conspirators.

Idealist thinkers, who believed that great ideas shaped the material world, held equally elitist theories that relegated the masses to either no role whatsoever in historical change, or to a completely passive role. For the Left Hegelians in Germany, for example, of whom Marx and Engels were members in the early 1840s, spirit (or ideas, or philosophy) was the active element, whereas the material, the "mass," was the passive element in social change, if it played any role at all.

The point is that most radicals adhered to the "great man" theory of history—every great event in history was brought about by the great ideas and great actions of great men. French radical nineteenth-century historian Augustin Thierry ridiculed this approach:

> It is highly singular that the historians stubbornly refused to attribute any spontaneity or creativity to the masses of people. If an entire people migrates and makes itself a new home, that means, our annalists and poets assert, that some hero has taken it into his head to found a new empire to add luster to his name; if a city is established, it is some prince that has given it life. The people, the citizens, are always material for the thinking of a single individual. Do you really wish to learn who founded an institution and who conceived a social enterprise? Search among those who really needed it; it was to them that the first idea of it, the wish to act, and a considerable part of the execution belonged.[13]

Historians and poets may write history, but it is great masses of people in motion—in particular, social classes—that make history.

Marx came to this conclusion in a series of notes, or "theses," he jotted down in 1845. First, he argued that the materialists who said that people were products of their circumstances, and that to change people you only had to change their circumstances, inevitably divided society into two parts: the passive majority and a thinking elite that could somehow stand outside society. Like the famous behavioral scientist B. F. Skinner, who set up various experiments to elicit certain predictable responses from his subjects, this minority would mold the passive majority by changing its circumstances. Of course, the problem with this view is that the people who are meant to change things are themselves products of their material environment, and so the whole theory breaks down.

To the idealists who argued that conditions didn't matter, and that only ideas were important, he argued that ideas without any connection to the real world were immaterial, and therefore incapable of changing social conditions. The validity of any idea about society could only be tested in practice—the practice of masses of people attempting to change society. The way Marx got around this dilemma was to say that historical change could only be conceived as the self-conscious activity of masses of people; that the oppressed changed their ideas, and their own conditions, through revolutionary action. "The coincidence of the changing of circumstances and of human activity or self-changing can be conceived and rationally understood only as *revolutionary practice*."[14]

Chapter Two

Marx's Materialist Method

Why theory matters

The last thesis that Marx jotted down in 1845 was this: "The philosophers have merely interpreted the world; the point, however, is to change it."[1] One way to interpret this statement is as an argument against theory. We don't need theory—that's for professors and intellectuals who like to debate to no particular end—we just need to fight for what we know is right. "You don't need a weatherman," goes the 1960s Bob Dylan song, "to know which way the wind blows."[2]

While people might declare that ideas about society are a waste of time, they wouldn't say the same thing about what we call the hard sciences. No one would ever say: Who needs physics? (Except maybe bored high school students.) All of our modern technology—from digital electronics to airplanes and computers—was developed on the basis of science.

Scientific theory helps us get beneath the surface appearance of things to understand the underlying laws that govern their behavior. Scientific theories are explanations about why and how things happen that are not apparent through immediate observation. "If we lived on a planet where nothing ever changed, there would be little to do," wrote science writer Carl Sagan. "There would be nothing to figure out. There would be no impetus for science. And if we lived in an unpredictable world, where things changed in random or complex ways, we would not be able to figure things out. Again, there would be no such thing as science. But we live in an in-between universe, where things change, but according to patterns, rules, or, as we call them, laws of nature."[3]

How do we know whether or not a theory is right or wrong? It has to be tested in practice. A scientific theory can be invalidated if it is falsified—that is, if examples or results are found that the theory cannot explain. In biology, a theory must be able to explain why things evolve in one way and not another. Wrong theories produce bad, if not useless, practical results; or they cannot explain every case they are meant to explain. Indeed, the proof of a scientific theory's soundness lies, with some exceptions, in its ability to predict behavior, whether practical experiments can reproduce what it predicts will happen, or whether the practical applications developed out of the theory actually work.

That isn't to say that science is completely neutral. Obviously, the fact that governments and businesses spend more time and money on things like nuclear weaponry than on curing disease tells us something about the way capitalism shapes scientific inquiry. Nevertheless, the whole purpose of science, for good or ill, is to assist in changing reality. Scientists, in other words, must be able to "interpret the world" in order to "change it." This holds true, perversely, also with the atomic bomb, if we replace "change" with "destroy."

What about society? Marx's little quip at the beginning was written as an attack on armchair thinkers, people who talked but did nothing. He didn't really think that there was no point interpreting the world—rather, he thought that there was no point interpreting the world unless you were trying to change it. Ideas divorced from practice are free to float in the stratosphere, where one is as good as the next—or are useless, as anyone who has been at a graduate school wine and cheese party can attest.

For the capitalists attempting to improve production techniques and outsell their competitor, science can be harnessed to suit their needs. But we live in a society that is divided into a small minority of very wealthy exploiters and a majority of people who work or starve. All societies that are divided into a minority class of exploiters and a majority class of exploited require for their functioning a set of ideas that reinforce class domination. "The ideas of the ruling class are in every epoch the ruling ideas, i.e. the class which is the ruling material force of society, is at the same time its ruling intellectual force,"[4] Marx and Engels wrote. "The class which has the means of material production at its disposal, has control at the same time over the means of mental production, so that thereby, generally speaking, the ideas of those who lack the means of mental production are subject to it. The ruling ideas are nothing more than the ideal expression of the dominant material relationships."[5]

The ruling, capitalist class (whom Marx and Engels referred to as the "bourgeoisie") certainly harnesses ideas to its needs. But it does so for the purpose of justifying its rule—not changing the unequal relations between rich and poor in society, but keeping them the way they are. The fact that the United States was founded on conquest (of Indians) and enslavement (of Africans), or that the legal system favors the rich over the poor, or that workers here had to go on strike to get an eight-hour day, is not going to be prominent in most high school textbooks. History reflects the "ruling ideology."

The "ruling ideas" are ideas meant to bolster the status quo, not explain or challenge it. An example of this would be the idea that strikes and social movements are caused by "outside agitators," or a minority of "troublemakers," a common refrain among employers and their political hirelings throughout the history of the U.S. labor movement. The argument conveys the idea that ordinary people are too happy with their lot to want to fight against their own oppression, but are gullible and therefore easily duped by "Machiavellian" leftists. The assumption is also "that the victims of injustice lack the wit or the will to challenge their superiors, that they are incapable of acting on their own grievance and rationally choosing their allies," writes radical British author Mike Marqusee.[6]

Historians and sociologists usually make more sophisticated arguments than this, but their sophistication is not necessarily an indication that they are any more insightful. Indeed, often less crude, more superficially impressive arguments are more useful in bolstering the status quo. Marx challenged the bourgeois (he used the word "bourgeois" interchangeably with capitalist) economists of his time, saying that for them, it wasn't a question of whether "this theorem or that was true, but whether it was useful to capital or harmful, expedient or inexpedient, politically dangerous or not."[7]

More than that, the social sciences routinely set out to discredit anyone who puts forth the idea that class and class struggle are central to history. Lenin put it this way:

> Throughout the civilized world the teachings of Marx evoke the utmost hostility and hatred of all bourgeois science (both official and liberal), which regards Marxism as a kind of "pernicious sect." And no other attitude is to be expected, for there can be no "impartial" social science in a society based on class struggle. In one way or another, *all* official and liberal science *defends* wage slavery, where Marxism has declared relentless war on wage slavery. To expect science to be impartial in a wage-slave society is as silly and naive as to expect impartiality from manufacturers on the ques-

> tion of whether workers' wages should be increased by decreasing the profits of capital.[8]

Insofar, Marx argued, as a real critical understanding of society represents a class, "it can only represent the class whose vocation in history is the overthrow of the capitalist mode of production and the final abolition of all classes—the proletariat."[9] By this Marx did not mean that to get an accurate answer to a question, you just need to walk up and ask a UPS worker. He meant that only movements of ordinary workers in struggle, seeking ways to challenge the world, require as a condition of success a real picture of the dynamics of society rather than the one presented on TV and in the history books.

But common sense tells us that truth is about impartiality, finding the golden mean between different positions. If you take a side, you can't be balanced, and therefore you can't get at the truth. Take the example of the debate in the courts and school boards over intelligent design—the view that life is a product of a supernatural creator rather than biological evolution. The media has often presented both sides as if they were part of a legitimate debate. The problem here is that this form of the presentation constitutes a surrender to the right-wing Christian advocates of intelligent design, whose entire strategy consists of attempting to push through local laws that permit "equal" treatment of intelligent design and Darwinian evolution in schools.

Intelligent design is in fact a more watered-down version of plain old Biblical creationism—the idea that a Christian God is responsible for the creation of all life and that evolution is an abomination. They pretend that intelligent design—a view that by definition cannot be tested because the Creator is supernatural and, therefore, outside the bounds of rational enquiry—is a scientific theory rather than a part of religious faith. By presenting intelligent design (religious dogma) as a legitimate contender with evolution (science), the media has in fact played straight into the hands of intelligent design's proponents.

The irony is that it is only by taking sides in a fight to change the world—on the side of the oppressed and exploited—will you have both the *need* and the *capacity* to understand how things work. For example, if as a worker I believe that bosses are reasonable people who are looking for ways to improve my wages, I will act accordingly: I'll go and ask politely at the manager's door for a raise. But I will quickly learn that my "theory" about the bosses won't get me very far. Employers raise wages in response to a labor shortage or to struggle, but—all other things being equal—they aren't interested in cutting into their own profits by increasing the wages of their workers.

Unfortunately, when looking at society, it is often accepted that one "theory" is as good as another. Imagine if physics were approached this way. You say the earth revolves around the sun, I say the sun revolves around the earth—who's to say what's correct? But if we are to intervene in society practically, and actually change it, "flat-earth" sociology won't do. We'll need to go beyond "common sense" ideas that help bolster the status quo—like "people are poor because there isn't enough to go around," "immigrants steal our jobs," "poor people are lazy," or "our government invades other countries to liberate people."

What is there to recommend one view of society over any other view? For Marx and Engels, the question of whether this or that view of the world was correct was something that had to be tested against experience. "The question whether objective truth can be attributed to human thinking," Marx wrote, "is not a question of theory but is a practical question.... Man must prove the truth, i.e., the reality and power, the this-worldliness of his thinking *in practice*."[10] Debating the truth or non-truth of any idea without reference to the real world was "purely a scholastic question."

Working-class people are not blank slates, but carry with them a variety of different, often contradictory ideas, some of which reflect the ruling ideas, and some which challenge them. For example, the same person who supports unions as a way to better conditions on the job may also hold racist ideas. Another may oppose racism, but accept sexist ideas about women. They may not be conscious that these ideas—some of which reinforce solidarity and liberation, others that reinforce division and oppression—are contradictory. The importance of clear ideas becomes more obvious in the course of mass action, when there are all kinds of debates about which way forward. The founder of Russian Marxism, Georgi Plekhanov, wrote, "without revolutionary theory there can be no revolutionary movement."[11]

By this he did not mean that we have to have all of our ideas sorted out before we can fight for a better world. What he did mean is that if our side—the side of the downtrodden, the mistreated, the exploited—is eventually to triumph and build a new society, it must have its own set of coherent ideas, its own worldview that counters that of the ruling class. A coherent worldview is shaped in part in the course of challenging capitalism, but it is also shaped by coming to grips with the historical experience of past struggles and by scientifically investigating the way our society works. "In the eyes of a philistine, a revolutionary point of view is virtually equivalent to an absence of scientific objectivity," observed Russian revolutionary Leon Trotsky.

> We think just the opposite: only a revolutionist—provided, of course, that he is equipped with the scientific method—is capable of laying bare the objective dynamics of the revolution. Apprehending thought is in general not contemplative, but active. The element of will is indispensable for penetrating the secrets of nature and society. Just as a surgeon, on whose scalpel a human life depends, distinguishes with extreme care the various tissues of an organism, so a revolutionist, if he has a serious attitude toward his task, is obliged with strict conscientiousness to analyze the structure of society, its functions and reflexes.[12]

Materialism and idealism

In the history of philosophy, idealism and materialism have very different meanings from their popular usage—where idealism means having unrealistic ideas (or unrealizable goals), and materialism refers to a desire to possess property and wealth. By that definition, Marx was an idealist and Bill Gates is a materialist.

According to their traditional usage in philosophical writing, idealism and materialism represent the two main divergent ways of looking at the world we live in. For the idealist, the mind—or the spirit, sometimes God—is the origin of all material things. The ancient Greek idealist philosopher Plato, for example, argued that the world and the things in it were determined by universal, logical categories. Therefore, every real tree was a copy derived from the universal, ideal category "tree." In fact, according to Plato, the universal ideal category was "real," whereas the material manifestation was merely a shadow, or weak copy, of the universal. Plato separated the mind from matter, and argued the former ruled over the latter.

Idealist thinking permeates much popular thought. For example, the idea that historical change comes about because great men (women don't usually get any credit) come along with great ideas, is widely accepted. But this doesn't explain why it is that anyone bothered to follow these leaders, or where the great ideas of these "great men" came from.

For the materialist, all of reality is based on matter, including mental activity, which is itself a result of the organization of matter in a particular way. Whereas the idealist places the mind above and outside of nature, the materialist argues that the mind itself is a product of natural developments. Minds cannot exist apart from the material world, and the material world existed long before any mind was able to experience it.

In this view, the abstract idea "tree" derives from our experience of actual trees. Universal categories are just generalizations that human beings made out of their experience of the real world. "It is not consciousness that determines life," wrote Marx, putting it another way, "but life that determines consciousness."[13]

One of the most common forms of idealism is the view that humans have unrestricted "free will"—the idea that individuals can do anything they set their mind to regardless of economic, social, and cultural obstacles placed in front of them. Materialists don't have to deny that human beings are sometimes responsible for what they do (although responsibility comes in degrees), or that human agency can sometimes be decisive in changing the course of history, to discount this idea.

The view that "you can beat poverty if you really try hard" implicitly accepts free will. Poverty, in this view, is not a social phenomenon caused by, for example, a factory closing or a chronic illness in the family (itself perhaps caused by some pollutant spewed into the air by some corporation). Rather, poverty is a personal failing.

The most famous example of this kind of thinking came from former U.S. president Ronald Reagan, who once argued that the "people who are sleeping on the grates ... the homeless ... are homeless, you might say, by choice."[14] The dramatic rise in homelessness in the 1980s naturally had nothing to do with the fact that Reagan halved the public housing budget and reduced federal spending to local governments.[15]

The flip side of this argument is that businessmen and wealthy professionals derive their social status from their brilliant personal qualities, not because of the silver spoons stuck into their mouths at birth.

No one has ever argued that companies go "bankrupt by choice." Yet every year, in spite of the wills of the individual businessmen involved, thousands do go bankrupt. The same applies to unemployment. Unemployment goes through cyclical rises and declines. It stretches logic to try and argue that a spike in unemployment is caused by a sudden case of mass laziness. The truth, as we shall show later, is that unemployment has economic causes that are beyond the control of individual workers or capitalists.

Marx and Engels ridiculed the view that ideas determine reality. "Once upon a time, a valiant fellow had the idea that men were drowned in water only because they were possessed with the idea of gravity," they wrote. "If they were to get this notion out of their heads," they could avoid drowning.[16] Behind the humor lay an important point:

Thought that bears no relationship to reality is impotent thought. The will to action is important, but if that will does not correspond to material possibilities, it doesn't count for anything. This can apply in obvious ways—willpower cannot overcome a shortage of food on a deserted island. Or it can apply in more subtle ways. Willpower alone cannot convince everyone at my workplace to walk out with me on strike.

What people say and think about themselves and the world must not be taken on its own merit, but must be judged in light of the underlying social and economic relations that govern their behavior. We must go beneath the surface of what often appear to be religious disputes, for example, to see that these conflicts express deeper class conflicts. "A distinction must be made," wrote Marx, "between the material transformation of the economic conditions of production … and the legal, political, religious, aesthetic or philosophic—in short, ideological forms in which men become conscious of this conflict and fight it out."[17]

Another popular idealist premise is that human behavior is shaped by universal morals. Ideas of right and wrong, that exist above society and above time, govern human behavior. This fails to address the fact that different societies had very different morals. For example, in ancient Greece, homosexual love was looked upon favorably, whereas in other societies it hasn't been.

A more current form of idealism is the idea that the international relations between states are not governed by military and economic competition, but by universal norms of human behavior: rules of trade, rules of war, and so on. All the glaring deviations in reality from these universal norms merely reflect that the real world is an imperfect copy of the ideal world from which it derives.

The abstract morality of good versus evil is used by opposing classes, and by opposing nations in wartime, to justify their own actions and condemn those of their opponents. The truth is, as Engels argued, people "consciously or unconsciously, derive their ethical ideas in the last resort from the practical relations on which their class position is based—from the economic relations in which they carry on production and exchange."[18] Morality, in the final instance, either justifies the domination of the ruling classes, or represents the oppressed classes' "indignation against this domination and the future interests of the oppressed."[19]

Sometimes the indignation manifests itself as a belief that the world should live up to the abstract moral ideas that various world leaders prattle on about. Sometimes it finds expression in the idea that we as individuals should live by a certain moral code. Many young people who are horrified by the inequalities of capitalism are motivated by a belief that one can change the world by changing one's own moral outlook and behavior. One need only reject greed and selfishness, and then impart this outlook to others. But this approach, though it might help its practitioner feel better about him/herself, doesn't change anything. Greed and selfishness are not the result of bad individual choices, but are engendered by the competitive and profit-driven nature of capitalism. A capitalist who is not greedy for profit is a capitalist who will lose out to his more greedy competitors.

The problem with the notion that it is only necessary to change people's ideas in order to change society is that this leaves the social structure of society intact. "This demand to change consciousness amounts to a demand to interpret the existing world in a different way, i.e., to recognize it by means of a different interpretation," Marx wrote of some German idealists of his day. In doing this "they are in no way combating the real existing world," but are "combating solely the phrases of this world."[20] The materialist view is exactly the opposite. Morals are derived from particular forms of human social organization. Capitalism breeds greed, not vice versa. In societies that foraged for food and shared it as a collective, greed was frowned upon because it disrupted the functioning of the group.

Marx and Engels subjected idealism itself to a materialist analysis, showing that it had historical roots in the separation of material and mental labor that came with the overall division of society into classes—those who engage in backbreaking work, and those who are free to engage in mental pursuits (priests, for example, in the earliest class societies). "From this moment onwards consciousness *can* really flatter itself that it is something other than consciousness of existing practice," wrote Marx and Engels, "that it *really* represents something without representing something real; from now on consciousness is in a position to emancipate itself from the world and to proceed to the formation of 'pure' theory, theology, philosophy, ethics, etc."[21]

Ideas are not suspended in air—they have real material roots. To understand why people think and behave the way they do, you must understand the way in which they work together to procure their means of existence. On this basis arises a superstructure of ideas and concepts that people form in their everyday intercourse to explain and influence the world around them.

Biological determinism: You can't change human nature

There is another kind of materialism that Marxism rejects outright, and that is the biological or genetic materialism that presents human behavior as determined either solely or primarily by our genetic inheritance. This line of reasoning, which goes back to such social Darwinists of the late nineteenth century as Sir Francis Galton and Herbert Spencer, presents us with the argument that human nature is the fixed and unchanging result of our biological makeup. Why do people behave the way they do? It's part of our genetic coding. Greed, selfishness, xenophobia, racism, male domination, violence, and war are all attributed to something innate to all of us. Needless to say, this is a very convenient argument for someone who is trying to uphold the status quo, for it places the blame for all sorts of nasty behavior on human traits that are beyond anyone's power to change.

The early advocates of social Darwinism, which could be summarized as "survival of the whitest and the richest," were blatant in their racism and disdain for the poor. In addition to arguing that white Anglo-Saxons were superior to the dark-skinned people of the world, Spencer also opposed universal education, free lunches for the indigent, and any laws regulating wages or working conditions.[22] These ideas went into decline briefly after the rise of Hitler, but began to revive in various forms starting in the 1960s, and culminated in the publication of *The Bell Curve* in 1994. In addition to arguing that people rise to the top of the society because they are intelligent, an attribute that they said was primarily based on genetic inheritance, the authors unabashedly argued that Blacks were inherently less intelligent than whites.[23]

The late Stephen Jay Gould rightly noted that these purportedly scientific ideas are ideology, not science, providing the justification for various right-wing policy initiatives that attack the poor and the oppressed. "Why struggle and spend to raise the unboostable IQ of races or social classes at the bottom of the economic ladder," he wrote. "Better simply to accept nature's unfortunate dictates and save a passel of federal funds; (we can then more easily sustain tax breaks for the wealthy!)? Why bother yourself about under-representation of disadvantaged groups in your honored and remunerative bailiwick if such absence records the diminished ability or general immorality, biologically imposed, of most members in the rejected group, and not the legacy or current reality of social prejudice?"[24]

The argument that our behavior is based on evolved genetic traits was presented most systematically by sociobiologist E. O. Wilson in the 1970s, and has since become widely accepted. "The most distinctive human qualities have emerged during the phase of social evolution that occurred through intertribal warfare and through genocide," Wilson asserted. "Among general social traits in human beings are aggressive dominance systems with males dominant over females."[25] Richard Lewontin, another Harvard geneticist, calls sociobiology "the latest and most mystified attempt to convince people that human life is pretty much what it has to be and perhaps even ought to be."[26] The method of sociobiology is to look around at the world as it is—our capitalist world—and from that distill a set of fundamental human traits that it claims apply to all human beings throughout history. These claimed universal traits, according to sociobiology—male dominance, hatred of strangers, systems of domination, competition for resources, even a hankering for religion—have their origin in our genes.

The modern incarnation of sociobiology, evolutionary psychology, claims that human beings possess genetically programmed behavior that developed over a long period of time in the Paleolithic era. But as biologist Steven Rose points out, in an argument that also applies to Wilson, "[T]he descriptions that evolutionary psychology offers of what human hunter-gatherer societies were like read little better than 'Just So' accounts, rather like those museum—and cartoon—montages of hunter-dad bringing home the meat while gatherer-mom tends the fireplace and kids.… There is a circularity about reading this version of the present into the past, and then claiming that this imagined past explains the present."[27]

These fashionable ideas, though continually offered as fact, have no scientific foundation. Search as they may, biologists will never find a war gene—because war isn't innate to humans any more than pacifism is. It's not that there is no biological basis for our behavior. But for every example of aggression in human behavior, we can also find examples of peaceful cooperation and sharing. Moreover, how these things are even defined depends on the historical and cultural setting. Neither violence nor sharing are genetically programmed—they are socially shaped and conditioned. As the evolutionary biologist Theodosius Dobzhansky noted, "Heredity does determine that a person can learn to speak a language or languages, but it does not determine which language he will learn or what he will say."[28]

If there is a fixed human nature, then how can it be that human societies have differed so much between different regions and historical times? How is it that some societies were egalitarian, sharing societies, while others were competitive and class-divided? How is it that some were warlike and violent, while others were relatively peaceful? How is it that some accorded women a high position, and others a subordinate one?

The French Jesuit missionary LeJeune, who lived among the Montagnais-Naskapi Indians on the Labrador coast of Canada in the early 1630s, for example, complained of them: "As they have neither political organization, nor offices, nor dignities, nor any authority, for they only obey their chief through the goodwill toward him, therefore they never kill each other to acquire these honors. Also, as they are contented with a mere living, not one of them gives himself to the Devil to acquire wealth."[29] The Jesuits who proselytized among this society considered it healthy to beat children into submission, while the Indians considered the practice barbaric.

Consider an incident described by Eleanor Burke Leacock in her excellent book *Myths of Male Dominance*. A French boy struck and injured a Montagnais boy. Alarmed, the Indians demanded gifts. But the French missionaries instead prepared to punish the French child by whipping him in front of the Indians. According to the report of a Jesuit, "One of the savages stripped himself entirely, threw his blanket over the child and cried to him that was going to do the whipping: 'Strike me if thou wilt, but thou shalt not strike him.' And thus the little one escaped."[30]

When the missionary tried to tell a Montagnais-Naskapi man that women should love only their husbands, so that men could be sure of who their children were, he responded: "Thou hast no sense. You French people love only your own children; but we all love all the children of our tribe."[31]

The "human nature" view of the world assumes that humans have a built-in nature—shaped genetically by their physical attributes—in the same way that other animals have a nature that determines their behavior. The wolf has sharp teeth to tear raw meat, and the bear has fur to keep warm, and fish have gills to breathe under water and special muscles adapted for swimming. But we humans have none of these *special* adaptations.

Our peculiar biological inheritance—in particular, our upright gait, larger brain size, opposable thumbs, and the capacity for language—gave us the ability to make tools to manipulate our environment cooperatively and to pass those skills on to our offspring. Humans can make fur coats, build shelter, and catch, grow, and cook food; i.e., we can create the things nature did not physically endow us with, things that allow us to exploit virtually every environment on the planet.

There is a human nature. But what makes us human—language, cooperative labor, and tool-making—are precisely the things that make human behavior so ever-changing and malleable. The point is, what makes humans distinct from other animals—though we are still animals—is that we possess an ability to artificially reproduce our means of existence, a fact which creates a plasticity of behavior that other animals do not possess. In short, we adapt culturally.

Human beings have changed relatively little genetically or biologically over the last forty thousand years. Yet our social forms of organization—the way that we organize ourselves to procure food, shelter, clothing, and other necessities—have changed tremendously, and in recent centuries, at an accelerating rate. It is this that accounts for the changing "nature" of humans—our morals, our ideas about the world and about ourselves—from one society to the next.

In attempting to attribute extremely variable human behavior throughout history to a relatively fixed constant—a genetically determined human nature—the biological materialists fall into the same trap as the idealists who believe that society is governed by universal ideals or norms. They are both incapable of explaining historical change and evolution.

Marx and Engels rejected both idealism and the old, static, deterministic materialism. If you recall, Marx criticized the French materialists' view that human beings were a product of their circumstances, because it was one-sided and left no room for human beings to shape their own history. These materialists always let idealism in the back door, in the form of a liberator standing somehow outside society. Marx and Engels' materialism was *dialectical.*

Dialectics? What the heck is that?

A lot of confusing ink has been spilled about this strange word, dialectics. People may have only a vague idea, if any, of what it is (something to do with an old German philosopher named Hegel, something to do with contradictions), but the question is of considerable importance. For the question of dialectics is about method—about how we go about looking at the world, how it works, and how it changes—and ultimately, how we can consciously transform it.

To put it most plainly, wrote Engels, dialectics is "nothing more than the science of the general laws of motion and development of nature, human society and thought."[32] That is, it is the form of thinking about the world which best corresponds to the way in which the processes of natural and social evolution work.

The ancient Greek philosopher Heraclitus is the first recorded thinker who stressed a dialectical view of the world. For Heraclitus, nothing was fixed, fast, or frozen. "Everything flows," he wrote. "Strife is the father of all things.... The fairest harmony is born of things different, and discord is what produces all things."[33] These are key concepts of the dialectic: Constant change and movement is the natural order of things, and change comes about through the conflict of contradictory forces ("strife").

The Marxist dialectic did come by way of a German philosopher by the name of George Frederick Hegel, who wrote his greatest works in the early part of the 1800s. His philosophy is extremely difficult to read, and though the young Marx, in a letter to his father in 1837, called Hegel's philosophy a "grotesque craggy melody,"[34] Marx was won over and became a disciple for a few years.

Hegel's ideas were a major breakthrough in philosophical thought. He developed his philosophy in the shadow of the French Revolution, and in many ways his philosophy of dialectics was an ideal expression of the spirit of that age—a period of almost unceasing conflict and change, of the death of old feudal relations and the birth of the new. At the heart of Hegel's dialectic was the idea that history was a process of the unfolding of the "absolute idea." Ideas and concepts were not static things, Hegel argued, but moved through contradiction in a continual process of development. To his dialectical approach to ideas Hegel counterposed what he called the "metaphysical" approach, which held that things were to be viewed as separate, static, without any contradiction. A is always A, B is always B, and A can never become B. But Hegel didn't just reject metaphysical thought. He argued that it had a value, within limits, but it stopped working as an approach once you started to analyze things in their movement and transformation.

The following quote will give you an idea of Hegel's approach. Here he's talking about the unfolding of philosophical ideas, but he uses an analogy from nature to make his point:

> The bud disappears in the bursting-forth of the blossom, and one might say that the former is refuted by the latter; similarly, when the fruit appears, the blossom is shown up in its turn as a false manifestation of the plant, and the fruit now emerges as the truth

> of it instead. These forms are not just distinguished from one another, they also supplant one another as mutually incompatible. Yet at the same time their fluid nature makes them moments of an organic unity in which they not only do not conflict, but in which each is as necessary as the other; and this mutual necessity alone constitutes the life of the whole.[35]

You could take the analogy even further back and say that the seed and the plant it can become seem to bear no resemblance. The seed goes through a series of stages of growth in which its old form is destroyed and a new form takes its place, yet through all its forms, it is still the same plant. Things can only be fully grasped not as separate, static entities, but as conflicting or contradictory elements of a unity or whole, a process involving birth, life, decay, and death. The contradictory elements combine in an appearance of fixity or stability, but those very same conflicting elements produce movement or development. In the process of this development, new forms burst forth and negate or supersede previous forms, yet are clearly also dependent for their development on those previous forms. That is the main idea of dialectics.

A dialectical approach sees change not simply as a series of quantitative changes that leaves the essence of the thing intact, but argues that quantitative changes can give way to qualitative leaps. The acorn transforms itself into an oak. A fertilized animal egg becomes a full-grown dog—yet the egg was not a little tiny microscopic dog that grew slowly to a big dog. An element, water for example, at different temperature points turns from a solid to a liquid, and from a liquid into a gas, and so on.

Finally, dialectics views fundamental change emerging from the fact that movement comes through contradictory forces acting against each other, creating an unstable unity. Dialectics therefore allows for temporary states of stability or equilibrium, but also for qualitative leaps or breaks in which the equilibrium breaks down and gives way to something new.

A good example from the natural world is biological evolution. Until the 1860s, species were considered immutable, each created separately by God. Yet this was based only on appearance. Closer study revealed that though species appear distinctly separate, they have evolved from each other over time. This cut against the idea that the world consisted of separate, unchanging pieces, or systems which moved in a stable, unchanging equilibrium of balance and harmony.

It's easy to see how these ideas influenced Marx. But Marx took over and transformed the dialectical method and applied it in a consistently materialist way to human history. In one of the prefaces he wrote to *Capital*, his most famous work, he makes clear his debt to Hegel. This is how he explains it:

> The mystification which the dialectic suffers in Hegel's hands by no means prevents him from being the first to present its general forms of motion in a comprehensive and conscious manner. With him it is standing on its head. It must be inverted, in order to discover the rational kernel within the mystical shell....
>
> In its rational form [the dialectic] is a scandal and an abomination to the bourgeoisie and its doctrinaire spokesmen, because it includes in its positive understanding of what exists a simultaneous recognition of its negation, its inevitable destruction; because it regards every historically developed form as being in a fluid state, in motion, and therefore grasps its transient aspects as well; and because it does not let itself be impressed by anything, being in its very essence critical and revolutionary.[36]

Hegel himself ended up as a defender of the conservative Prussian state, but at the heart of his philosophy nevertheless was a radical concept: as Engels noted, the idea that "all that exists deserves to perish."[37]

So, the dialectic involves change, movement. But it isn't simply the gradual change, like erosion of a riverbank over millions of years—sometimes a catastrophic flood can do what slow erosion took eons to accomplish. The dialectical model says that things can be in temporary equilibrium, but they are never static and unchanging. Indeed, the equilibrium is always formed by the interaction of conflicting, or contradictory elements, which break apart at a certain threshold. This is how the Russian Marxist Trotsky summed up the dialectic:

> Hegel's logic is the logic of evolution. Only one must not forget that the concept of "evolution" itself has been completely corrupted and emasculated by university professors and liberal writers to mean peaceful "progress." Whoever has come to understand that evolution proceeds through the struggle of antagonistic forces; that a slow accumulation of changes at a certain moment explodes the old shell and brings about a catastrophe, revolution; whoever has learned finally to apply the general laws of evolution to thinking itself, he is a dialectician, as distinguished from vulgar evolutionists. Dialectic training of the mind, as necessary to a revolutionary fighter as finger exercises to a pianist, demands approaching all problems as *processes* and not as motionless categories. Whereas vulgar evolutionists, who limit themselves generally to recognizing evolution in only certain spheres, content themselves in all other questions with the banalities of "common sense."[38]

Chapter Three

The Marxist View of History

The materialist conception of history

We have established that Marxism does not view history as something that is governed either by eternal ideas or by some biologically fixed conception of human nature. Just as life has evolved, so has human history, since evolution is really just change through time. But what governs that change?

"The writers of history," wrote Marx, "have so far paid very little attention to the development of material production, which is the basis of all social life, and therefore of real history."[1] What was important for Marx was not "what is made but how, and by what instruments of labor, that distinguishes different economic epochs."[2]

Marx called this view of human history "the materialist conception of history." It began with the idea that social change and social progress are determined, first and foremost, by the ways in which human beings come together to produce their means of survival. "Men can be distinguished from animals by consciousness, by religion or anything else you like," wrote Marx and Engels. "They themselves begin to distinguish themselves from animals as soon as they begin to produce their means of subsistence."[3]

Marx's basic premise was that the way people organized with each other to produce their subsistence was dependent on the type of productive technology they had, and that the type of productive methods in turn determined the kind of social organization they could have: "In the social production of their existence, men inevitably enter into definite relations, which are independent of their will, namely relations of production appropriate to a given stage in the development of their material forces of production. The totality of these relations of production constitutes the economic structure of society, the real foundation, on which arises a legal and political superstructure and to which correspond definite forms of social consciousness."[4] Each stage of human development, with its corresponding "mode of production," has its own distinct economic laws of motion, which are independent of the wills of those caught up in it. But changes in the way production takes place produced new forms of social relations and corresponding cultural, political, and legal changes.

Each mode of production— foraging, horticulture, slavery, feudalism, capitalism—had its own set of social relations, that is, the social arrangements by which people interacted in production and reproduction of their lives. Each had its dominant, exploiting class and its oppressed, exploited class. (The exception is in gatherer-hunter societies, where there were not class divisions, as we shall see.)

The transformation from one mode of production to another was not smooth or automatic. On the contrary, the social relations established at each stage of development acted as a block against the development of new relations, restricting the further advancement of society. Each ruling class would at first act to lead society forward, then, as their rule progressed, would act to prevent any changes to the system from which they benefited. They would move from becoming a class that was historically progressive into a class that was historically regressive. (By "progressive" or "regressive" Marx simply meant whether a particular mode of production advanced the development of society's productive forces, and therefore humanity's control over its destiny, or retarded it.)

In each phase of human history, this contradiction between what Marx called the "forces of production" (the productive power of society) and the "relations of production" (the form of social organization under which production took place) grew to a point at which there would begin "an epoch of social revolution," in which these contradictions, manifested in an antagonism between contending classes, would burst forth.[5] Then the clash of ideas, organizations, and classes would determine whether society moved forward or backward. "At a certain stage of their development," Marx continued, "the material productive forces of society come in conflict with the existing relations of production, or—this merely expresses the same thing in legal terms—with the property relations within the framework of which they have operated hitherto. From forms of development of the productive forces these relations turn into their fetters."[6] In short, molecular economic changes produced economic contradictions, which in turn produced social and political conflicts—class struggle—in which the old relations were overthrown and replaced by new ones.

The most poetic and succinct description of this process is found in the first section of the *Communist Manifesto*: "The history of all hitherto existing society is the history of class struggles. Freeman and slave, patrician and plebian, lord and serf, guild-master and journeyman, in a word, oppressor and oppressed, stood in constant opposition to one another, carried on an uninterrupted, now hidden, now open fight, a fight that each time ended, either in a revolutionary reconstitution of society at large, or in the common ruin of the contending classes."[7]

By rejecting the idealist idea that people can achieve whatever they "will," Marx didn't embrace "determinism"—the idea that human beings are slaves to the blind forces of history—or that the revolutionary transformation of society was as inevitable as the sun rising every morning. For Marx, history consisted, in essence, of the changes brought about by human beings in the process of producing their existence. In a now famous passage, Marx argued that people "make their own history." "But," he added, "they do not make it just as they please; they do not make it under circumstances chosen by themselves, but under circumstances directly encountered, given and transmitted from the past."[8]

History is not something that "happens," like a meteor shower or a thunderstorm, but is the activity of real people interacting and clashing with each other. But the limits of human activity are always circumscribed by the material constraint placed on them by the way in which they are compelled to obtain their existence at a given level of production. This dictates a certain social division of labor and ways in which people relate to each other. The weight of the old customs and ideas corresponding to that level of development also press on those attempting to challenge the old. So long as humankind does not have complete conscious mastery over production, full freedom is impossible. Humans act with purpose, with will, but their individual intentions interact in such a way as to produce outcomes that are not consciously willed. This contradiction becomes most pronounced in capitalist society, in which individual wills appear powerless over the blind workings of the market. But once humanity has created a means of production that can provide for the needs of humanity, the necessity of a division of society into classes is abolished, and the basis of a society based upon the conscious mastery of production and distribution becomes possible for the first time. A society democratically and consciously planned by the associated producers, on the basis of the application of the most sophisticated scientific knowledge, has long been within our grasp.

The socialists who followed Marx and Engels tended to read into Marx and Engels' historical materialism a kind of schematic list of stages that every society must pass through according to its level of economic development. Stalinism took this to the height of absurdity and turned Marxism into its opposite. Instead of being a guide for workers to achieve liberation, it became, in Stalin's hands an ideological screen that justified his dictatorship over the proletariat.

Marx castigated those who caricatured his argument, seeking to "metamorphose my historical sketch of the genesis of capitalism in Western Europe into a historico-philosophical theory of general development, imposed by fate on all peoples, whatever the historical circumstances in which they are placed."[9]

But the materialist understanding of history is not like the law of gravity. We know that anything we drop in a vacuum, where there is no friction or wind resistance, falls at the same rate. Human history's welter of variables cannot be isolated in that way, but can only be observed in their messy totality. Natural events are blind, i.e., they involve no intervention by any conscious will. Human history, on the other hand, involves people, or groups of people, acting together or in conflict to achieve definite, more or less conscious goals.[10] Yet in spite of—or perhaps because of—those competing wills, history produces results neither intended nor foreseen by its participants. There are, in other words, driving material forces beneath the surface that shape the consciousness of historical actors and also shape and limit the scope and character of their actions.

Material conditions do not predetermine what will happen in history; they merely indicate the constraints on what is possible at any given moment. A certain set of social arrangements give rise to a corresponding set of ideas. But that does not mean that ideas are merely a passive reflection of material relations. Ideas can act back on those relations to change them—provided they are ideas that correspond to what is materially possible at that moment, and that those ideas embrace a sufficient number of people to effect a social change.

Engels felt compelled on more than one occasion to clarify to both critics and supporters that his and Marx's materialism was not mechanical or one-sided:

> According to the materialist conception of history, the ultimately determining element in history is the production and reproduction of real life. Other than this neither Marx nor I have ever asserted. Hence if somebody twists this into saying that the economic element is the only determining one, he transforms that proposition into a meaningless, abstract, senseless phrase. The economic situation is the basis, but the various elements of the superstructure—political forms of the class struggle and its results, to wit: constitutions established by the victorious class after a successful battle, etc., juridical forms, and even the reflexes of all these actual struggles in the brains of the participants, political, juristic, philosophical theories, religious views and their further development into systems of dogmas—also exercise their influence upon the course of the historical struggles and in many cases preponderate in determining their form. There is an interaction of all these elements in which, amid all the endless host of accidents (that is, of things and events whose inner interconnection is so remote or so impossible of proof that we can regard it as non-existent, as negligible), the economic movement finally asserts itself as necessary.[11]

The rise of class inequality

In an English preface to one of his most important works, *Socialism: Utopian and Scientific,* Engels summed up succinctly what he and Marx meant by "historical materialism": "I use … the term 'historical materialism' … to designate that view of the course of history which seeks the ultimate cause and the great moving power of all important historic events in the economic development of society, in the changes in the modes of production and exchange, in the consequent division of society into distinct classes, and in the struggles of these classes against one another."[12]

Marx and Engels' materialist account of historical change placed class division and class struggle at its heart. But Engels added an important addendum to the famous phrase in the *Communist Manifesto* that "the history of all hitherto existing society is the history of class struggles."[13] He noted that this was true only for written history. For most of our existence as a species, humans lived as the Montagnais-Naskapi did—without any class division. For tens of thousands of years, humans knew "no soldiers, no gendarmes or police, no nobles [or] kings, no prisons."[14] People decided how long to work, and all things beyond personal possessions were communally owned and shared in what some have called "primitive communism."

The Jesuit historian Pierre Charlevoix, who lived among Indians in French Canada in the early 1700s, wrote in his *History of New*

France: "The fraternal disposition of the Redskins doubtless comes in part from the fact that mine and thine, those icy words, as St. John Chrysostom calls them, are as yet unknown to the savages. The care that they take of orphans, widows, and the infirm, the hospitality they practice in so admirable a manner, are but a consequence of their view that everything ought to be common for all men."[15]

The Iroquois Indians, who engaged in a simple form of agriculture and hunting, were fairly egalitarian. "All quarrels and disputes are settled by the whole body of those concerned," Engels wrote of the Iroquois. "There can be no poor or needy—the communistic household and gens [clan or group of families] know their obligation toward the aged, the sick, and those disabled in war. All are free and equal—including the women. There is as of yet no room for slaves, nor, as a rule, for the subjugation of alien tribes."[16]

The status of women in communal societies was far higher than in class societies that followed. Among the Iroquois, a woman could dissolve her marriage simply by placing her husband's belongings outside the household door. "No matter how many children, or whatever goods [the husband] might have in the house, he might at any time be ordered to pick up his blanket and budge; and after such orders it would not be healthful for him to attempt to disobey," wrote the anthropologist Louis Henry Morgan, who studied the Iroquois in the 1870s.[17] This was due in part to the fact that women in Iroquois society did most of the labor in the fields (having previously been the gatherers, and therefore knowing the most about edible plants), which accounted for more of the group's food than did hunting.

Subsequent anthropological research has reinforced Morgan's and Engels' view that most societies that foraged for food—as well as many societies that engaged in simple agriculture (sometimes called "horticulture")—were free of class division and women's inequality. Such societies had no need for a group of people who were elevated above society and ruling over it.

Why, then, if people lived for so long without bosses or cops, did class divisions ever emerge at all? Starting about ten thousand years ago, some societies, as a result of the depletion of their food sources, moved to domesticating plants and animals instead of foraging for plants and hunting animals. This is commonly known as the Neolithic revolution. Foraging people had already gathered an enormous amount of knowledge about the plants they gathered. In foraging societies, the small bands necessarily produced only for immediate needs, with little thought of creating a surplus very much above their immediate needs. When food became scarce in one area, they simply picked up and moved elsewhere.

Some studies of modern foraging societies show that far from engaging in a brutish, relentless struggle for existence, people only spent on average something like two to five hours a day procuring subsistence.[18] A 1960s study calculated that "!Kung Bushmen of Dobe, despite their harsh environment, devote from twelve to nineteen hours a week to getting food."[19] And the !Kung had been pushed to more marginal lands from the regions more abundant in food where their ancestors had thrived.

The depletion of these plants because of over-harvesting as populations increased, or perhaps some climatic change, prompted some societies to turn to food domestication. Once people began to produce their food rather than just forage for it, they could sustain bigger populations that could stay in one place. In turn, this new, growing, more sedentary population had need of a surplus store of food as a hedge against disasters. (There were cases in which the food supply in an area was so abundant—through fishing, for example—that it allowed for the development of larger, sedentary populations as well.)

Early agricultural societies therefore tended to reward those who worked the hardest to increase food production. The prestige of these "redistributor" chiefs—called in some cultures "big men"—rested on their ability to produce, and exhort their followers to produce and give away more than anyone else. Still, their status as providers placed them in control of society's surplus. As the surplus grew, such chiefs could take some of the extra surplus and use it to pay for specialists—craftsmen, priests, servants, and warriors.[20]

"Under certain circumstances," writes anthropologist Marvin Harris,

> the exercise of power by the redistributor and his closest followers on the one side, and by the ordinary food producers on the other, became so unbalanced that, for all intents and purposes, the redistributor chiefs constituted the principal coercive force in social life. When this happened, contributions to the central store ceased to be voluntary contributions. "They became taxes. Farmlands and natural resources ceased to be elements of rightful access. They became dispensations. And redistributors ceased to be chiefs. They became kings.[21]

In other words, a figure that begins as a giver turns into its opposite, a taker—that is, an exploiter.

This was one possible path toward the emergence of classes. Classes arose in different ways, but always for the same underlying reason. In ancient India, for example, the first state evolved from those individuals "responsible for the collective maintenance of irrigation throughout the river valleys."[22] Elsewhere, the first class division was between masters and slaves—the expansion of the old family structure to include war captives who could produce extra wealth. In any case, classes emerged on the basis that "production had developed so far that the labor-power of a man could now produce more than was necessary for its mere maintenance."[23]

Once agriculture was established, society became capable of producing a surplus over and above what was needed for subsistence. But that surplus was only possible on the basis of the hard toil of the majority, and could only sustain a small minority who were freed from that labor. Class division was a necessary result of society's low level of productivity. As Engels put it, "So long as the total social labor only yields a produce which but slightly exceeds that barely necessary for the existence of all; so long, therefore, as labor engages all or almost all the time of the great majority of the members of society—so long, of necessity, this society is divided into classes. Side by side with the great majority … arises a class freed from directly productive labor, which looks after the general affairs of society."[24]

Classes are therefore defined by their relationship to the production and control of society's wealth, and in particular, the surplus product. Each ruling class used its position of control over the surplus to increase its own wealth and power over those it exploited—that is, to maximize the appropriation of surplus wealth. In any society, discover who appropriates and controls the surplus wealth produced in society and you have discovered the ruling class of that society. Find the class that produces the surplus wealth for the ruling class of a particular society, and you have found the exploited class.

Human progress—the advance of our ability to produce an expanding surplus over and above our basic needs—was impossible without the rise of class society. But the rise of class society has meant that every advance in human productive power has been made at the expense of the majority of humanity. "The power of these naturally evolved communities had to be broken," Engels wrote of pre-class societies,

> and it was broken. But it was broken by influences which from the outset appear to us as a degradation, a fall from the simple moral grandeur of the old [pre-class] society. The lowest interests—base greed, brutal sensuality, sordid avarice, selfish plunder of common

> possessions—usher in the new, civilized society, class society; the most outrageous means—theft, rape, deceit and treachery—undermine and topple the old, classless gentile society. And the new society, during all the 2,500 years of its existence, has never been anything but the development of the small minority at the expense of the exploited and oppressed great majority.[25]

The rise of class society also necessitated the development of another institution which is often portrayed as something eternal and "natural" to all human societies: the state, "a public power distinct from the mass of the people," wrote Engels.[26] This special coercive power wasn't necessary in a classless society, where the general male adult population could be armed because they shared common interests. But once you have a division into classes, there needs to be a body that can moderate class conflict, and keep it from threatening the economic interests of the dominant class. Wrote Engels, "This power, arisen out of society, but placing itself above it and increasingly alienating itself from it, is the state."[27] The state, in other words, is at its core a political institution that concentrates in its hands the coercive power of society and removes as much as possible the means of coercion from the majority exploited class.

The most popular reason given for the existence of this "public power" is that without it human nature is such that everyone would be at each other's throats. "During the time men live without a common power to keep them all in awe," wrote the seventeenth-century philosopher Thomas Hobbes, a great supporter of monarchy, "they are in that condition which is called war; and such a war as is of every man against every man."[28] In short, the state is a referee in a social brawl. But once it is acknowledged that a coercive state apparatus did not emerge until very late in human history, then this view can be seen for what it really is—more of a justification for state power than a real explanation of it.

Hobbes merely observed superficially that the state regulates conflict. The truth is that it arises to regulate a certain kind of conflict—class conflict, itself a historical product. But that doesn't mean that the state is an impartial referee. It always rigs the game in favor of the wealthy classes in such a way that it wins most of the time. As Engels put it:

> As the state arose from the need to keep class antagonisms in check, but also arose in the thick of the fight between the classes, it is normally the state of the most powerful, economically ruling class, which by its means becomes also the politically ruling class, and so acquires new means of holding down and exploiting the oppressed class. The ancient state was, above all, the state of the

> slave-owners for holding down the slaves, just as the feudal state was the organ of the nobility for holding down the peasant serfs and bondsmen, and the modern representative state is the instrument for exploiting wage-labor by capital.[29]

The rise of capitalism: greed unbounded

"Long, long ago there were two sorts of people; one, the diligent, intelligent and above all frugal elite; the other, lazy rascals, spending their substance, and more, in riotous living." This "insipid childishness," this historical fairy tale, wrote Marx, is what usually passes as an explanation as to why capitalist society is divided between the very rich and the rest of us. The true explanation is far less flattering to the so-called elite. "It is a notorious fact that conquest, enslavement, robbery, murder, in short, force, play the greatest part" in the rise of capitalism.[30]

All class societies are defined by the fact that there is a majority that works to keep a minority in idleness—a majority that slogs away and a minority that skims all the extra wealth over and above the subsistence needs of the majority. As Marx wrote, "Wherever a part of society possesses the monopoly of the means of production, the worker, free or unfree, must add to the labor-time necessary for his own maintenance an extra quantity of labor-time in order to produce the means of subsistence for the owner of the means of production, whether this proprietor be an … Etruscan theocrat, a civis romanus, a Norman baron, an American slave-owner, a Wallachian boyar, a modern landlord or capitalist."[31] Each class society has its own character, defined by the form that the exploitation takes, "the form in which … surplus labor is in each case extorted from the immediate producer, the worker."[32]

Under slavery and feudalism, the way in which a surplus was extracted was completely transparent. Anything produced over and above the costs of purchasing the slave and maintaining him (which varied depending on whether the owner profited more from working the slave to death or stretching his service out longer) was taken by the slaveowner as surplus product. The feudal peasant or serf was required either to hand over a portion of his crop to the lord and/or the state in rent, tithes, or taxes, or to perform unpaid labor (called "corvee") for the lord. The vast majority of the population produced what they needed to live on rather than buying it from others.

Whereas serf and slave labor was to varying degrees forced or bonded labor, modern capitalism is dependent on "free labor." This sweet-sounding term, however, disguises a bitter truth. The "free" does not only refer to the fact that the wage worker is no longer owned body and soul like a slave, or tied to the same land like a serf. Marx noted that "free" also means the worker is free of any possession of land or tools or any guaranteed means of livelihood, and therefore compelled on pain of destitution to hire him- or herself out piecemeal, "unencumbered," as Marx facetiously wrote, "by any means of production of their own."[33]

Whereas in previous societies trade was secondary, if not marginal, capitalism is the first system of production in which all economic intercourse involves the buying and selling of commodities and where other forms are marginal. But capitalism is also more than that. It is a system where the labor itself—or a person's capacity to work—becomes a commodity that can be bought and sold on the market. Under feudalism, people were tied to the land or owned their own tools and workshops. A condition for capitalism to develop fully, then, was the separation—by force, fraud, and legal sanction—of the direct producers from land and tools on one side, and the concentration of all the land and instruments of production in the hands of a few rich capitalists on the other.

There were several sources from which the capitalist class came: from merchants, who amassed great wealth from the trade in commodities, including spices, cloth, and slaves; from peasants, who were able to buy land and become capitalist farmers; and from master craftsmen in the towns, who "transformed themselves into small capitalists, and, by gradually extending their exploitation of wage-labor and the corresponding accumulation, into 'capitalists.'"[34] Far more important in the development of the bourgeoisie (or capitalist class), though, were the merchants, who moved beyond pure buying and selling to become full-fledged capitalists, that is, exploiters of labor as well as sellers of commodities. First, they "put out" material to artisans and laborers to be worked up, initially in the home or in small, scattered workshops, where the material would be made into finished commodities and sold for a profit. Later, these merchants would bring the laborers under one roof to work—the precursor of the modern factory.

This process was dependent upon two developments—the ability of merchants to amass fortunes in order to build larger capitalistic enterprises, and the availability of a labor force for these new enterprises. A period of "primitive accumulation" (or "original expropriation," as Marx also called it) was necessary, involving "the expropriation of the agricultural producer, of the peasant, from the soil" (as well as the destruction of the old skilled handicrafts of the villages and farms). The merchants were also able to build up their immense fortunes through conquest and forced labor in the colonies, with considerable aid from the state.[35]

The new class of wage workers was created by forcible theft of the common lands that the peasants had depended on for their livelihood. English landed gentry and big farmers, for example, taking advantage of the high price of wool, simply "enclosed" common lands, claiming them for their own, and turned them into sheep pastures. Soldiers were sent to drive tenants and small landholders by force from land they had tilled for centuries. Laws were then enacted in the fifteenth and sixteenth centuries that punished unlicensed begging and vagrancy with whipping, imprisonment, and, for a third offense, death.[36] "Thus were agricultural folk forcibly expropriated from the soil," wrote Marx, "driven from their homes, turned into vagabonds, and then whipped, branded and tortured by grotesquely terroristic laws into accepting the necessary discipline for the system of wage labor."[37]

In the history of capitalism, this process has never been repeated in exactly the same way. In colonial America, for example, the issue was not how to "free up" peasants to be workers, because there weren't any peasants to be had. Moreover, free immigrants tended to seek land rather than work in the towns and cities. Any employer that wanted to get around paying the relatively high wages that such a tight labor market allowed looked in two directions, both involving forced labor. Initially, the colonies imported indentured servants from Europe—people who signed a contract compelling them to work for several years for a master in exchange for passage.

In the South (and in the Caribbean), a system of plantation exploitation based on the use of slaves from Africa became the preferred method for securing a cheap and plentiful supply of labor. Alongside the creation of this new class of "free" laborers came the development of unfree labor in the New World. "In fact," noted Marx, "the veiled slavery of the wage-workers in Europe needed, for its pedestal, slavery pure and simple in the new world."[38]

Marx and Engels' condensed description of the rise of the bourgeoisie and of a world market in the *Communist Manifesto* emphasizes capitalism's dynamism, explaining how exploration, the discovery of the New World, and the spread of colonies gave a tremendous boost to commerce and industry.[39] But these proceedings, wrote Marx in *Capital*, were in truth "written in the annals of mankind in letters of blood and fire."[40] "The discovery of gold and silver in America," wrote Marx,

> the extirpation, enslavement and entombment in mines of the indigenous population, the beginnings of the conquest and plunder

> of the East Indies, the turning of Africa into a warren for the commercial hunting of black-skins, are all things which characterized the dawn of the era of capitalist production. These idyllic proceedings are the chief moments of primitive accumulation.[41]

The development of capitalism spurred the growth of mass industry and an integrated world market. Through sheer economic weight, and also by outright force, capitalism compelled the world to follow in its own image. "In one word, for exploitation, veiled by religious and political illusions," Marx and Engels wrote in the *Manifesto*, "it has substituted naked, shameless, direct, brutal exploitation."[42] Profit at any cost became the all-consuming, driving force of all economic activity. In *Capital*, Marx cites a trade unionist's chilling observation made in 1860:

> With adequate profit, capital is very bold. A certain 10 per cent will ensure its employment anywhere; 20 per cent certain will produce eagerness; 50 per cent positive audacity; 100 per cent will make it ready to trample on all human laws; 300 per cent, and there is not a crime at which it will scruple, nor a risk it will not run, even to the chance of its owner being hanged. If turbulence and strife will bring a profit, it will freely encourage both. Smuggling and the slave-trade have amply proved all that is here stated.[43]

Abundance and the end of inequality

Notwithstanding the "sordid avarice" and "selfish plunder" of class society, human productivity has advanced. As Marx and Engels so brilliantly summarized in the *Manifesto*, the rise of capitalism has created a world market, where each part of the world is dependent on the other; it has concentrated populations in large cities, subordinating the country to the town; and it has, by the development of centralized and expanded, machine-based mass production, created productive forces that far surpass all previous societies. The bourgeoisie "cannot exist without constantly revolutionizing the instruments of production, and thereby the relations of production, and with them the whole relations of society."[44]

Abundance is the first material premise that makes socialism more than just a utopian dream and makes its achievement really possible. As Engels explained:

> It is precisely this industrial revolution which has raised the productive power of human labor to such a high level that—for the first time in the history of humanity—the possibility exists, given a rational division of labor among all, to produce not only enough for the plentiful consumption of all members of society and for an abundant reserve fund, but also to leave each individual sufficient

> leisure so that what is really worth preserving in historically inherited culture—science, art, human relations—is not only preserved, but converted from a monopoly of the ruling class into the common property of the whole of society, and further developed.[45]

The decisive point for Engels is that this abundance has removed every excuse for the existence of a handful of exploiters, or for any kind of privation. Indeed, the existence of a ruling class has now long been a positive hindrance on human development.

Organized rationally, modern technology would lessen the burden of toil and free up the majority to participate fully in the running of society, by limiting "the labor-time of each individual member to such an extent that all have enough free time left to take part in the general—both theoretical and practical—affairs of society."[46]

Chapter Four

Marxist Economics: How Capitalism Works, and How It Doesn't

For most people, economics is a mystery better left unsolved. Economists are viewed alternatively as geniuses or snake oil salesmen. Either way, economics is dismal, boring, hard to understand, and ultimately a waste of time—something for snobby professors or wealthy investors, but not for us. Marx rescued economics from the economists and turned it into a tool for explaining inequality, exploitation, and crisis—as well as a way to end all three. At the heart of Marx's understanding of the economics of capitalism is the "labor theory of value." This concept is the foundation for the whole edifice of his theory of capitalism.

The labor theory of value

At the beginning of his most important work, *Capital,* Marx described capitalist wealth as an "immense accumulation of commodities."[1] In order to get a handle on how capitalism worked, Marx began with this basic cell of the capitalist organism—the commodity—and worked from here, adding more features to present a systematic picture of the whole. It is similar to the method used by scientists, who, if they want to figure out a problem, devise an experiment that eliminates as many variable factors as possible to isolate the phenomenon they want to investigate. They then work their way through a series of approximations, back to the real world. In one respect, Marx started this way because he wanted to isolate key factors of the system and then put them back together to show how they worked in their interaction and movement.

Another reason, however, was that he wanted to show how the appearance of "equal exchange" of commodities in the market camouflaged inequality and exploitation. At its most superficial level, capitalism can be described as a system in which production of commodities for the market becomes the dominant form. The problem for most economic analyses is that they don't get beyond this level.

Commodities, Marx argued, have a dual character, having both "use value" and "exchange value." Like all products of human labor, they have use values, that is, they possess some useful quality for the individual or society in question. The commodity could be something that could be directly consumed, like food, or it could be a tool, like a spear or a hammer. A commodity must be useful to some potential buyer—it must have use value—or it cannot be sold. Yet it also has an exchange value, that is, it can exchange for other commodities in particular proportions. Commodities, however, are clearly not exchanged according to their degree of usefulness. On a scale of survival, food is more important than cars, but that's not how their relative prices are set. Nor is weight a measure. I can't exchange a pound of wheat for a pound of silver. Yet there must be some quantitative relation that all commodities have. "Despite their motley appearance," Marx noted, commodities "have a common denominator."[2]

That common denominator is human labor. Almost all commodities are products of labor. Commodities exchange according to how much labor-time they take to produce. In the real world they don't, but Marx begins by constructing a simplified model of the economy for the reason already noted. Marx argued that the action of buying and selling mass quantities of commodities in the market reduced them, behind the backs of the producers, to quantities of abstract labor-time. The value of a commodity, that is, how much of it can be exchanged for another commodity, is determined by the amount of labor-time necessary to produce it. "Necessary labor-time" simply means the amount of time something should take to make, more or less, using prevailing techniques of production. If, for example, I build a kitchen cabinet with my hands in a day, when a cabinet of the same quality can be built in a factory in an hour, I can't sell mine for twenty-four times the price of the factory-made cabinet. A great portion of the time it took me to build the cabinet is therefore not "socially necessary" labor; it is, as far as the market is concerned, wasted labor.

The value of one commodity becomes expressed in a certain quantity of another commodity. This explains why, for example, a car is more valuable than a radio, or a computer is more expensive than a pencil. One took more time to make than the other.

Marx was influenced by the new economic analyses of the world presented by political economists like Adam Smith and David Ricardo. Writing in a period before the political triumph of the bourgeoisie, these economists wrote with a scientific rigor and honesty that later economists did not possess. "The value of a commodity," wrote Ricardo, "depends on the relative quantity of labor which is necessary for its production."[3]

This "labor theory of value" was dropped by later economists and replaced with the idea that value is equal to price, and price is determined by a commodity's relative scarcity or abundance. The idea that labor is the measure of value was too dangerous because it acknowledged that labor is the most important source of wealth under capitalism. But as Marx pointed out, supply and demand "regulate nothing but the temporary *fluctuations* of market prices. They will explain to you why the market price of a commodity rises above or sinks below its *value*, but they can never account for the *value* itself."[4] In other words, while the price of a shoe and the price of a shoestring might fluctuate, shoes always cost more than shoestrings because shoes embody more labor than shoestrings.

Of course, you can't look at a commodity—a car or a book or a shoe—and find any exchange value. All you'll see is that it is a useful object fashioned by human hands. That's because value isn't really a quality that any object has. Value is not really a thing, but a historically evolved relation between human beings that takes "the fantastic form of a relation between things."[5] Marx called the way in which capitalist society appears to imbue objects with characteristics they do not materially possess "the fetishism of commodities."[6] Value is a meaningless category outside of market relations, that is, outside a society in which independent, separate producers of commodities meet each other in the marketplace. All human societies produce useful things, but not all societies produce them for exchange, that is, as items to be bought and sold.

There is nothing quite as wonderful as money

"Yellow, glittering, precious gold," says Timon in Shakespeare's *Timon of Athens,* has the power to "make black white" and "foul fair," "wrong right, base noble, old young," and even make the "coward valiant."[7]

Money seems to possess mystical powers—pieces of paper or of metal which confer on their bearer the power to convert them into real objects of need or want. It has become a kind of fetish or idol that we bow down to. We are so accustomed to money's role in society that it appears to be the natural state of human society. But there's nothing magical about money. Indeed, while the Spanish conquistadors killed for gold because it was the quintessential form of money, in Inca society the metal was used for ornamentation.

"All the illusions of the monetary system," wrote Marx, "arise from the failure to perceive that money, though a physical object with distinct properties, represents a social relation of production."[8] What does that mean? Money arises first as a means of exchanging commodities between independent producers. In a community where all goods are produced and shared in common, everyone contributes their work as they can, and everyone takes out what they need from the common storehouses. Such a society does not need money, because there is no exchange of commodities taking place.

The earliest exchange took the form of barter. Different communities exchanged surplus products they did not need for goods produced somewhere else that they needed but could not produce themselves. One community would take some surplus salt and trade it to a community that needed it, in exchange for that other community's surplus obsidian or fur pelts, for example. The barter would be roughly based on the amount of labor it took for each community to produce its particular product. This kind of barter existed probably even in the earliest hunter-gatherer societies. But it was incidental trade, not essential to a group's survival. To put it another way, most of the use values a society produced never became commodities, but were directly consumed without being exchanged. As Marx wrote in *Capital*, a "relationship of reciprocal isolation," that is, a society of independent producers, "does not exist for the members of a primitive community of natural origin, whether it takes the form of a patriarchal family, an ancient Indian commune or an Inca State. The exchange of commodities begins where communities have their boundaries, at their points of contact with other communities."[9]

At first trade is incidental and haphazard, but then becomes regular and habitual, and on that basis communities can calculate roughly how much one sort of thing will exchange for another. Further economic development that comes with the accumulation of an agricultural surplus leads to a greater division of labor between agriculture and the manufacture of weapons, tools, and luxuries, for example. This in turn gives rise to more commodity exchange, not just between communities, but also within them—to the rise of a market for various goods, in other words. As trade becomes more regular, some kind of medium became necessary to facilitate exchange—a commodity that could be used to buy all other commodities, agreed upon by all. At first it was usually whatever moveable commodity was most coveted and in abundance: cattle, horses, shell beads, and later, with the development of metal work, precious metals like silver and gold.

It should be kept in mind, however, that only with the rise of capitalism did commodity production—production for the market—become the dominant form of production. In ancient Rome, for example, where the landowning class accumulated enormous estates that exploited great slave gangs, trade accounted for a small fraction of overall revenue.

Because of their malleable character, gold and, to a lesser degree, silver became the preeminent money commodities. States began producing silver or gold coins in various weights, stamped with the face of a particular ruler.

There is nothing magical about gold. It is a commodity like all others, whose value is measured by how much labor-time is necessary to produce it. By convention, it became what Marx called the "universal equivalent."[10] We could, by agreement, make shoestrings money, and then all prices would be quoted in shoestrings. The problem is that it would take too many shoestrings to buy something valuable, and so it's not a practical commodity to use as money. For related reasons, lead never became money. Lead money would require that we throw away our wallets for wheelbarrows.

The mystery of money is compounded by the fact that, as capitalism developed, money as a means of circulation and exchange was replaced by paper symbols of money, and coins debased with cheaper metals. But these coins and paper symbols were originally named after the gold or silver weights they were supposed to be symbols for (a pound note, for example, originally represented one pound of sterling silver). That paper notes are ultimately symbols of real value is demonstrated clearly by the fact that if a government prints money at will, its value depreciates.

In modern capitalist society, where everything can be bought and sold, money's historical origins are completely invisible, and it appears to possess a power independent of human will. "Men are henceforth related to each other in their social process of production in a purely atomistic way," wrote Marx of capitalism. "Their own relations of production therefore assume a material shape which is independent of their control and their conscious individual action. This situation is manifested first by the fact that the products of men's labor universally take on the form of commodities. The riddle of the money fetish is therefore the riddle of the commodity fetish, now become visible and dazzling to our eyes."[11]

Moses and the profits

Today, scarcely a few hundred years after the rise of industrial capitalism, the market has become such a normal feature of economic life that it is hard to conceive of any other economic mode of existence. Yet on the scale of human history it is a recent phenomenon. That has never stopped economists from projecting capitalist relations of production into the distant past. Marx ridiculed one economist who discovered the "origins of capital" in the "first stone which the savage flings at the wild animal he pursues."[12] The famous eighteenth-century economist Adam Smith put it most famously when he wrote of the "propensity in human nature" to "truck, barter and exchange."[13]

Goods can be collectively or individually produced, and they can be shared in common rather than exchanged. If I make myself an omelet, it is not a commodity. If I sell the omelet, it becomes a commodity. If I have a dinner party and make food for twenty guests, I have not made any commodities, because I am giving the food away. But if I invest in a restaurant, hire cooks and waiters, and sell food to twenty people, then we have capitalist food production, that is, production and sale for profit.

In addition to seeing trade as eternal, bourgeois economists also try to argue that the purpose of the capitalist market is simply to facilitate the distribution of products. The famous American economist Paul Samuelson described economics as "the study of how men [sic] and society end up choosing … to employ scarce resources … to produce various commodities and distribute them for consumption."[14]

The main things to note here are that, one, Samuelson equates economics with commodity production, and two, he sees the capitalist market as simply a distribution mechanism. The early economists, like Adam Smith and David Ricardo, were far more honest in their appraisal of the capitalist system that was growing up around them than its later apologists like Samuelson. "It may very justly be said," Adam Smith explained in one of his lectures, "that the people who clothe the whole world are in rags themselves"—an observation that could be made today as much as in the eighteenth century.[15]

Samuelson fails to define the most important thing that distinguishes capitalism from all previous forms of production—that it is a system whose main drive is profit-making. "Use-value," that is, the production and distribution of useful things, wrote Marx, "must therefore never be treated as the immediate aim of the capitalist."[16] All societies, to survive, must produce and distribute useful things. The question is, what is the specific form in which this happens and how does it change?

Samuelson would only be right if capitalism were a system of independent producers whose sole purpose for bringing their wares to market was to get other things (of equal value) they needed but did not produce. I make a pair of shoes, sell them for money, and use the money to buy some carrots you produced in your garden. Marx simplified this economic circuit with the formula C-M-C (commodity-money-commodity), or selling in order to buy. It is true that this describes in a way what most of us do—we sell (our labor) in order to buy (our necessities).

But for capitalists the purpose of selling is not to end up with other things of equal value. That would be a waste of time. The aim is to end up with more than what you started with. Capital, after all, is, in Marx's aphorism, "self-expanding value."[17] Though capitalists must produce something useful to someone in order to find a market for it, they are selling it merely for its value, i.e., for the profit it can bring them. Capitalists buy in order to sell. Marx described the basic circuit of capital M-C-M' (money-commodity-money), the M' representing the original investment plus the extra value realized after sale, or "surplus value."

To his contemporaries, who argued along the same lines as Samuelson would many years later, Marx had this admonishment:

> It must never be forgotten, that in capitalist production what matters is not the immediate use-value but the exchange value and, in particular, the expansion of surplus value. This is the driving motive of capitalist production, and it is a pretty conception that—in order to reason away the contradictions of capitalist production—abstracts from its very basis and depicts it as a production aiming at the direct satisfaction of the consumption of the producers.[18]

"Nothing will come of nothing"[19]

We have already shown how in a market economy commodities are exchanged as equivalents, that is, according to how much labor-time they contain. Yet, if equal values exchange on the market, according to the amount of labor-time they embody, where does profit come from? How is it that something can be sold for more than it was purchased for?

Perhaps that's all profit is—setting a price above cost. But if everyone selling commodities simply marked up the cost of their products, they would have to pay the inflated prices of other sellers who were doing the same thing. The nominal price of everything might go up, but the relative value of each thing wouldn't change, and no one would gain. In other words, the markups would cancel each other out, and still there would be no extra value. To use Marx's terms, no "surplus value" is added to commodities during the process of circulation. Surplus value has to come from somewhere else—in the process of production.

As already discussed, the historical evolution of capitalism not only involves a division of labor in which isolated individuals produce for the market, but also the separation of the means of production—the tools, machinery, and physical plant necessary for production—from the mass of workers. Once this separation takes place, the majority, the working class, are forced to sell their labor power to the minority, the capitalist class that has concentrated these means of production into its hands. And the owners of these means of production also, therefore, own the products of labor and the proceeds from their sale.

As Marx jokingly related, the marketplace where goods are exchanged is seen as "a very Eden of the innate rights of man" where "alone rule Freedom, Equality, [and] Property," because each "exchange equivalent for equivalent."[20] The exchange between labor and capital, where workers are forced by their very survival needs to seek employment, is portrayed as a fair exchange between two equal partners.

But if the value of a commodity is determined by the amount of necessary labor-time embodied in it, then what is the value of labor? Here we have to make a distinction between the value of labor expended (i.e., as it is contained in an amount of work or product), and the value of someone's capacity to labor. Marx argued that the value of this particular commodity, labor power, is equal not to what a worker can produce, but to the labor-time necessary to make up what it costs to keep a worker and a worker's family alive and functioning—the cost of producing, and reproducing, labor power. Marx put it this way:

> Like that of every other commodity, its value [labor power] is determined by the quantity of labor necessary to produce it.... A certain mass of necessaries must be consumed by a man to grow up and maintain his life. But the man, like the machine, will wear out, and must be replaced by another man. Beside the mass of necessaries required for *his own* maintenance, he wants another amount of necessaries to bring up a certain quota of children that are to replace him on the labor market and to perpetuate the race of laborers. Moreover, to develop his laboring power, and acquire a given skill, another amount of values must be spent. For our pur-

pose it suffices to consider only *average* labor, the costs of whose education and development are vanishing magnitude.[21]

In order to set their workplaces into motion, capitalists must bring together means of production (machinery and raw materials) and labor power, by purchasing them on the market. The workers, using the machinery, then work up the raw materials into a finished product to be sold. The capitalist totals the cost of the used-up raw materials together with the amount of incremental wear and tear and includes it in the final cost of the product. These things are products of past labor, and as they are used up they pass their value onto the new product.

But new labor-time is needed to work up the final product by current, living labor, and this also goes into the final value of the product. In other words, the value of a commodity is made up of two parts—"constant capital," or what Marx called "accumulated labor," passed on by the machinery (which adds its value as the machine wears out) and raw materials to make the product; and "variable capital," or what Marx called "living labor," which is added by workers in the immediate process of production. The capitalists pay for all the value added by accumulated, or "dead," labor—but only part of the value added by living labor. If a capitalist sold a product by the cost of wages plus materials and machinery wear and tear, there would of course be no profit—the capitalist would merely get back what he or she paid out.

It is, Marx noted, a "piece of good luck" that labor's use is greater than "what the capitalist pays for that use."[22] The value of labor power—that is, wages—is less than the value of output that this labor can produce. Put another way, workers produce enough value to cover the cost of their wages (variable capital) in just a part of the working day. The labor performed for the rest of the working day does not have to be paid for—it is "surplus labor," which produces "surplus value," and therefore when the product is sold, this unpaid portion goes into the pocket of the capitalists.

So the source of surplus value—and thus profits—is unpaid labor. The appearance of equality in the market, whereby a capitalist buys labor at a "fair price," as we now see, hides good, old-fashioned exploitation. Capitalists don't really care whether they're producing steel girders or computers, green beans or golf balls—as long as they end up with more money than when they started. And they can't do that without exploitation.

Bourgeois economists squirm around this fact. They have long tried to portray profit as the capitalist's "reward" for being a capitalist, for being so kind as to employ people who otherwise would starve, and for "risk-taking." Profit, according to the nineteenth-century economist John Stuart Mill, writing in 1848, represents a "recompense" for the capitalist's "forbearing to consume his capital for his own uses"—his "remuneration for abstinence."[23] According to this logic, if the capitalist is going to be so altruistic as to skimp on his own needs in order to invest his hard-earned capital, he should get a little back in return. Yet Mill is forced to admit that the surplus that accrues to capitalists must come from somewhere. "The cause of profit," he acknowledges, "is that labor produces more than is required for its support."[24] When put this plainly, it is hard to argue with.

The capitalist's "reward," in fact, results from workers' "forbearing to consume" the fruits of their own labor. Whether capitalists reinvest the surplus to expand production, or whether they spend it on their own personal luxury—and they do both in extravagant proportions—they are making use of wealth they did not produce. It is not abstinence on the part of the bosses, but on the part of the workers, that explains profit.

Competition: the big fish eat the small fish

"The bourgeoisie," wrote Marx, "cannot exist without constantly revolutionizing the instruments of production, and thereby the relations of production, and with them the whole relations of society."[25] Capitalists invest money to make more money, to make a profit. Their aim is "the unceasing movement of profit-making," as Marx put it.[26]

To make money, capitalists must sell their products on the market. There must be a demand for them. Yet individual capitalists don't control the market; rather, the market controls them. There is no central control, no planning in the economy as a whole—only the anarchy of the market, where individual producers are forced to compete with one another for market share, and only know once they've brought their products to market whether they will sell or not. This competition is what drives capitalists to continually revolutionize the means of production—to reduce production costs in order to cheapen their product and outsell their competitors. On pain of being driven into extinction by their competitors, capitalists must be able not only to sell most of what they produce, they must be able to sell it at a profit. In turn, they must be able to reinvest a part of this profit to expand production and beat out their competitors. As Marx wrote, "Accumulate, accumulate! That is Moses and the prophets! … Therefore, save, save, *i.e.*, reconvert the greatest possible portion of surplus-value, or surplus-product into capital! Accumulation for accumulation's sake, production for production's sake: by this formula classical economy expressed the historical mission of the bourgeoisie."[27]

Capitalists do this in two ways. First, they fight to lower wages as much as possible, to the barest minimum if they can get away with it. The smaller the portion of investment that goes to wages, the bigger the portion of a day's labor that goes unpaid and therefore counts as surplus value. Another way to do this is to make workers work longer hours for the same pay.

In the early days of capitalism, low wages and impossibly long hours (not to mention child labor) were the norm. But as capitalism developed, workers began organizing and winning a shorter working day, and many capitalists came to realize that if workers were going to successfully reproduce and raise the next generation of workers, they couldn't be worked to death through twelve-, fourteen-, or sixteen-hour workdays.

Capitalists increasingly turned to finding ways to increase productivity—the output per worker per hour. They did this first by making workers work harder to produce more in less time. "Taylorism," or the misnamed "scientific management"—named after Frederick Winslow Taylor, an early-twentieth-century engineer devoted to improving industrial efficiency—was all about managers observing workers and timing their movements in order to eliminate all "dead time" and "superfluous motion." The aim was to turn the worker into a streamlined automaton.[28] Capitalists think that by paying wages they earn the right not only to set a worker to work, but to determine the way in which the work is performed. A worker's own ingenuity in finding the most efficient way to perform a task, which he or she naturally uses to lighten the burden of labor, is taken by capitalist managers and used to squeeze out every last drop of work. One author describes the militarized methods of "scientific management" used on workers at United Parcel Service: "As every UPS employee works, every motion, every step, every turn has been studied, measured and timed. Drivers must work exactly according to UPS methods: enter the truck with the right foot, not the left; carry the package with the left arm, not the right; carry the truck keys on the little finger of the right hand, and on no other finger." One worker tells of how his wife calls him a "UPS robot."[29]

Bosses also squeeze out more work by investing in more and more productive machinery, thereby cutting down the cost per unit of production and undercutting the competition by underselling it. Going back to the labor theory of value, if machinery cuts down the time it takes to produce something, the product's value will go down. It is this that permits the capitalist to sell at or below the value of the competition. With each new invention, some capitalists will go bankrupt and others will adopt the new technology, wiping out the advantage of the capitalist who introduced it first. Then the whole process starts again.

Over the history of capitalism, productivity has soared astronomically compared to the sluggish pace of technological change in previous societies. "From the beginning of the nineteenth century to the end of the twentieth," writes economic historian Michel Baud, "worldwide per capita production was multiplied by a factor of six; since world population during this time span rose from one billion to six billion, we may estimate that total world production was multiplied by a factor of thirty-six."[30]

To give some examples, between 1973 and 1990, according to one study, world machine productivity increased by more than 50 percent.[31] Over the past three decades, changes in steel production methods have reduced by as much as 90 percent the time it takes to produce a ton of steel.[32]

Another result of capitalist competition is that individual capitals get bigger and bigger, not only by growing in size as profits are reinvested in bigger and more productive operations, but also because the big fish swallow the little fish. This happens by bigger firms buying out smaller ones, and by profitable enterprises buying out and scooping up ones that have failed. "One capitalist always kills many,"[33] as Marx wrote in *Capital,* calling this process the concentration (bigger units) and centralization (fewer units) of capital. This process doesn't mean that small businesses disappear, but it does mean that they become less and less economically significant. According to economist Michael Zweig, in the United States in 1995, 1.5 percent of businesses employed 34 percent of the manufacturing workforce. Ninety-six percent of manufacturing corporations took in only 12 percent of revenue, whereas the 1,134 largest corporations, less than 0.5 percent of all manufacturing corporations, "took in 71 percent of all manufacturing corporations' revenue and 83 percent of the profit."[34]

What therefore began as more or less "free" competition, over time, has led toward the growth of trusts, cartels, and monopolies, where a small number of huge corporations control an entire market. This process took off dramatically among the leading capitalist nations—

the United States, Britain, Germany, France, and Japan—in the late 1800s. For example, a wave of mass mergers during "the 1890s produced significant industrial concentration. For the U.S. economy as a whole there were over 3,000 mergers during 1898-1902. In 1901, US Steel Corporation was formed through a series of mergers involving about 165 separate companies. It became the world's first billion-dollar company and controlled over 60 percent of the U.S. steel market."[35]

But as these capitalist concerns grew, they became so large that they were driven beyond national boundaries, more and more into the creation of an integrated world market. Capitalism is the first economic system that is truly a world system that draws all corners of the planet into its "cash nexus."[36]

Capitalism creates tremendous wealth unheard of in previous times, but it does so in such a way as to deny the wealth it creates to the majority it exploits. In theory, the growth of machine-based manufacturing should be a means to lessen the burden of work, shorten the workday, and provide everyone with jobs. Instead, "Machinery in itself shortens the hours of labor, but when employed by capital it lengthens them; … in itself it lightens labor, but when employed by capital it heightens its intensity; … in itself is a victory of man over the forces of nature but in the hands of capital it makes man the slave of those forces; … in itself it increases the wealth of the producers, but in the hands of capital it makes them into paupers."[37]

Urban planner and historian Lewis Mumford, though no Marxist, could see how the vast gulf between the promise of technological progress and its capitalist application was a glaring contradiction at the heart of the system: "Those machines whose output was so great that all men might be clothed; those new methods of agriculture and new agricultural implements which promised crops so big that all men might be fed—the very instruments that were to give the whole community the basis of a good life, turned out, for the vast majority of people who possessed neither capital nor land, to be nothing short of instruments of torture."[38]

From its inception, capitalism has depended on there being a pool of unemployed and semi-unemployed workers that could be drawn on when growth is on the upswing, and tossed into the streets when growth slows down. This unemployed "reserve army" varies from country to country, but nowhere is it below 6 or 7 percent of the population, and in most places it is far larger. The growth of capitalism creates jobs—a fact frequently touted by presidents and pundits. However, over the long haul, capitalism is also a job-killer, as a result of the shrinking of the role of labor in the production process. Unemployment is an inbuilt feature of capitalism, one which capitalists depend on to discipline workers who have jobs. Instead of lowering everyone's hours and providing jobs for all, capitalism maximizes the hours and intensity of work, using the threat of unemployment, or the threat that other workers can always be hired for less, as a means for keeping the working class in check. In other words, the very process that improves productivity, and therefore the potential for a greater standard of living and less work for all, becomes under capitalism a means to increase exploitation at the worker's expense.

The crisis of overproduction

The unplanned, explosive growth that takes place under capitalism does not happen smoothly. It is accompanied by periodic crises that lead to mass bankruptcies and unemployment. From Marx's day to the present, the system has been prone to sudden periods in which growth gives way to stagnation and even decline, economic crises that "put the existence of the entire bourgeois society on trial, each time more threateningly."[39] These crises, absurdly, are not caused by shortages, like a crop failure or some other disaster. They are crises of *overproduction*. "Society suddenly finds itself put back into a state of momentary barbarism," wrote Marx and Engels in the *Manifesto*. "And why? Because there is too much civilization, too much means of subsistence, too much industry, too much commerce."[40]

Economic crises underline the fact that in our society production is not for human need, but for profit. Crises happen because capitalists can't sell their goods profitably, not because there aren't millions who could use the "overproduced" goods. Eight hundred million people go hungry every year. Yet economists can speak of a "grain glut" or a "pork glut." Steel is used to make so many essential products that literally hundreds of millions of people desperately need, yet the financial press can talk of a "steel glut." Millions can be homeless, yet there can be talk of a "real estate glut."

Supply and demand under capitalism have nothing to do with human need. In India, for example, 200 million people are malnourished. Yet in 1995, India exported $625 million worth of wheat and $1.3 billion worth of rice (a total of 5 million metric tons).[41] Profit alone "determines the expansion or contraction of production, instead of the proportion between production and social needs, the needs of socially developed human beings.... Production comes to a standstill not at the point where needs are satisfied, but rather where the production and realization of profit impose this."[42] Workers are reminded of this dynamic with each new crisis of overproduction—such as the laid-off workers at Enron in 2001, who were driven away from the front of company headquarters in Houston by mounted police. However, capitalism is actually a system of "constant *underproduction*," insofar as it fails to meet the basic needs of millions of people.[43] There cannot seriously be any talk of overproduction so long as the needs of the majority are not properly met.

A rational system based upon planned production would make use of the tremendous advances we have made in science and technology to first ensure that food, shelter, clothing, and adequate transportation were provided for all. As long as people need such things, there cannot be, in rational terms, "overproduction." But capitalism is anything but rational from that standpoint.

What causes these crises? Capitalist crises arise from the unplanned nature of the system. Overproduction of commodities is a regular feature of a system in which production and distribution are regulated not by a plan but blindly through the market. Because individual capitalists or corporations produce without knowing in advance what they can sell, and moreover, because they strive to expand production and capture more market share, there is a built-in tendency for capitalists "to produce without regard to the limits of the market."[44] Crisis—that is, a disruption in the process of production and circulation—takes place in the same way that trains become held up, one behind the other, if too many are launched on the same line. In fact, it is only through crisis, ultimately, that the system is able to restore some balance in the economy. One is a condition of the other.

This is not how mainstream economists see it. In flush times, bourgeois economists offer upbeat forecasts of endless prosperity ahead. "American industry and business have reached that status of well-being," wrote one economist not long before the Wall Street crash in 1929, "where it no longer has to fear a recurrence of the radical spreads from prosperity to depression that formerly afflicted business and industry."[45] Similarly effervescent claims were made during the Clinton boom of the 1990s: "The big, bad business cycle has been tamed," proclaimed the *Wall Street Journal* in 1996.[46]

But during the 1990s, boom did give way to bust, starting with a group of Asian economies and then spreading worldwide. In the first half of the decade, billions of dollars in investment flowed into the Asian "tiger" economies, fueling a boom in export-led growth that led economists to declare an Asian "miracle." But when exports slumped, these countries—Thailand, Indonesia, South Korea, Malaysia, and the Philippines—found themselves unable to repay massive loans extended to them by the International Monetary Fund (IMF) and other institutions, money they had borrowed on the assumption that sales would continue to grow. "Then, in 1997," noted the *Financial Times*, "came the panic: the net inflow turned into an estimated outflow of $12 billion. The swing in the net supply of private capital was $105 billion in just one year, a staggering 10 percent of the combined pre-crisis gross domestic product of the five countries."[47] Indonesia was devastated by waves of bankruptcies, and 20 million people were tossed out of their jobs—in a country that was already suffering from a staggering 38 percent unemployment rate.[48]

The Asian crisis then spread globally, to Russia, Latin America, and the United States. According to Joel Geier, "World trade declined for the first time since the Second World War," and in the United States, three million manufacturing jobs were wiped out. "In no other recession since the 1930s had there been so many, or such massive, corporate bankruptcies: Global Crossing, Enron, Conseco, WorldCom, Bethlehem Steel, United Airlines, Roadway, Budget Rent-A-Car, K Mart and Montgomery Ward, among others."[49]

Typically, economists failed to predict the crisis. One of the more serious economic commentators, Paul Krugman, explained to an audience of bankers in Hong Kong: "I was 90 percent wrong about what was going to happen to Asia. However, everyone else was 150 percent wrong—they saw only the 'miracle,' and none of the risks."[50] This wishing away of crisis goes back to the eighteenth- and early-nineteenth-century economists like J. B. Say and James Mill, who said that supply creates its own demand. There can be no "superfluity of commodities," argued Mill, because everything that is produced will find a buyer.[51] Marx was scornful of this idea. "Nothing can be more childish," wrote Karl Marx in *Capital,* "than the dogma that, because every sale is a purchase and every purchase a sale, therefore the circulation of commodities necessarily implies an equilibrium of sale and purchase."[52] It may be a comforting idea, but it hardly accords with reality, where economic crisis, at its core, consists precisely in the rupture between purchase and sale.

The cycle of boom and bust begins with an upswing or boom—periods of unrestrained growth in which capital investments in new technology and labor spur growth, more and more workers are hired, more and more goods are sold, and more and more profits are raked in. Capitalism's periodic crisis of every ten years or so is in part caused by the system's tendency toward this hyped-up, unplanned growth. But like a partygoer who has had too much fun, there is always the inevitable crash, hangover, and morning blues. "Business is always thoroughly sound, and the campaign in fullest swing, until the sudden intervention of the collapse," wrote Marx.[53]

As capitalism reaches the height of its boom phase, prices and wages start to go up in response to the increasing demand for labor and goods. Hungry for profits, capitalists borrow huge sums of money from banks and other lenders in order to get in on the profit bonanza, thereby taking on huge debts that they expect to pay off from windfall profits. Debt, in other words, helps prolong the boom by offering cheap money to investors; but it sets them up for bigger falls once the crisis hits, because it creates an intricate financial chain, that, if broken, threatens a financial crisis.

As the Polish-born Marxist Rosa Luxemburg wrote in her famous book *Reform or Revolution*, "When the inner tendency of capitalist production to extend boundlessly strikes against the restricted dimensions of private property, credit appears as a means of surmounting these limits in a particular capitalist manner."[54] Yet credit does so by extending production beyond the limits of the market, that is, beyond the point at which goods can be sold profitably. In addition, credit allows for more extensive market speculation—buying and selling based on price fluctuations. Credit ties capitalist investors together in a web of relations, so that when some capitalists go bankrupt, it threatens the health of the whole system. "Credit," wrote Luxemburg, "instead of being an instrument for the suppression or the attenuation of crises, is on the contrary a particularly mighty instrument for the formation of crises."[55]

As increasing costs eat into profits, and capitalists begin to worry about their profit rates, they begin to cut back on investments, producing first a crisis in what Marx called "department one," the department that makes the means of production (producer goods). Workers are then laid off in this sector, which restricts consumption and begins to produce a slump in sales in department two, the production of means of consumption (consumer goods).[56] Banks and other lenders begin calling in loans and refusing to grant new loans, which leads to bankruptcies, more layoffs, more slumps in sales, and so on in a vicious downward spiral. Crises can be mild or harsh, producing either stagnation or a decline in production (negative growth) for a shorter or longer period. But they always lead to mass layoffs, and therefore increased misery, for the working class and the poor.

"How are the relations corresponding to a 'healthy' movement of capitalist production to be restored?"[57] Marx asked. Growth can only be restored after a certain amount of capital is destroyed or drastically devalued and profit rates are restored. This happens in a number of ways. First, unemployment brought on by the crisis allows the employers to drastically lower wages without fear of retaliation. Second, the machinery and physical plant of bankrupt businesses is either destroyed or devalued. Some of the oldest, least productive plant and equipment are simply tossed on the scrap heap. The rest can still be operated, but not profitably by their owners, whose investments can't be recouped because prices are too low. The capitalists that have survived the crisis best now swoop in and buy up on the cheap the unprofitable or bankrupt businesses. The cheaper capital and wage costs mean that the remaining capitalists can once again begin to operate profitably. Then the whole cycle begins again.

Each economic crisis accelerates the centralization and concentration of capital, the big fish eating the small fish (or the profitable fish eating the bankrupt fish). State intervention can of course sometimes alter the character or the impact of the boom-bust cycle. For example, states can manipulate the supply of money or try to influence interest rates in order to make it easier or harder for capitalists to get loans. But these manipulations, because they attack the symptoms rather than the causes, cannot eliminate crises.

Capitalism's Achilles' heel

Underlying the cyclical crisis is a longer-term tendency for capitalist growth to produce relatively diminishing returns, a tendency for the rate of profit—how much money is made over and above investment costs—to fall over time.

We have already seen that the need to increase market share compels each capitalist to invest in technology that reduces the amount of labor-time necessary to produce a particular commodity, and therefore its cost. The invention, for example, of the oxygen furnace to replace the open hearth furnace in the 1960s reduced the time it took to melt iron from ten hours to forty-five minutes. Over the past thirty years, the number of man-hours required to produce a ton of steel has dropped by 90 percent among many U.S. manufacturers.[58] The capitalist who is the first to use labor-saving technology is able to undersell his or her competitors—at least until the competitors adopt the same methods. This boosts profits in the short term, but over time it shrinks the role of the very element in the production process that produces profit—labor. How can we explain this?

The working day can be divided into two parts—the paid and unpaid portion, as described earlier. Marx called that portion of the day in which workers produce the equivalent of their own wages "necessary labor," and that portion of the day in which they work for the bosses' profits "surplus labor." In product terms, a portion of the product when sold covers wages, the cost of materials, and the wearing down of machinery, and the other portion is extra, surplus value. Marx called the ratio of surplus labor-time to necessary labor-time "the rate of exploitation."

For example, if I work an eight-hour day, and it only takes four hours to make up the cost of my wages for the day, then I am working four hours of unpaid, surplus labor-time, which makes for a rate of exploitation of four hours to four hours, or 100 percent.

This rate of exploitation under capitalism is constantly increasing, because with increased productivity, the amount of time necessary to reproduce the necessities of workers goes down, leaving a greater portion of the day a grant of free labor to the capitalist. In other words, the time in the workday needed to replace the value of a worker's wage tends to go down, and the amount of unpaid labor as a result tends to go up. As a result of this, workers can actually receive a higher wage and still be more exploited than a worker who receives a lower wage. The reason this is true is because as productivity goes up, and more wealth is produced, a worker may receive more in absolute terms (i.e., in terms of purchasing power), but may receive less relative wealth, i.e., compared to what the boss is raking in.

As capitalism advances and grows, as it becomes more and more productive, the proportion between what a capitalist spends on technology and machinery ("constant capital") and what a capitalist spends on wages ("variable capital") grows. As productivity increases, labor becomes a relatively smaller and smaller component of production, and machinery a relatively larger and larger component. As capitalism advances, fewer and fewer workers set greater and greater amounts of machinery into motion.

For example, changes in the productivity of printing mean that today a few people operating presses that fill an entire warehouse can print tens of thousands of newspapers in a matter of hours. One result of this is that as capitalism grows and requires less labor to produce more goods, more and more workers become "superfluous."

This poses a problem, however. Since labor is the source of surplus value, its shrinking role in production means that surplus value, as a percentage of the total capital, also shrinks. Capitalists measure their success not by the rate of exploitation, but by the rate of profit—that is, by how much extra value they're getting compared to their total expenditure, which includes not only wages, but the costs of machinery and materials. Investing in new machinery leads over time to an increasing ratio of expenditure on machinery compared to labor. Since unpaid labor is the source of surplus value, even an increase in the rate of exploitation can't counteract this tendency for the rate of profit to fall.

Ironically, the very process that capitalists employ to outbid their competitors and raise their short-term profit rates tends over time to run down the general rate of profit. If this tendency played out to its logical conclusion, the system would simply grind down to a snail's pace and eventually seize up (capitalists would stop investing). But there are counteracting influences on falling profits that prevent it from reaching this point. Wages can be lowered below their value, and workers can be made to work harder. New inventions can not only reduce the amount of labor a given amount of capital sets in motion, it can also cheapen the means of production and therefore reduce the cost of investment. And finally, as we have seen, the devaluation of capital brought about by crisis also reduces the cost of inputs.

The decline in profits can also be offset by siphoning off some of the funds that could be used to invest in new machinery, using them instead to invest in luxury goods, financial speculation, or military spending. In the decades following the Second World War, for example, high levels of U.S. government spending on the arms race siphoned off money that otherwise would have led to accelerated growth, and by moderating the rate of economic expansion, prolonged the postwar boom. But this "permanent arms economy" could only forestall crisis, not prevent its eventual reemergence.[59] At a certain point, the diversion of funds toward military spending acted as a weight dragging down the United States in relation to its European and Japanese competitors, who, under the U.S.–NATO military umbrella, were able to invest in more advanced production techniques and expand in the private sector, without bearing the same cost of military expenditure. What first began as a means to prolong the postwar boom became over time a financial burden that intensified the crisis when it finally came in the 1970s.

Like all living systems that go through cycles, the cycles of capitalism's birth are different from the cycles in its old age. This is true for two reasons. The first reason is that competitive capitalism, over time, has turned into its opposite, monopoly capitalism. The relatively freer competition of early capitalism between smaller competing firms has given way to the concentration and centralization of capital into ever-larger units, and the merging of competing firms has in turn created a situation in which a small number of giant firms control entire industries, not just within nations, but internationally. Within international conglomerates, there is greater and greater planning, but anarchy still reigns in the world market as a whole. The character of competition between these giant firms becomes in some ways more regulated, involving greater and greater amounts of state intervention. But this is only because the potential impact of crises under these circumstances can be more severe.

Crises become crises not of one country, but of the world market as a whole, because competition takes place between giant international firms whose operations span the globe. States that only have control of one patch of territory find it harder and harder to affect world economic policy through their manipulation of currency and interest rates, let alone the economy on their own national turf.

But that doesn't mean that capitalism will simply collapse under its own weight as an old house crashes down from rot—an idea some have incorrectly attributed to Marxism. Challenging this idea, Trotsky, in comparing capitalism in its birth, maturation, and decay to the "the breathing of a human organism," nevertheless reminds us that capitalism, unlike human beings, does not die of "natural" causes, but only if the working class overthrows it:

> A man keeps drawing breath until he dies, but a youth, an adult and a dying man each breathe in a different way and the body's health may be judged by the breathing. But nonetheless a human being keeps breathing until death. Similarly with capitalism. The oscillation of these waves, these ups and downs are inevitable so long as capitalism is not snuffed out by the victorious proletariat.[60]

Chapter Five

No Power Greater—the Working Class

We have discussed two conditions that make socialism both possible and necessary. One is the tremendous abundance that has eliminated the social basis for inequality and want. The other is the yawning contradiction of capitalism that gives rise to periodic economic crises. The third is the existence of an exploited class that can, through its own collective action, usher in a new society.

"The mystics of the Middle Ages who dreamed of the coming millennium were already conscious of the injustice of class antagonisms," wrote Engels. But the possibility for bringing about a real millennium lies in the fact that "modern large-scale industry has called into being … a proletariat, a class which for the first time in history can demand the abolition, not of this or that particular class organization, or of this or that particular class privilege, but of classes themselves."[1]

The struggle between classes is as old as class society itself. The first recorded strike took place in the twelfth century BC under the reign of Ramses III. Building workers in Thebes who hadn't received their wages (paid in grain) walked off the job and took refuge in a temple until their demands were met. They also engaged in the first recorded sit-in.[2] According to historian W. W. Tarn, "strikes, an old Egyptian custom, were numerous; not merely riots in which the manager got beaten, but regular withdrawals of labor."[3]

More common in pre-capitalist societies, however, were struggles of peasants and slaves. Marx's favorite historical figure was the Thracian gladiator-slave Spartacus, who led seventy thousand slaves against the Roman Empire in 73 BC and destroyed several Roman armies before he was defeated.[4] Peasant rebellions were numerous in ancient China as well as in feudal Europe. Wat Tyler led a great peasant revolt in England in 1381 against attempts by the landlords to push them into serfdom, but it too was crushed.

What all these struggles have in common is that they could not impose their own social order on society because the material conditions did not exist for the elimination of exploitation. As A. L. Morton, author of the *People's History of England*, notes, "The peasants could combine for long enough to terrorize the ruling class but had no means of exercising a permanent control over the policy of government."[5] Sooner or later, the peasants would have to disperse and return to their land, leaving state power to others.

But the rise of capitalism and modern industry gathered a new class together into sizable workplaces, concentrated in large urban centers. That class is the modern working class, "that class in society which lives entirely from the sale of its labor and does not draw profit from any kind of capital."[6]

Work under capitalism becomes a completely alienating experience, where workers control neither the form nor the pace of their work, nor the fruits of their own labor. Under capitalism, work dominates the worker, rather than the other way around. Forced to work at the pace of the line, the machine, the stopwatch, or the manager, workers become alienated from their own intellectual and physical potential. Every advance in labor productivity appears to the workers as merely a means to increase the despotism of the workplace over them. In Marx's biting phrase, the worker is degraded to "the level of an appendage to the machine."[7] Work becomes not something fulfilling, "not the satisfaction of a need but a mere *means* to satisfy needs outside itself."[8] Workers come to dread work, doing it only because without it they and their families could not survive.

But workers are not merely victims. By "throwing great masses in one spot," wrote Engels, capitalism "gives to the proletarians a consciousness of their own strength."[9] The large workplaces—factories, hospitals, warehouses, offices—in which workers form part of an integrated whole, teach workers a collective discipline and cooperation that can be turned to their own advantage. Workers learn by their own experience that, in the words of American socialist Eugene Debs, "There is no escape for you from wage slavery by yourself, but while you cannot alone break your fetters," you can bring about change "if you will unite with all other workers who are in the same position that you are."[10]

The key weapon of collective action for workers is the strike. Workers may be dependent on the capitalist for a job, but the capitalist is dependent on workers for profit. "Without our brain and muscle, not a single wheel would turn" goes the popular labor song "Solidarity Forever."[11] When labor organizes and refuses to work, the wheels of industry cease to turn, and the bosses' source of profits dries up. Thus, strikes spark fear into capitalists because they are a reminder, to quote Lenin, that "it is the workers and not they who are the real masters."[12]

Workers first engage in strikes because they are the only means to secure immediate redress from their employer. But as an act of collective solidarity, striking helps workers identify their common interests with the whole working class—it helps them to attain class consciousness.

The significance of strikes cannot simply be measured by their immediate results, but by the way in which they build workers' confidence in themselves and increase their fighting spirit. "Every strike," wrote Lenin, "reminds the workers that their position is not hopeless, that they are not alone."

> See what a tremendous effect strikes have both on the strikers themselves and on the workers at neighboring or nearby factories or at factories in the same industry. In normal, peaceful times the worker does his job without a murmur, does not contradict the employer, and does not discuss his condition. In times of strikes he states his demands in a loud voice, he reminds the employers of all their abuses, he claims his rights, he does not think of himself and his wages alone, he thinks of all his workmates who have downed tools together with him and who stand up for the workers' cause, fearing no privations.[13]

As capitalist production becomes more centralized and concentrated, workers become powerful beyond their numbers. If productive power is concentrated, so is the impact on the system when workers withdraw from production. A strike of transport workers can shut down an entire city, even an entire country. A strike of thousands of workers in a factory that produces some essential part can shut down an entire industry. Workers are strategically placed at the heart of production and can therefore have a bigger impact in struggle than previously oppressed classes.

All previous revolutions merely replaced one kind of exploitation with another, one ruling class with another. But by the virtue of its collective social weight, the working class is the first exploited class in history with the capacity to reorder society in the interests of the majority. Workers can't divide up the factories, the hospitals, and the offices and share them out individually as peasants would the land—one person takes a steel furnace, another a lathe, another a heart monitoring machine. You can't parcel out an assembly line. The only way workers can abolish the conditions of exploitation is to collectivize and socialize the means of production and distribution.

But how do workers move from collective workplace action to actually challenging the entire edifice of capitalism? "In depicting the most general phases of the development of the proletariat," summarizes the *Manifesto,* "we traced the more or less veiled civil war, raging within existing society, up to the point where that war breaks out into open revolution, and where the violent overthrow of the bourgeoisie lays the foundation for the sway of the proletariat."[14] Real flesh was put on this poetic passage by the experience of the class struggle itself.

How Parisian workers taught Marx

In her book *Marxism and Freedom*, Raya Dunayevskaya reproves those who praise Marx's genius as though it got its impulse "from the sheer development of his own thoughts instead of from living workers changing living reality by their actions."[15] Marx and Engels, like the great Marxists who followed them, did not develop their ideas in a vacuum, but always in close contact with the class struggle.

"The first step in the revolution by the working class," Marx and Engels wrote in the *Communist Manifesto,* "is to raise the proletariat to the position of ruling class—to win the battle of democracy."[16] But there hadn't yet been any experience of what a successful workers' revolution would look like when they penned these words. The Paris Commune of 1871 gave them their answer. Before then, it might have been possible to argue that "winning the battle of democracy" would simply mean workers taking over the existing state machine—that is, getting workers' candidates elected to political office. But what the Paris Commune taught Marx and Engels was that "the working class cannot simply lay hold of the ready-made state machine and wield it for its own purposes."[17]

Why? We have already noted that the state is a product of class division. So long as society is divided into classes, a state is necessary to keep the exploited in check. In every prior revolution the rule of one class had been replaced by another, but the state remained—the bureaucracy and armed forces simply being transferred from the defeated to the victorious classes. Indeed, the bourgeois revolutions of the seventeenth and eighteenth centuries produced even more bureaucratically top-heavy, centralized states than the feudal society, with larger armed forces, too. "At the same pace at which the progress of modern industry developed, widened, intensified the class antagonism between capital and labor," Marx explained, "the state power assumed more and more the character of the national power of capital over labor, of a public force organized for social enslavement, of an engine of class despotism."[18]

In March of 1871, the workers of Paris, organized into the Parisian National Guard, defeated troops sent by France's leader, Louis Thiers, to disarm them. Thiers had just been elected head of France's new republic after Napoleon's Second Empire was disastrously defeated in a war with the Prussian army. The peace terms required France to disarm and allow Prussian troops to march into Paris.

But the Parisian working class refused to give up their arms. The workers rallied heroically around the National Guard militias, defeating Thiers' troops and compelling the bourgeoisie, their armed forces, and their political apparatus to flee Paris for Versailles.

The Paris Commune was elected on March 26, 1871, and remained in power for only two months. Fatefully, it didn't follow up its victory by pursuing and disarming Thiers' troops when they were retreating from Paris, nor did it attempt to spread the Commune to other cities in France. This gave Thiers the breathing space to reorganize at Versailles and eventually fight his way back into Paris. The Communards were crushed in an orgy of violence that took thirty thousand workers' lives.

Many socialists looked upon the Commune as a foolhardy exercise. Marx understood the Commune's weaknesses, but he leapt to its support, delivering a series of searing lectures in defense of Parisian workers and outlining the lasting significance of the Commune. It had abolished conscription and the standing army; it decreed the separation of church and state; it began to devise plans to reopen factories under the control of the workers in them; and it abolished night work for bakers. But these achievements were minimal compared to the most important achievement of the Commune. It was, argued Marx, "essentially a working class government, the product of the struggle of the producing against the appropriating class, the political form at last discovered under which to work out the economical emancipation of labor."[19]

The Communards turned direct suffrage into an instrument of the real rule of society by the majority. "Instead of deciding once in three or six years which member of the ruling class was to misrepresent the people in Parliament," wrote Marx in his brilliant work *The Civil War in France,* "universal suffrage was to serve the people, constituted in Communes."[20] One of the weaknesses of the Commune that Marx failed to note, however, was that suffrage was not universal—women were not given the right to vote. Nevertheless, one of the striking things about the Commune was the leading role played by working women both in its creation and in its defense. Wrote one reactionary opponent of the Commune, "During the final days [of the Commune], all of those bellicose viragos held out longer than the men did behind the barricades.... Many of them were arrested, with powder-blackened hands and shoulders bruised by the recoil of their rifles; they were still palpitating from the overstimulation of battle."[21]

Marx elaborated on what made the Commune so unique. First, elected delegates to the Commune were workers themselves, "revocable at short terms" and paid at "workman's wages." Moreover, the Commune wasn't set up to be a parliamentary talk shop, but "a working ... body, executive and legislative at the same time." The police—under the bourgeoisie a special force standing apart from society and enforcing the interests of the rich—were "turned into the responsible, and at all times revocable, agent of the Commune."[22]

Much has been made about the fact that Marx and Engels used the term "dictatorship of the proletariat" to refer to a workers' government—as if they meant rule by an individual or a minority. But they considered all forms of class rule, at bottom, dictatorships of one class over another. Engels answered this charge best when he said: "Of late, the Social-Democratic philistine has once more been filled with wholesome terror at the words: Dictatorship of the Proletariat. Well and good, gentlemen, do you want to know what this dictatorship looks like? Look at the Paris Commune. That was the Dictatorship of the Proletariat."[23]

Though it lasted only two months, the Paris Commune represented the first time workers had ever taken power. Its first lesson was that because the state exists as a repressive apparatus to maintain the power of the capitalists (a machine for the suppression of one class by another), it cannot simply be "seized" by workers, but must be dismantled and replaced by direct workers' democracy based on recallable delegates elected by workers themselves.[24]

In order to prevent the old order from regaining power, and in order to begin to implement a new social and economic program, workers need their *own* state, that is, the organization of the majority to suppress the minority. Only when class antagonisms are completely suppressed can society do away with the state. Thus by setting up a "commune state," workers abolish the basis on which classes—and the state upon which they rely—survive. "The state," Engels concluded,

> is nothing but a machine for the oppression of one class by another, and indeed in the democratic republic no less than in the monarchy; and at best an evil inherited by the proletariat after its victorious struggle for class supremacy whose worst sides the victorious proletariat, just like the Commune, cannot avoid having to lop off at once as much as possible until such time as a generation reared in new, free social conditions is able to throw the entire lumber of the state on the scrap-heap.[25]

The importance, and limits, of unions

The working class cannot achieve even the most minimal advance without organizing. The bosses have their civic organizations and their manufacturers' associations, and they have at their disposal a centralized state apparatus. Workers must have their own organizations if they are to fight back. The most elementary form of workers' organization is the union. Unions are training grounds that give workers confidence in their own collective power of resistance. They are the first line of defense for workers against attempts by capitalists to continually push down wages and conditions to their lowest possible level. Unions, to quote Eugene Debs, "have been a moral stimulus as well as a material aid to the worker," promoting "the class-conscious solidarity of the working class."[26]

Marx defended the importance of unions, but he also pointed out their limitations. "Trade unions," he wrote, "work well as centers of resistance against the encroachments of capital." However, "they fail generally from limiting themselves to a guerrilla war against the effects of the existing system, instead of simultaneously trying to change it, instead of using their organized forces as a lever for the final emancipation of the working class, the ultimate abolition of the wage system."[27]

Unions seek to change the terms of wage slavery, not to abolish it. The way unions are organized mirrors this reality. First of all, unions don't organize workers as an entire class—but by their particular crafts or industries. Unions therefore overcome some of the divisions imposed by capitalism—but they also reflect these divisions.

Unions require a full-time officialdom whose job is to negotiate with the employers. These leaders may come from the ranks, but their social position changes. Union officials no longer work and experience the same hardships as the workers they represent; their salary is dependent on members' dues, and is generally higher (in some cases a lot higher) than the workers they represent. Paradoxically, an organization created to advance workers' interests produces a leadership that can sometimes be a brake on the struggles that are necessary to advance those interests.

The German revolutionary Rosa Luxemburg, writing more than one hundred years ago, summed up the general outlook of this layer.

> The specialization of professional activity as trade-union leaders, as well as the naturally restricted horizon which is bound up with disconnected economic struggles in a peaceful period, leads only too easily, amongst trade-union officials, to bureaucratism and a certain narrowness of outlook. Both, however, express themselves in a whole series of tendencies which may be fateful in the highest degree for the future of the trade-union movement. There is first of all the overvaluation of the organization, which from a means has gradually been changed into an end in itself, a precious thing, to which the interests of the struggles should be subordinated. From this also comes that openly admitted need for peace which shrinks from great risks and presumed dangers to the stability of the trade-unions.[28]

This explains why workers of different unions experience the same things from their leaders—a reluctance to "risk" the organization in serious confrontations with employers, the tendency to prefer "peaceful" negotiation over a strike, the preference for limited strikes over bigger, more general confrontations. In many cases, union officials become so separated from the rank and file, so bloated with high salaries and so accustomed to hobnobbing with employers, that they are incapable of defending their own members.

This doesn't mean that union leaders can't or won't fight. Caught between the interests of the rank and file and the employers, union leaders are sometimes forced to lead battles simply to defend their organization. But by inclination they lean toward organizational conservatism, trying to harmonize the interests of labor and capital. The American trade union officialdom, wrote Debs, "are at once the leaders of labor and the lieutenants of capital, and who, in their dual role, find it more and more difficult to harmonize the conflicting interests of the class of whom they are the leaders and the class of whom they are the lieutenants."[29]

Unions more often than not tend to reinforce the separation between economic struggle and political struggle. Particularly in the United States, "pure and simple" unionism, which focuses only on economic issues, is rife. The strongest weapon of the unions—the strike—is reserved for economic issues, and even then is resorted to only reluctantly. Walkouts that make political demands on the government—for a shorter workday, against child labor, to oppose a war—are practically nonexistent. Instead, politics is typically restricted to union leaders mobilizing their members to vote for a bourgeois candidate.

These shortcomings in the U.S. labor movement have weakened and thinned its ranks in the teeth of employer attacks so that today the majority of workers are not members of unions. As in the 1930s, mass unionizing drives from below will be a necessary development in the reemergence of workers' struggle.

Two of the most important questions for the workers' movement therefore are: One, how can it move past the limitations of its own trade union leadership whenever the latter betrays workers' real interests; and two, how can the working class overcome "sectionalism," the splitting up of workers into separate parts on the basis of differences of wage levels, skill, industry, and trade, and develop forms of organization that mobilize and unite the working class as a whole? Unless workers are united as a class, they cannot challenge the system.

The role of socialists in the unions and in workplaces flows from this analysis. First, socialists support and promote the building of unions as elementary organizations of struggle. Second, socialists promote union democracy and shop-floor representation as the best means of mobilizing the real power of the unions—their rank and file. Third, socialists support union officials who are more willing to fight, while understanding that the nature of unions puts limits on how far these officials will go. Fourth, socialists have to build the confidence and organization of the rank and file to act, if necessary, independently of union officials. Finally, socialists need to organize groups of rank and file militants in various workplaces who are capable of linking together workers in different industries and struggles—so they can move from separate battles toward class-wide confrontations and, ultimately, to challenging the system as a whole.

Workers' councils: the modern form of workers' power

The undeveloped state of industry in Paris in 1871 meant that workers' delegates were elected to the Commune by neighborhood and out of the Parisian National Guard militias, which were dominated by workers. The Commune, though its delegates were elected based on geography, ended up being a de facto workers' organization because well-to-do Parisians had fled the city.

In later revolutions, after industrialization created bigger concentrations of workers in workplaces and urban centers, workers would create organs of struggle that were based on delegates elected from workplaces. The workers' council, or soviet ("council" in Russian), was first established during the 1905 revolution, as a strike committee in St. Petersburg, made up of elected delegates from the different factories, set up to coordinate a general strike. Though originally an organ of struggle, it soon came to be seen by workers and peasants all over Russia as an alternative center of governmental power.

In his description of the 1905 revolution, Leon Trotsky, who was elected president of the Petersburg Soviet, tells a story of how a clerk from an outlying province wrote a letter complaining of his mistreatment by a prince, addressing the envelope to "The Workers' Government, Petersburg"—and it was delivered.[30]

Workers created soviets again in the 1917 revolution—on a ratio of one delegate per one thousand workers. The soviets pulled along behind them all the oppressed and downtrodden. Soviets also spread to soldiers, sailors, and poor peasants. "No political body more sensitive and responsible to the popular will was ever invented," wrote the radical U.S. journalist John Reed of the Russian soviets he witnessed in 1918.[31] This was a superior form of organization to the trade unions because the soviets brought together workers across industries, uniting them nationally as a class. They were capable therefore of uniting and leading the whole class in struggle, and of leading all of the oppressed and poor peasants behind them.

But soviets were not some peculiar Russian invention. Similar institutions have sprung up time and time again, in all parts of the world, during periods of mass upheaval. The workers' councils in Germany in 1918, the factory councils in Italy in 1920, the workers' councils in Hungary in 1956, the *cordones* in Chile in 1973, the workers' *shoras* of the Iranian revolution of 1979, the "inter-factory committees" of Solidarnosc in Poland in 1980—all these are cases where workers, in the heat of mass struggle, created mass democratic organizations of struggle embracing the whole class, and basing themselves on workplaces as centers of workers' power. In every case, these institutions were set up to aid workers in both their political and economic battles. They didn't always get to the point where the movement became fully conscious of its potential to be an alternative to the old state, but in every case these council organizations represented a "dual power," the incipient power of the working class to reorganize the whole of society on democratic lines.

In the United States, the class struggle has at times been explosive and violent, but workers have never reached a point where council-type organizations have been created on a national scale. But there have been glimpses. In the mid-1930s, during the biggest rank and file strike wave in U.S. history, workers throughout the country, following the lead of auto workers in Flint, Michigan, sat down and occupied their workplaces to demand union recognition. By the end of 1937, almost half a million workers had participated in sit-down strikes.[32]

In Seattle in 1919, almost all the city's workers struck in solidarity with thirty-five thousand long shore workers who had previously struck for higher pay. A strike committee was formed of elected representatives from each of the 101 striking union locals. The strike committee discussed not only issues of how to conduct the strike, but how to keep basic services running during the strike, like emergency health care and milk delivery. The general strike naturally raised the practical issues of workers' control of production and distribution. An editorial written by Anna Louise Strong on the eve of the strike expressed the potential:

> Labor will not only SHUT DOWN the industries, but labor will REOPEN, under the management of the appropriate trades, such activities as are needed to preserve public health and public peace. If the strike continues, Labor may feel led to avoid public suffering by reopening more and more activities, UNDER ITS OWN MANAGEMENT.[33]

The strike ended, under pressure from conservative union leaders, in six days. Nevertheless, it posed in embryo the question of who runs society and in what way.

A workers' council is even more democratic and representative than a strike committee based upon union delegates, since it brings together delegates elected from different workplaces. But for committees of workers' delegates to go from being an embryo of a new society to being an alternative government, they must not only become a national form of organization that embraces the majority of workers in the cities and towns, they must also be able to do away with the old state structure, as Marx and Engels pointed out in their writings about the Paris Commune. These soviet-type organizations begin as organs of struggle that help coordinate the fight, but they can become the basis of a new way of organizing society.

We want no condescending saviors

The 1871 rules of the International Workingman's Association, written by Marx, declared: "The emancipation of the working class must be conquered by the working classes themselves."[34] They cannot be freed by liberal reformers. They cannot be freed by a heroic band of guerrillas. They cannot be freed by a small band of terrorists with dynamite. And they cannot be freed by any party or group that stands above or outside their own struggles. The English version of the anthem of the international socialist movement puts the same idea in the negative:

> No savior from on high delivers
> No faith have we in prince or peer
> Our own right hand the chains must shiver
> Chains of hatred, greed and fear[35]

Eugene Debs urged workers in his speeches to fight for themselves and not wait for someone to fight for them. "I cannot do it for you, and I want to be frank enough to say that I would not if I could. For if I could do it for you," he stressed, "somebody else could undo it for you."[36]

Marx's phrase underscored an idea that was fundamentally different from a whole number of radical and socialist ideas current then, and which in various forms are still current now. These ideas can be roughly placed under the category "substitutionism." In Marxist terms, any group, class, or party that substitutes its own activity for that of the class it claims to emancipate, that acts as a proxy in the name of and on behalf of the working class and the oppressed, is substitutionist.

In the early days of capitalism, when the working class was in formation, and had yet to systematically assert itself in collective struggle, substitutionism was historically inevitable. The utopian socialists, for example, substituted their own schemes for a better world for workers' own struggles, seeing workers not as the creators of the new world, but merely its beneficiaries.

Marx and Engels also contended with the conspiratorial radicalism of the French socialist August Blanqui and the Russian anarchist

Mikhail Bakunin. Engels criticized the Blanquist belief that "a small well-organized minority should attempt a revolutionary uprising at the right moment," that would "carry the mass of the people" with them.[37] Marx and Engels likewise rejected Bakunin's elitist notion that a secret society of "a hundred powerfully and seriously allied revolutionaries" acting secretly "like invisible pilots in the thick of the popular tempest," could act as the spark for a Europe-wide revolution.[38] Marx criticized these revolutionaries for substituting their urgent desire for revolution with the practical conditions and patient work necessary for its realization. "What childish naiveté," he complained, "to advance impatience as a convincing theoretical argument!"[39] But what Marx and Engels took issue with above all in these radical schemes was the way in which the actions of minorities were meant to replace the self-activity of ordinary people acting to free themselves from their chains.

Leon Trotsky made the same case against individual acts of terrorism. Even the smallest strike, sit-in, or street protest can boost the self-confidence of workers, whereas an individual act of violence or terror has the opposite effect. "In our eyes," wrote Trotsky,

> individual terror is inadmissible precisely because it belittles the role of the masses in their own consciousness, reconciles them to their powerlessness, and turns their eyes and hopes towards a great avenger and liberator who some day will come and accomplish his mission.[40]

Trapped by their own circumstances?

According to the sixteenth-century French essayist Michel de Montaigne, when three Indians from the coast of Brazil paid a visit to Charles IX of France in 1562, someone asked them "what they thought of all this" and "what they had been the most amazed by" during their stay in France. The Indians, who knew no class division in their own society, "have an idiom in their language which calls all men 'halves' of one another," and they observed that French society was divided into very unequal "halves." They noticed, wrote Montaigne, that

> there were among us men fully bloated with all sorts of comforts while their halves were begging at their doors emaciated with poverty and hunger: they found it odd that those destitute halves should put up with such injustice and did not take the others by the throat or set fire to their houses.[41]

Transported to the United States in the twenty-first century, the Native Americans might have the same question. They would see a society where the richest fifth of Americans have nine times more wealth than the poorest fifth. Why don't the vast majority, whose labor makes such obscene wealth possible, take the 1 percent "by the throat, or set fire to their houses"? The answer, of course, is that rebellions and revolutions have occurred throughout history. However, it must be admitted that the oppressed are not in a permanent state of rebellion—otherwise capitalism would have already been overthrown.

The answer that is usually given as to why workers have yet to achieve socialism is a very depressing one. In George Orwell's *1984*, the main character, Winston, a low-level government bureaucrat beaten down by the all-seeing, all-knowing dictatorship of "Big Brother," understands that the "proles"—the working class of Oceania—are the only hope if the system is to be overthrown. "They needed only to rise up and shake themselves like a horse shaking off flies," Winston imagines.[42] But Winston is full of despair, because apparently this is completely impossible. As he wanders through the streets of a working-class district, he hears loud shouts in the distance, imagining that it might be a protest—only to find a group of women fighting over a saucepan.

"Heavy physical work," wrote Orwell of the proles, "the care of home and children, petty quarrels with neighbors, films, football, beer, and, above all, gambling filled up the horizon of their minds."[43] In his secret diary, Winston describes the apparent dilemma that makes a workers' revolution impossible: "Until they become conscious they will never rebel, and until after they have rebelled they cannot become conscious."[44]

It is no accident that *1984* is part of practically every high school curriculum. It reinforces what is a widespread prejudice in the United States: that workers are too divided, too distracted by "bread and circuses," and too mentally limited to change the world. This bad caricature of the working class is widespread. It is an elitist view, to be sure, often argued by educated middle-class professionals and a ruling class who look down upon workers and think of themselves as too "cultured" and "intelligent" to ever be duped or hoodwinked—except when it comes to blindly accepting the idea that the meek cannot inherit the earth.

The truth is that workers hold all sorts of ideas about the world they live in. Some of those ideas express a rejection of the status quo; others express acceptance of it. The system is buttressed ideologically—on television, radio, in schools, in the newspapers, from the pulpit. Workers are encouraged to accept the ruling ideology—that poverty, greed, racism, inequality, and war are products of immutable human nature; that workers are too uneducated, too stupid to run society; that only the well-born can rule; that revolutions end in tyranny; and that this, as Preceptor Pangloss, the "oracle" of a baron, tells us in Voltaire's *Candide*, is the "best of all possible worlds."[45]

One reason that ruling ideas can take hold at all is simply inertia—the inherent conservatism built into a set of human social relations once they are established. "Society does not change its institutions as need arises, the way a mechanic changes his instruments," wrote Trotsky. "On the contrary, society actually takes the institutions which hang upon it as given once for all."[46] The state is always prepared to resort to legal repression and even armed force if it is threatened. But for much of the time, force isn't necessary to maintain order. So long as a majority of people give their passive consent to the status quo, force isn't necessary.

In order to change society, workers must become conscious of their position as the oppressed class and organize themselves as a class to fight for their own interests. According to Orwell's Winston, this is impossible. According to historical experience, it is not. Consciousness is not static or fixed simply because the bosses wish it were. Workers are not automatons that accept all the ruling ideas of society without question. If that were true, all radical change would be impossible. Workers accept the everyday "common sense" ideas—that is, ideas that reinforce existing conditions—as well as ideas that challenge them. To quote the Italian revolutionary Antonio Gramsci, a worker actually carries in his or her head two contradictory consciousnesses, "One which is implicit in his activity and which in reality unites him with all his fellow-workers in the practical transformation of the real world; and one, superficially explicit or verbal, which he has inherited from the past and uncritically absorbed."[47]

This contradiction is a reflection of the fact that capitalism both divides and unites workers, that is, it brings them together in large numbers and at the same time fosters competition between them. "Competition separates individuals from one another, not only the bourgeois but still more the workers," wrote Marx and Engels,

> in spite of the fact that it brings them together. Hence it is a long time before these individuals can unite.... To demand the opposite would be tantamount to demanding that competition should not exist in this definite epoch of history, or that the individuals should banish from their minds relationships over which *in their isolation* they have no control.[48]

Workers are forced to fight back—to stop a wage or benefit cut, to fight against a draconian labor law, or (for undocumented workers) to fight for amnesty. Hal Draper, a U.S. socialist who wrote an excellent series of books on Marx's ideas, wrote,

> To engage in class struggle it is not necessary to "believe in" the class struggle any more than it is necessary to believe in Newton in order to fall from an airplane.... The working class moves toward class struggle insofar as capitalism fails to satisfy its economic and social needs and aspirations, not insofar as it is told about struggle by Marxists.[49]

In the course of struggle, the gap between workers' own experience and the ruling ideas widens to the point where workers begin to reject them—the ruling ideas begin to break down. In big struggles, these ideas break down very quickly. "A strike," wrote Lenin, "opens the eyes of the workers to the nature, not only of the capitalists, but of the government and the laws as well."[50] The important thing is that a group of workers decide to take action. When they do, their experience opens their eyes to the truth, which in turn gives them more confidence to fight. Workers who strike quickly learn that the police and courts are set up against them and for the employers—and also that the press defends employers and tries to present workers' interests in a bad light. One struggle gives heart to others to struggle, and one struggle piggybacks on another.

It is the fight against suffering and exploitation, rather than suffering itself, that transforms consciousness. In isolation or defeat, workers are more easily prone to turn their suffering and bitterness on each other, or on scapegoats. But the experience of struggle teaches solidarity to workers, calling into question divisions of race, sex, and nationality that are deliberately fostered between them by the ruling class. They learn that whenever the employers or the state can pit them against each other they are weak; and when they unite, they are strong. They learn that if any part of the working class or oppressed is held down, it makes it easier for the bosses to hold all workers down.

Socialism doesn't come about through education. No matter how much propaganda socialists put out, it wouldn't be enough to convince everyone to be socialists. This would of course be preferable—we'd simply send out a series of chain letters explaining why we need to reorganize society along rational lines, and eventually we'd reach everyone. Revolution wouldn't be necessary because the vast majority would simply say to the exploiting minority, "Your time is up." Unfortunately, it doesn't work that way. For one thing, the bourgeoisie has control of the mass media and can always reach more people.

In fact, it is primarily struggle that teaches. As Lenin noted:

> When bourgeois gentry and their uncritical echoers, the social reformists, talk about the "education of the masses," they usually mean something schoolmasterly, pedantic....
>
> The real education of the masses can never be separated from their independent political, and especially revolutionary, struggle. Only struggle educates the exploited class. Only struggle discloses to it the magnitude of its own power, widens its horizon, enhances its abilities, clarifies its mind, forges its will.[51]

It was this concept that prompted Marx to remark, "Every step of real movement is more important than a dozen programs."[52] That is why in periods of relative calm, when there is little struggle, the possibility of fundamental change seems remote. But beneath the inertia are molecular processes that are creating the dry conditions in which a spark can ignite the tinder and cause a conflagration.

It is in fact partly the natural conservatism of mind—the way in which people cling to old ideas long after they make sense—that gives rise to social explosions. As Trotsky concluded from his participation in the Russian Revolution,

> The swift changes of mass views and moods in an epoch of revolution ... derive not from the flexibility and mobility of man's mind, but just the opposite, from its deep conservatism. The chronic lag of ideas and relations behind new objective conditions, right up to the moment when the latter crash over people in the form of a catastrophe, is what creates in a period of revolution that leaping movement of ideas and passions which seems to the police mind a mere result of the activities of "demagogues."[53]

A statement issued by the founding meeting of the united Shoras (Iranian workers' councils) in March 1979, after the fall of the Shah, shows the way in which revolutionary struggle raises the working class up and makes it the natural leader of all the oppressed. "We the workers of Iran," the statement began, "through our strikes, sit-ins and demonstrations, overthrew the Shah." Workers of Iran put up with privation and death "in order to create an Iran free from repression, free of exploitation. We made the revolution in order to end unemployment and homelessness, to replace the SAVAK [the Shah's secret police]-oriented Syndicate with independent workers' Shoras, formed by the workers of each factory for their own economic and political needs." Among the statement's demands were free health care, housing benefits, an end to the intervention of armed forces to break up strikes, and free nursery services at work.[54]

Farrell Dobbs, a Trotskyist worker who played a leading role in the 1934 Minneapolis Teamsters' strike, one of the most important rank and file–led strikes of the era, answered the naysayers against workers' capacity for struggle like this:

> Wiseacres of the day spoke pontifically about the "passivity" of the working class, never understanding that the seeming docility of the workers at a given time is a relative thing. If workers are more or less holding their own in daily life and expecting that they can get ahead slowly, they won't tend to radicalize. Things are different when they are losing ground and the future looks precarious to them. Then a change begins to occur in their attitude, which is not always immediately apparent. The tinder of discontent begins to pile up. Any spark can light it, and once lit, the fire can spread rapidly.[55]

Chapter Six

Democracy, Reform, and Revolution

Earlier we discussed the Hobbesian idea that the state is there to prevent a war of each against all. The "Hobbes lite" view, appropriate to modern liberal theories about democracy, is that the state's role is to balance various competing interests—business, labor, women, minorities, immigrants, farmers, consumers, and so on. In this view, sometimes called pluralism, the role of the state is to reconcile various competing interests so that "all the active and legitimate groups in the population can make themselves heard at some crucial stage in the process of decision."[1] The state in this view is a neutral body standing above society and arbitrating between competing interests. The U.S. government, our history books tell us, has a system of "checks and balances" that guarantees this fairness.

But does this view correspond to reality? For things to really work this way, the various groups would need to have more or less equal clout. But this view of power obscures the fact that in a capitalist society some interest groups are more "legitimate" than others. Pluralism disguises the fact that society contains a fundamental *class* divide, and that the basis of political power is economic rather than geographic or territorial. The fact that most people over eighteen can vote in this country does not mean that we all have an equal say or equal power. "One man, one vote is, apparently, the be-all and end-all of democracy," observed the late British socialist journalist Paul Foot. "One man may own six newspapers, two television stations and six factories. Another may earn 20 pounds a week, 7 pounds of which goes in rent and 13 of which has to make do for his family. Each has one vote. But are they equally represented in society?"[2]

In the United States, wealth is concentrated at the top. According to a 1999 United for a Fair Economy study, the top 1 percent of households has more wealth than the bottom 94 percent combined—holding nearly half of all financial wealth.[3] Since then, the disparities have only widened. In 2003, the top 1 percent of households owned 57.5 percent of corporate wealth, while the poorest fifth owned .6 percent.[4] In a society based upon massive concentrations of wealth on the one end, and poverty and low wages on the other, one billionaire has far more political clout than even millions of workers, as far as voting goes. The economic pecking order determines the political pecking order.

Marx developed a far more accurate theory of the state than the pluralists, arguing in the *Communist Manifesto* that, "the executive of the modern state is but a committee for managing the common affairs of the whole bourgeoisie."[5] That doesn't mean that the state directly represents the interests of each individual capitalist. Sometimes it sacrifices the interests of some businesses over others. But overall, it manages the "common affairs" of the wealthiest class.

Of all the various groups that seek "access" to government, therefore, the ones that get the biggest hearing are the wealthiest. And here we are not only speaking of individuals, but of colossal institutions—banking conglomerates, giant corporations, and so on—less than 1 percent of which controls two-thirds of the corporate assets of the entire U.S. economy.[6] "Parliamentarism," wrote the socialist Paul Lafargue, "is a system of government in which the people acquires the illusion that it is controlling the forces of the country itself, when, in reality, the actual power is concentrated in the hands of the bourgeoisie."[7]

The ruling capitalist class exercises its dominance over the state in a number of ways. First of all, as is fitting of a society based upon the market, politicians are bought and sold to the highest bidder—hence the billion-dollar corporate lobbying industry in Washington, the international capital of influence peddling. Occasionally the outright bribery becomes so blatant and widespread that politicians are forced to cry "disgrace," hang a few scapegoats out to dry, and pass laws that promise to stamp out corruption for good. But soon new legal loopholes are discovered (or created), and the whole filthy process begins again. Secondly, the entire system is set up so that it is impossible to run even a local candidacy without enormous sums of money.

Capitalists don't need direct control of the state for it to act more or less in their interests. As Michael Parenti, in his book *Democracy for the Few,* notes:

> Because business controls the very economy of the nation, government perforce enters into a unique and intimate relationship with it. The health of the capitalist economy is treated by policymakers as a necessary condition for the health for the nation, and since it happens that the economy is in the hands of large investors, then presumably government's service to the public is best accomplished by service to the investors. The goals of business (rapid growth, high profits, and secure markets) become the goals of government, and the "national interest" becomes identified with the dominant capitalist interests.[8]

What concerns capitalists most is ensuring that nothing interferes with their ability to make money. They are more or less content with any state that can guarantee this, whether it is a democratic republic, a constitutional monarchy, or—if necessary to holding popular resistance in check—a military dictatorship. Capitalists will even put up with a fascist dictatorship, like Hitler's, if such a state promises to prevent revolution. But even the most democratic government sets up legal loopholes that permit it to suspend democratic rights when "national security" is threatened. In 1851, Karl Marx noted that the French Constitution "guarantees liberty," save for "exceptions made by law." "For each paragraph of the constitution contains its own antithesis, its own Upper and Lower House, namely, liberty in the general phrase, abrogation of liberty in the marginal note."[9] The marginal note comes in handy during periods of civil unrest or wartime, as a means to suppress dissent.

The Patriot Act, passed by the second Bush administration not long after the September 11 attacks, is the most recent version of what Marx described. But it has plenty of antecedents in U.S. history. The Alien and Sedition Acts of 1798 gave the government the right to imprison or deport any "alien" considered a threat to the U.S. government, and made any spoken or printed criticism of the government, or opposition to any of its laws, punishable by two years in prison. The Espionage Act of 1917 "made it a felony to make 'false statements' or statements that might cause 'insubordination' or 'disloyalty' in the armed services or statements that could 'obstruct' enlistment into the armed services."[10] The Sedition Act of 1918 made it a crime in wartime to use "disloyal, profane, scurrilous, or abusive language" about the United States government, its flag, or its armed forces.[11] The Smith Act of 1940—used in 1941 to prosecute and imprison eighteen members of the Socialist

Workers' Party—made advocating or organizing for the overthrow of the government punishable by up to twenty years in prison.[12]

Thousands of socialists and anarchists—including both native-born and immigrant workers—were spied on, imprisoned, deported, beaten, tortured, and otherwise abused during the First World War. Montana's Sedition Law, which became the prototype of the national law, imprisoned dozens of Montanans under its statutes, which included making it a crime to speak German. One of the biggest backers of the law was Anaconda Copper Mining Company, who saw the law as a means to quell labor unrest.[13] The U.S. ruling class's contempt for genuine freedom of speech was summed up by the Mexican anarchist Enrique Flores Magón, who served three years in U.S. prisons between 1918 and 1920 for publishing a radical newspaper: "[T]his ill-called Country of Liberty has now converted into a crime punishable by twenty years in the Penitentiary anyone who preaches free thought and free speech." This statement earned him deportation back to Mexico.[14] Eugene Debs, in his antiwar Canton Speech (which also landed him in jail), sarcastically remarked, "it is extremely dangerous to exercise the constitutional right of free speech in a country fighting to make democracy free for the world."[15]

Ordinary workers have had to fight for what limited democracy capitalism is willing to grant every step of the way. In Britain, the working class had to organize mass protests in order to win complete universal male suffrage without property restrictions—and women didn't win the right to vote in the United States and Britain until the twentieth century. Long after slavery was abolished in the United States, millions of Blacks in the South—and many poor whites—were denied the right to vote. Many ruling classes were at first fearful that complete universal suffrage might threaten their rule. But universal suffrage, as well as formal equality, free speech, and a number of other important democratic rights, turned out not to be such a grave threat to capitalism after all.

Freedom of the press comes most readily to those who have the millions of dollars necessary to own one. There is formal legal equality in many societies, but the poor are the law's most common victims. The nineteenth-century French writer Anatole France has a character in one of his books, the poet Choulette, who mocks the "the majestic quality of the law which prohibits the wealthy as well as the poor from sleeping under the bridges, from begging in the streets, and from stealing bread."[16] Debs joked that in the United States, the "judicial nets are so adjusted as to catch the minnows and let the whales slip through."[17] A shoe fitter, a socialist who participated in the 1877 St. Louis General Strike, put a fine point on this double standard: "A man who stole a single rail is called a thief, while he who stole a railway is a gentleman."[18]

The formal equality expressed in the law hides extreme inequality—the most egregious modern example being the 1986 law establishing a hundred-to-one disparity of sentencing between convictions for crack vs. cocaine possession, crack being the drug of the poor, cocaine of the more affluent. Under the law, possession of 500 grams of cocaine is punishable by the same prison time as possession of 5 grams of crack; possession of 5 kilos of cocaine or 50 grams of crack results in the same prison sentence.[19]

True, capitalists who get caught defrauding other capitalists are sometimes punished by the state, as were the heads of WorldCom and Enron, in order to placate other capitalists but also to demonstrate that the judicial system "works." But often the punishment is just ineffectual wrist-slapping. When a conglomerate of companies, including General Motors, Standard Oil, and Firestone, conspired to rip up the electric trolley system across the nation in the mid-1930s and get cities to convert to GM buses and cars, a judge fined each company five thousand dollars, and a handful of executives a dollar each. By 1955, the corporations had destroyed 88 percent of the country's electric trolley system. In the words of one former executive, this example "suggests that the larger the crime, the more the boundaries between 'crime' and 'business as usual' begin to blur. As Atlanta mayor and former United Nations ambassador Andrew Young once said, 'Nothing is illegal if 100 businessmen decide to do it.'"[20]

A major portion of the state—the military, police, and intelligence agencies, the state bureaucracy, and much of the judiciary—isn't even subject to elections. The voting population doesn't make crucial decisions like whether or not to go to war, make treaties, or conclude trade agreements. We don't get to vote on military spending or what kind of health care system we have.

And of course there is no workplace democracy. At work, the employer is a despot, setting the nature and pace of work, and hiring and firing at will (especially if there is no union). If we don't like our pay, benefits, or working conditions, we can't fire our boss or vote to change anything. We're told instead, "If you don't like it, go someplace else and work." This is the limit of our "freedom" as workers, even though we spend at the very least half of our waking life at work.

Virtually every important decision that affects our lives is set beyond the reach of the majority. Parliamentary democracy—in which we choose unaccountable misrepresentatives every two, four, or six years—has been very successful in providing the illusion of real democracy in a society where a small number of very wealthy people and the bureaucrats who serve them make all the important decisions. Workers have an interest in fighting for the freest and most complete democracy; whereas the employing class aims to stunt and curtail democracy, and, when necessary, even eliminates it.

The Democratic Party and the limits of reformism in the United States

Illusions in the Democratic Party as a party of the people have been the great Achilles heel of the left in the United States. Throughout much of the country's history, the Democratic Party has positioned itself as a popular alternative to the more conservative, blatantly pro-capitalist Republican Party. Both parties, however, are intimately tied and committed to capitalism. "Part of the reason that the U.S. 'survival of the fittest' periods of economic restructuring are so relentless rests on the performance of the Democrats as history's second-most enthusiastic capitalist party," writes former right-wing pundit Kevin Phillips. "They do not interfere much with capitalism's momentum, but wait for the excesses and the inevitable populist reaction."[21]

The two-party system has been tremendously successful in preventing the emergence of any successful third-party challenges, from the left or the right. As far back as 1893, Engels astutely observed that the formation of a workers' party in the United States was hindered by a "Constitution … which makes it appear as though every vote were lost that is cast for a candidate not put up by one of the two governing parties."[22] His description of the U.S. political system as consisting of "two great gangs of speculators, who alternately take possession of the state power and exploit it by the most corrupt means and for the most corrupt ends," reads like it was written yesterday.[23]

Both parties have always been funded by big business, both are supporters of overseas conquest, and both have used troops to quell strikes. Before the Civil Rights movement, moreover, the Democratic Party was the party of Jim Crow segregation. In his Socialist Party campaign speeches Debs constantly hammered on these truths. "If the Democratic Party is the 'friend of labor' any more than the Republican Party," he said in 1900, "why is its platform dumb in the presence of Cœur d'Alene?" Debs was referring to an 1892 strike of Colorado miners where, after company guards killed five strikers, the miners marched the guards and strikebreakers out of town. The strike was broken when the governor sent in fifteen hundred troops and locked up six hundred strikers in a stockade prison. "What has the Democratic Party to say about the 'property and educational qualifications' in North Carolina and Louisiana, and the proposed general disfranchisement of the negro race in the southern states?" asked Debs. "The differences between the Republican and Democratic parties involve no issue, no principle in which the working class have any interest."[24]

The New Deal and Civil Rights eras are the touchstones today for those who argue that the Democrats lead a party of the people. In the 1930s, the Democrat Franklin Delano Roosevelt, warily eyeing the mass working-class upsurge that led to the formation of the Congress of Industrial Unions (CIO), presented himself as both a friend of labor and a savior of capitalism. "Those who have property fail to realize," he wrote to Supreme Court justice Felix Frankfurter, "that I am the best friend the profit system ever had."[25] During the course of the Civil Rights movement, Southern Democrats deserted the party. Northern liberal Democrats were always one step *behind* the Civil Rights movement, eager to wind down the struggle (which they feared) and win the voting allegiance of enfranchised Blacks (which they coveted).

The populist rhetoric of the Democrats is designed to take the fire out of any move to form a radical third party. Alarmed by the growth of the Populist Party, for example, which received 1.4 million votes in the 1894 mid-term elections, the Democratic Party fielded William Jennings Bryan as its presidential candidate in 1896. Bryan breathed populist rhetoric in order to win over Populist Party supporters. Democratic leaders also diligently cultivated the "fusionist" wing of the Populists, which proposed merging the two parties.

At its 1896 convention, the Populists voted to endorse Bryan as their candidate. Populist leader Tom Watson knew this signaled the end of populism, writing, "Populists cannot denounce the sins of the two old parties and yet go into political copartnership with them. The moment we make a treaty the war must cease … and when we cease our war upon the two old parties, we have no longer any excuse for living."[26] Watson warned, "Fusion means the Populist Party will play Jonah, and they [the Democrats] will play the whale."[27] Watson was right. The decision to back Bryan effectively killed the Populist Party.

The absence of any radical working-class or left political parties is one of the secrets of the relative stability of bourgeois politics in the

United States historically, narrowing at election time the choice, for workers and the poor, to one between two evils. The history of the two-party system shows that electing the lesser evil demobilizes mass struggle by putting the masses' faith in the actions of bourgeois politicians. It lowers the political level of the movement, too, because it compels activists to become apologists for a party that does not represent their interests.

If the lesser evil wins, his (so far there have been no women presidents) policies in office are glaringly different from his campaign rhetoric. The most famous case of this was Lyndon Johnson, who won the presidential race in 1964 on a promise to end the war, but then sent five hundred thousand troops to Vietnam. This was a particularly egregious case because it turns out Johnson had secret plans to send more troops to Vietnam before he won the election.[28]

The two parties represent the liberal and conservative wings of the same capitalist class. What unites them—their commitment to serving the interests of capital—is far more important than their differences. That is why Clinton supported neoliberal free trade policies, just as Bush does now. That is why Clinton ended up pushing through Republican-style welfare reform that drastically slashed welfare for the poor.

Marx and Engels had much to teach on the value of the left and progressives running their own candidates. In 1886, the Central Labor Union in New York formed the Independent Labor Party of New York and Vicinity in order to participate in New York City's mayoral race. The new party chose single-tax advocate Henry George as its candidate. George himself was not from the labor movement, but was a middle-class populist. He had recently written a popular book, *Progress and Poverty*, which advocated a single tax on landed property as a panacea to solve society's ills.

In a hotly contested race in which the ruling class pulled out all the stops to prevent a Labor Party victory, George came in second in a three-way race, with 31 percent of the vote. Writing from Europe, Engels was positive about the election:

> In a country that has newly entered the movement, the first really crucial step is the formation by the workers of an independent political party, no matter how, so long as it is distinguishable as a labor party.... That the first program of this party should still be muddle-headed and extremely inadequate, that it should have picked Henry George for its figurehead, are unavoidable if merely transitory evils. The masses must have time and opportunity to evolve; and they will not get that opportunity unless they have a movement of their own—no matter what its form, providing it is

> their own movement—in which they are impelled onwards by their own mistakes and learn by bitter experience.[29]

We must have a politically independent movement of our own—a lesson we still need to learn in the United States today.

What about the oft-repeated argument that voting for left candidates "steals" votes from liberals and helps the right wing into power? According to this logic, there is no good time to break from the Democratic Party. The working class and the poor are doomed in perpetuity to vote for a party that does not truly represent their interests. Every election time we hear the argument that it is the "most important election of our lifetime," and that the right can only be defeated by electing the lesser evil. "The ultimate intention of all such phrases," wrote Marx, "is to dupe the working class."[30]

If I tie a rope to the fender of a car sinking into a muddy lake, but the car pulls me into the muck instead, it is clear who is doing the pulling and who is being pulled. The repeated attempts by the left in America to capture or move the Democratic Party leftward follows this pattern. Misplaced support on the left for the Democratic Party has meant that our side is unable to use elections to count our forces. Worse, presidential elections disorient and disorganize our side. Liberals spend a great deal of time convincing activists to tone down the criticism, to refrain from struggle in the lead-up to the election, so as not to embarrass or undermine the Democratic candidate. Depending on the state of the class struggle, some more liberal Democrats may even offer verbal support for some of the demands of the social movements. But in the end their purpose is to bring anyone leaning away from the Democrats back into the fold. On election day, they will be asked to vote for the more conservative Democratic candidate who has been chosen for his or her "electability." Dennis Kucinich ran a long-shot primary campaign in the 2004 presidential election that raised opposition to the occupation of Iraq and the Patriot Act and support for universal health care. He ran not to win, but to corral leftists and progressives into the party. When it came time to choose the Democratic presidential candidate, he pressured all his supporters to vote for John Kerry, a pro-occupation, pro–Patriot Act, anti–universal health care centrist. "The Democratic Party created third parties by running to the middle," explained Kucinich during his campaign. "What I'm trying to do is to go back to the big tent so that everyone who felt alienated could come back through my candidacy."[31]

The practical result of not presenting a real left pole at election time is to permit a rightward drift of the general political climate in which both the liberal and conservative bourgeois candidates feel absolutely no pressure from the left. This "politics of realism" or of "the possible," therefore, make the prospects for building an independent movement capable of achieving real radical change more remote.

The logic of lesser-evilism, both in the electoral sphere and in the realm of struggle, is always to narrow, constrict, and moderate demands, to accept anything so long as it is not the worst alternative. "[Y]ou can't fight the victory of the rightmost forces," argued Hal Draper, "by sacrificing your own independent strength to support elements just the next step away from them."[32] But that is precisely the argument made by liberals.

Eugene Wagner, a Michigan attorney who served on the board of the National Coalition to Abolish the Death Penalty (NCADP), makes a typical argument. Death penalty opponents shouldn't support "illegal" civil disobedience protests, he insists, because it might drive away important affiliates, expose the organization to criminal proceedings, and give "aid and comfort to many of our opponents in spreading the false and pernicious idea that abolition of the death penalty is based on radical left-wing principles."[33] This is miles away from any idea that abolishing the death penalty is a struggle that must be taken to the streets, or that it is a class issue, part of a general attack on the poor and working class. On the contrary, many abolitionist lawyers believe that demonstrations actually hurt a prisoner's chance of finding justice: "You'll anger the prosecutor or judge." The ultimate logic of this argument is that the best way to fight for reforms is not to fight at all–you'll anger those in power and there will be a backlash.

This was the message of the "paper of record" toward the immigrant rights protests that swept the country, culminating in boycotts, walkouts, and marches involving a few million people across the country on May 1, 2006. "Sleeping giants can, and should, get moving," the *New York Times* editorial graciously granted to a movement it had no power to stop, "But they should tread carefully." The *Times* editors warned that the protests were a "perilous business," suggesting instead of boycotts and strikes "delicate consensus building" to avoid antagonizing the immigrant-bashing right or sending "students the wrong message about the importance of education."[34] As if mass action to achieve social reform were not educational or effective! Liberals have a long history of preaching to mass movements to tread delicately so as not to "provoke" reaction. Naturally, there is no danger of a backlash if the oppressed never fight back. To those who cautioned the Civil Rights movement to "wait," Martin Luther King Jr. replied, "We know through painful experience that freedom is never voluntarily given by the oppressor; it must be demanded by the oppressed."[35]

Talking about a revolution

Our schoolbooks would like us to believe that social change must always be gradual and peaceful. Sudden, abrupt changes are seen as disruptions of a "normal" functioning society. "Respectable" society looks upon mass protest, civil disobedience, strikes, disruption, and revolution with horror. But fundamental social change rarely comes gradually. Industrial unions didn't come to this country by the gradual addition, year after year, of a few new unions. On the contrary, mass industrial unionism came in an explosion of organizing and mass strikes over a period of about five years, from 1934 to 1938. The gains of the Civil Rights movement were achieved through heroic civil disobedience and mass protest in the face of systematic racist terror.

While governments caution the governed to act peacefully and refrain from drastic action, they themselves reserve the right to use overwhelming force. There was nothing gradual about the invasion of Iraq. Moreover, the modern capitalist class rose to power on the basis of revolutionary violence—the heirs of 1776 are no exception. Gradualness and big leaps are complementary and contradictory aspects of history, one preparing the conditions for the other. As Trotsky wrote,

> For us it is enough to know that gradualness in various spheres of life go hand in hand with catastrophes, breaks and upward and downward leaps. The long process of competition between two states *gradually* prepares for war, the discontent of exploited workers *gradually* prepares a strike, the bad management of a bank *gradually* prepares a bankruptcy.[36]

We could add, the perpetual poisoning of the planet gradually leads to environmental catastrophe.

Revolution is the ultimate social leap—a period when the gradual accumulation of mass bitterness and anger of the exploited and oppressed coalesces and bursts forth into a mass movement to overturn existing social relations and replace them with new ones. A few days of revolutionary upheaval bring more change than decades of "normal" development. Rulers and systems that seemed invincible and immovable are suddenly unceremoniously toppled. Revolution is not an aberration in an otherwise smoothly functioning society. "Force," wrote

Engels, can play "a revolutionary role.... In the words of Marx, it is the midwife of a very old society pregnant with a new one, it is the instrument with the aid of which social movement forces its way through and shatters the dead, fossilized political forms."[37]

The last three centuries have been filled not only with wars, but also with revolutions and near-revolutions. A list of only some of these gives us an idea of the scope of revolutionary upheaval since the dawn of modern capitalism—the American Revolution (1776–87), the French Revolution (1789–94), the U.S. Civil War (1861–65), the European revolutions of 1848, the Russian Revolutions (1905 and 1917), the German Revolution (1918–23), China (1925–27), the Spanish Civil War (1936–39), the Hungarian Revolution (1956), Chile (1973), Portugal (1974–75), Iran (1979), Poland's Solidarnosc uprising (1980–81). This partial list is enough to put to rest the notion that revolutions are rare or unusual occurrences. What is striking in all the twentieth-century revolutions is the central role of mass strikes and of working-class self-organization in the form of elected councils of workers' delegates, by whatever name they are called.

You can't skin a tiger paw by paw

There have always been moderates in the socialist movement that have made the case for peaceful reform, rather than revolution, as the most "realistic" way to achieve socialism. The German Social Democratic "revisionists" in the early twentieth century (social democracy was the name given to socialist parties at the time) are the best known. Their leading spokesperson, Eduard Bernstein, argued that capitalism, no longer crisis-prone, was softening class antagonisms by slowly improving workers' living standards. The growth of trade unions and cooperatives, and above all winning a socialist majority in parliament, were all that was needed—and if they didn't frighten away businesses by moving in too radical a direction, German Social Democrats could slowly but surely bring about socialism. Socialism was no longer an economic, but rather a moral, imperative, and as such could also be appealing to the well-to-do.

Bernstein's famous dictum was that "the ultimate aim of socialism is nothing, but the movement is everything."[38] But "revisionism"—named for its revising of Marx's revolutionary doctrine—also had a peculiar conception of just what the "movement" was. It denigrated the importance of struggle, such as strikes and street protests. These were seen as too disruptive, too threatening to the bourgeoisie, whom the reformists hoped to placate by only demanding incremental change. (For the record, Bernstein also supported colonialism, defending the right of "civilized peoples to act" as "the guardians of the uncivilized."[39])

There are two problems with this view of socialism. The first is that in this scenario, workers do not liberate themselves. They depend on others to make changes on their behalf. Class struggle plays no role, except as a means to exert pressure on the top. Workers do not learn through their own action how to construct a new world. They are at best a mere stage army, or, worse, a passive voting bloc. But the second—and most important—problem with reformism is that it doesn't work, for the simple reason that those who hold power won't give it up voluntarily or peacefully. "No privileged class," wrote Albert Rhys Williams, a witness to the 1917 revolution in Russia, "voluntarily resigns any of its privileges. No class steeped in tradition discards the old and gladly embraces the new."[40] If socialism is really to be the expropriation of wealth and the socialization of production, that means depriving the bosses of their power and taking away their wealth and their ability to extort any more wealth. Whether you propose to do this in small installments or all at once, the ruling class will resist with all their might. Or as the British historian R. H. Tawney put it, "Onions can be eaten leaf by leaf, but you cannot skin a live tiger paw by paw."[41]

When Southern U.S. slaveholders found their monopoly of political power undermined in Washington as a result of the creation of non–slave states in the 1850s, they resorted to secession and war to protect their economic and political power. Even assuming socialists could gain a majority of elected positions in government, they would still face a "pro-slavery" rebellion—an all-out effort by the capitalist class to ensure that such a government either acquiesced to their interests or was swept aside. That is why they have police, armies, and prisons. The purpose of armed force is to act as a last line of defense against any attempt to challenge capitalism.

There are times when even formal democracy becomes too threatening to the powers that be—as the many military coups around the world show. Rosa Luxemburg pointed this out at the turn of the twentieth century:

> In this society, the representative institutions, democratic in form, are in content the instruments of the interests of the ruling class. This manifests itself in a tangible fashion in the fact that as soon as democracy shows the tendency to negate its class character and become transformed into an instrument of the real interests of the

population, the democratic forms are sacrificed by the bourgeoisie and its state representatives.[42]

This is certainly what happened in Chile in 1973. The electoral victory of the Popular Unity socialist government gave encouragement to a series of mass strikes, along with factory and land takeovers. President Salvador Allende preached a peaceful, constitutional "Chilean road" to socialism, attempting at every turn to restrain the mass movement in order to prove his commitment to "constitutionalism." He brought military generals into his cabinet (including Pinochet, the man who would soon lead the coup against him), assuring the populace that the officers respected the constitution. He signed a "statute of guarantees" not to touch the armed forces, or the legal and educational systems, and authorized the army to conduct searches of factories to confiscate arms workers were stockpiling to defend themselves against fascist gangs.[43]

Unfortunately, Chile's wealthy were committed to the constitution only insofar as it guaranteed their rule. Fearing the growing working-class movement, they threw their support behind a brutal military coup. Under the command of General Augusto Pinochet, the army murdered Allende in the presidential palace and crushed the workers' movement in blood. Allende's constitutionalism merely disoriented the mass movement, allowing General Pinochet the breathing room he needed to destroy it.

Communist Parties (CPs) throughout the world at that time, who long before had abandoned revolutionary Marxism under the tutelage of Stalinist Russia in the 1930s and 1940s, drew deeply conservative conclusions from Allende's defeat. The problem was not that Allende disarmed the workers' movement and opened the door to defeat, but that the class struggle had gone too far and had thereby provoked the reaction. "The tragic Chilean experience has demonstrated," fretted Italian CP leader Enrico Berlinguer, "how the anti-democratic reaction tends to become more violent and ferocious when popular forces begin to conquer the fundamental levers of power in society and the state."[44] Berlinguer's conclusion was that the working class should compromise with capitalism rather than try to conquer fundamental power. "Liberalism has always said to the workers that by their class struggle they 'provoke' the reaction," wrote Trotsky. "The reformists repeated this accusation against the Marxists.... These accusations reduced themselves, in the final analysis, to the profound thought that if the oppressed ... balk, the oppressors will not be obliged to beat them."[45]

Marx and Engels were sharply critical of what they called "parliamentary cretinism," the tendency to place all hopes for social change on parliamentary institutions.[46] They ridiculed Social Democrats who, while putting off socialism "as an heirloom for their children," focus attention on "all sorts of trifles, tinkering away at the capitalist social order so that at least something should appear to be done without at the same time alarming the bourgeoisie."[47] Marx and Engels were not opposed to electoral campaigns. But for them, elections were good opportunities for revolutionaries to "bring before the public their revolutionary attitude."[48] They heaped scorn on socialists who saw their task as getting "educated" men elected in order to represent workers' interests from above. "We cannot co-operate," they snapped in an angry circular to German socialist leaders, "with men who say openly that the workers are too uneducated to emancipate themselves, and must first be emancipated from above by philanthropic members of the upper and lower middle classes."[49] The whole process of seeking electoral victory at all costs created a trend among the reformists to broaden their mass appeal by toning down their politics. Instead of politics being guided by principles, reformism fell into opportunism—what Rosa Luxemburg described as "sacrificing the basic principles of class struggle for momentary advantage."[50]

This has certainly been the experience of socialist parties that have been elected to office throughout history. Instead of challenging capitalism, they have ended up as its apologists, adapting to it rather than transforming it. During the First World War, the leaders of the German Social Democratic Party—along with the leaders of the other main socialist parties in Europe—cast their support for their "own" government's war effort, completely abandoning the principle of working-class internationalism laid down in the *Communist Manifesto*. "For this system, not one man, not one penny," had once been the party's slogan.[51] Reformists had degraded Marxism from a movement of revolutionary internationalism into one of national reformism. The German socialist Karl Kautsky offered as an excuse for European socialism's collapse into opportunism that the Socialist International "is essentially an instrument of peace," and therefore ineffective in wartime.[52] "The global historical appeal of the *Communist Manifesto* undergoes a fundamental revision," wrote Luxemburg in 1915, "and, as amended … now reads: proletarians of all countries, unite in peacetime and cut each other's throats in war!"[53]

There are more recent examples. French socialists François Mitterrand in the 1980s and Lionel Jospin in the 1990s implemented policies that helped to gut France's social safety net—and enabled the

French bosses' system to stay profitable.[54]

Mitterrand's election to the presidency in 1981 initially struck fear into French capitalists. He quickly allayed them by embarking on a series of austerity measures that included a wage freeze and a plan for restructuring French industry designed to weaken the unions and, in the words of Daniel Singer, "sacrifice many of their conquests on the altar of flexibility."[55] Mitterrand, like Bill Clinton in the 1990s, was able to push through a series of conservative measures without provoking the same level of working-class resistance that would have resulted had a right-wing government attempted to impose them. Along with this went a new ultra-moderate image. "To say that French socialism had mellowed is an understatement," wrote Singer. "The concepts of class and capitalism, even the very word *socialism,* had disappeared from their vocabulary."[56] For this, capital was eternally grateful. The French stock exchange, the Bourse, rose at twice the rate of the New York Stock Exchange during Mitterrand's presidency. "When Mitterrand was elected," according to Singer, "he was viewed with suspicion. Five years later, when the defeated socialists were leaving the government, the lonely president was being hailed unanimously by the *Economist,* the *Financial Times,* and the *Wall Street Journal* as a wise statesmen, having done yeoman service for the left, for France, and for the Western world."[57]

If the old social democrats shared with Stalinism an identification of socialism with the state, modern socialist parties in Europe have even dropped the pretense of being for any kind of socialism. After the Second World War, European social democratic parties were advocates of a "mixed economy," somewhere between the market and state ownership of the means of production. In the era of neoliberalism, they abandoned a commitment even to state "socialism." Instead, they now argue for a "third way," and have become open supporters of neoliberal austerity policies aimed at cutting the social wage and eroding labor rights.[58] In this way they have cut themselves off more and more from their former working-class supporters.

Reformism would only work if the state were a neutral body, an empty vessel to be filled up by whichever party gets into office. Luxemburg, in her epitaph on the failure of reformism, noted that those who favor legislative reform over social revolution "do not really choose a more tranquil, calmer and slower road to the same goal, but a different goal. Instead of a stand for the establishment of a new society they take a stand for the surface modifications of the old society."[59]

It is important to remember, however, that rejecting *reformism* is not the same as rejecting *reforms,* and in particular, the fight for reforms. It is precisely through struggles for immediate demands—over wages, working conditions, and for political and social improvements—that workers are able to develop consciousness of their own power, as well as the confidence born of collective action, to move toward revolutionary action. Struggle changes consciousness. That is why the fight for reforms has the potential to go further; because once in struggle, the horizons of workers expand beyond their immediate conditions. The possibility of another world looms more closely on the horizon.

But the struggle for reforms cannot be equated with revolution. In a revolution, that is, in a period of mass upheaval and social convulsion, consciousness is transformed on a mass scale. This transformation is both a condition and a result of revolution. As Marx and Engels wrote:

> Both for the production on a mass scale of this communist consciousness, and for the success of the cause itself, the alteration of men on a mass scale is necessary, an alteration which can only take place in a practical movement, a revolution; this revolution is necessary, therefore, not only because the ruling class cannot be overthrown in any other way, but also because the class overthrowing it can only in a revolution succeed in ridding itself of all the muck of ages and become fitted to found society anew.[60]

What does a revolution look like?

A social revolution is not a military coup by a handful of plotters, nor is it simply a change of personnel at the top as a result of mass protests. Mass protest can overthrow a government—as we've seen many times in Latin America. But often the overthrow has only put another leader in power without changing the fundamental class relations in society. Unless the state is overturned and conditions are created for the creation of new social relations, a political rather than a social revolution has taken place.

Trotsky described socialist revolution as "the direct interference of the masses in historic events ... the forcible entrance of the masses into the realm of rulership over their own destiny."[61] The question of revolution always boils down to a contest for power in which a new class imposes a new order on the ruins of the old by deposing the old ruling class. We know that the state often resorts to violence even when the struggle is not revolutionary—witness the way U.S. police come out in full riot gear every time a peaceful antiwar protest is organized. Imagine what they might do if millions of workers attempted to seize control of the factories, hospitals, and schools to run them democratically. Perhaps that's why socialists are often confronted with the question, isn't the state too powerful to challenge?

This seems to be an unsolvable paradox. Piecemeal reforms are incapable of transforming society, and yet revolution will be met with superior force—and defeated. Perhaps the best we can hope for are minor changes that don't threaten the power of bosses. This is wrong on two counts. First of all, the more militant and united the struggle, the greater the chances that even minor reforms will be successful. Second, there are plenty of examples of powerful regimes falling under the weight of mass revolt that before their fall seemed impregnable. No one predicted the fall of the Shah of Iran—protected by his dreaded secret police—in 1978. The Western press treated the Eastern European states as impregnable fortresses of Stalinist tyranny before they fell in 1989.

The view that the state is all-powerful is based on a misconception of what revolutions are and the conditions that give rise to them. Revolutions succeed not because those who are rebelling have superior arms. If that were a requirement, a revolution could never win. Revolutionary situations arise only when millions of ordinary people become convinced that society can't continue in the old way, and when there are splits and confusion at the top over how to restore order and overcome the crisis. As Lenin wrote,

> To the Marxist it is indisputable that a revolution is impossible without a revolutionary situation; furthermore, it is not every revolutionary situation that leads to revolution. What, generally speaking, are the symptoms of a revolutionary situation? … (1) when it is impossible for the ruling classes to maintain their rule without any change; when there is a crisis, in one form or another, among the "upper classes," a crisis in the policy of the ruling class, leading to a fissure through which the discontent and indignation of the oppressed classes burst forth. For a revolution to take place, it is usually insufficient for "the lower classes not to want" to live in the old way; it is also necessary that "the upper classes should be unable" to live in the old way; (2) when the suffering and want of the oppressed classes have grown more acute than usual; (3) when, as a consequence of the above causes, there is a considerable increase in the activity of the masses, who uncomplainingly allow themselves to be robbed in "peace time," but, in turbulent times, are drawn both by all the circumstances of the crisis *and by the "upper classes" themselves* into independent historical action.[62]

For a period, a rising movement can throw the state and the ruling class it represents onto the defensive. Divisions develop at the top over how to restore order—should reforms be granted to mollify the movement, or should repression be used, or both? Reforms are granted. Instead of stopping the movement, placating it, the reforms embolden the movement, which draws into its train all of the oppressed and exploited—women, national minorities, and others.

Sections of the ruling class and the military begin to debate the possibility of restoring order by force, i.e., by physically crushing the rising. Reactionary forces begin testing the defenses of the movement, probing for its weakest spots. Society balances on a knife's edge. Will the old order reimpose itself, or will new social forces seize power? This is the essence of all revolutionary situations. Of course, if those leading the movement are able to channel the struggle into reforms that do not fundamentally challenge the status quo, then it is possible that the movement can be defused before it reaches revolutionary proportions. When this happens, as it did after the May 1968 general strike in France, for example, the movement subsides and the old order is able to restore itself. But if workers are convinced that they can and must move forward, then the only two choices are: a dispersal of the old state power by the united working class, leading millions behind it, or the suppression of the movement.

A necessary feature of every revolutionary situation is "dual power," the existence of popular forms of power—workers' councils—alongside the old state. But "dual power" cannot last. In all revolutionary situations, either society moves forward, to the establishment of a new state based upon workers' councils or some similar form of direct democracy, or backward to the destruction of the workers' organizations and the reestablishment of capitalist order.

The formation of workers' councils of some sort is a precondition for socialism. But whether workers win or not is a question of power. The working class can only become the new power if it disperses the old power. For that, the working class must not only be organized, it must have behind it the majority of the oppressed and whole sections of the middle class. And it must also be armed and ready to defend its control of workplaces and the streets. Force must decide in the end because as we've already pointed out, the ruling class will use the utmost force to stay in power.

Trotsky wrote after his experience as president of the main workers' council in Petrograd in the 1905 Russian Revolution:

> In struggle it is extremely important to weaken the enemy. That is what a strike does. At the same time a strike brings the army of the revolution to its feet. But neither the one nor the other, in itself,

> creates a state revolution. The power still has to be snatched from the old rulers and handed over to the revolution. That is the fundamental task. A general strike only creates the necessary preconditions; it is quite inadequate for achieving the task itself. At a certain moment in revolution the crucial question becomes: on which side are the soldiers—their sympathies and their bayonets?[63]

In mass upheavals, the weakest link of the ruling class is the armed forces. Repression can only work if soldiers are disciplined to carry out their orders. But in circumstances of great social upheaval, this isn't a foregone conclusion—because most soldiers are themselves workers. If this were not true, revolutions could never win. A mass movement can fight for the hearts and minds of soldiers, thereby splitting the military and winning soldiers to the side of revolution. The "all-powerful" state then becomes temporarily paralyzed because it cannot rely on its own armed forces. But the movement must be strong enough and provide a clear program that convinces the soldiers that the movement can win. This is what happened in the 1917 revolution in Russia. Trotsky describes in his classic *History of the Russian Revolution* how in the midst of mass street demonstrations, even the crack Cossacks sent to suppress protests winked as workers dived under their horses, and regular soldiers turned their guns on the police when they attacked the crowds.[64]

During the 1877 great railroad rebellion in the United States, the first mass national strike wave in U.S. history, many of the local militias refused to attack striking railroad workers. A local Pennsylvania militia was sent out to crush a strike on the Philadelphia and Reading Railroad after workers seized control of company property. The militia men made it clear that they would report for duty, but "if ordered to fire, they will lay down their arms; that they are workingmen and do not desire to kill other workingmen."[65]

The late British Marxist Tony Cliff described a similar process during the 1975 Portuguese Revolution.

> The families living in the shantytown of Bairro da Boavista in the outskirts of Lisbon took over a housing estate that had stood empty for three years.... An army company ... was deployed to force the families back to the corrugated lean-tos of the shantytown. The officer in charge ... went straight to what he thought was the weakest link, an old widow who had just moved with her six sons to a two-bedroom flat with electricity. She replied: "You better shoot me right here. All my life I have had the earth for a floor. At least I will die on a proper floor." The officer stood there for a moment. Outside, the men, women and children who had assembled to resist any eviction were speaking to the soldiers:

"This could be your shantytown! Remember that you, too, are the people! Turn the guns on the speculators and not on your brothers and sisters!" The officer understood, and, taking the company with him, left the estate.[66]

Between labor and capital

Workers and bosses are not the only classes under capitalism. There are the chronically destitute—people who live in abject poverty who cannot find steady work, or any work at all, some of whom turn to petty crime to survive. In addition, between labor and capital there is a middle class that consists of professionals, managers, and small businesspeople—sometimes referred to as the petty bourgeoisie. The upper end of this layer shares more in common in its lifestyle and outlook with the capitalist class. The lower end, in terms of salary and working conditions, has more in common with the working class. As a whole, the middle class vacillates between the two main classes. Strictly speaking, the middle class is not a class in the sense that is used in reference to workers and bosses. Its conditions are too heterogeneous. Loosely speaking, it is all those who are either small-scale exploiters, control the labor of others, or rely on their professional skills and education to draw a large salary.

As a small businessperson, a shopkeeper identifies with the capitalists; as someone who labors long hours to make ends meet, the shop owner has more in common with wage workers. If the class outlook of the working class is collectivist, the class outlook of the middle class is individualist. Its whole class position reinforces not collective interest and collective action, but advancement through individual pluck and ability.

This isn't only true of small businesspeople, whose material conditions tend to reinforce the idea of individual merit, but is especially true of the "intelligentsia"—academics and professionals such as lawyers and doctors. Their whole educational and life experience reinforces individualism. This individualist ideology is encouraged also among certain types of white collar workers—teachers and civil servants, for example—to convince them that they are "professionals" rather than workers. But these workers find that they must do all the same things other workers do—organize, strike, fight back—in order to protect their job conditions and living standards. And so their own experience tends to contradict the myth of their "professionalism" and individualism. It is this very sense of individualism that ties the middle classes to capitalism.

"The writer does not have to get up when the alarm sounds," wrote Trotsky,

> behind the doctor's back stands no supervisor, the lawyer's pockets are not searched when he leaves the court. But in return, he is compelled to sell not his mere labor power, not just the tension of his muscles, but his entire personality as a human being—and not through fear but through conscientiousness. As a result, these people don't want to see and cannot see that their professional frock-coat is nothing but a prisoner's uniform of better cut than ordinary.[67]

Hence when well-educated academics muse about how workers are too "well off" to want real change, they are oblivious to the fact that this is a more apt description of their own class position. The working class, though bombarded with propaganda about the sacredness of the individual, has a different class experience. "A worker," contrasts Trotsky, "comes to socialism as a part of a whole, along with his class, from which he has no prospect of escaping. He is even pleased with the feeling of his moral unity with the mass, which makes him more confident and stronger."[68]

Middle-class radicalism, whatever particular form it takes, tends toward a rejection of class conflict, replacing it with a sense of commitment to improving humanity in general on the basis of moral imperatives, which often translates into moral preaching. The middle-class German "True Socialists," contemporaries of Marx, in rejecting French-style class struggle, "felt conscious of having overcome 'French one-sidedness.'" Their defanged brand of socialism, commented Marx and Engels, represented "not true requirements, but the requirements of Truth; not the interests of the proletariat, but the interests of Human Nature, of Man in general, who belongs to no class, has no reality, who exists only in the misty realm of philosophical fantasy."[69]

The petty bourgeoisie is an in-between class, "a class shading off into the bourgeoisie or the proletariat," writes Hal Draper, citing Engels. "One 'in which the interests of the two classes are simultaneously mutually blunted.' In consequence the petty-bourgeois 'imagines himself elevated above class antagonism generally.'"[70]

The middle class is incapable of offering its own solution to the problems of capitalism. In the battle for socialism, it can only play an auxiliary role. It can be drawn into struggle in times of deep-seated crisis. At times, anger or despair draw sections of the middle class to the right—as in Germany in the 1930s, or in Europe today, where sections of the middle class are drawn to the far right. It can also be drawn to the left—as in Argentina where sections of the middle class joined workers and the unemployed to bring down the government in

2001. But it is also more volatile, and quicker to abandon the fight. While the working class and sections of the middle class can together bring down a government, only working-class leadership in the movement can lead the struggle to a new society.

Why workers must lead

Workers have time and again brought their concentrated power to bear in bringing down unpopular, oppressive regimes. The tremendous power of Black workers in South Africa was the most important factor in the downfall of apartheid—the system of racial separation and white supremacy. Strikes by Iranian oil workers were key to bringing down the Shah of Iran in 1979; in 2003, miners in Bolivia played an important role in bringing down hated neoliberal president Gonzalo Sánchez de Lozada.[71] Yet in all these cases, while workers may have plowed the ground, others gathered the fruits of victory, or succeeded in limiting the horizons of change. The struggle in most cases united a variety of different social and class forces that were agreed on what they opposed, but not on what they were for.

In South Africa, a combination of armed struggle, mass protest, and strikes—under the leadership of the African National Congress (ANC)—was able to finally bring an end to apartheid. The ANC's 1955 Freedom Charter stated, "South Africa belongs to all who live in it—Black and White." But the ANC was not prepared to go beyond this basic democratic goal. The charter, insisted the ANC's chief leader Nelson Mandela, aimed not at socialism but rather "the transfer of power … to all the people of this country, be they workers, peasants, professional men or petty bourgeoisie." As for capitalism—the ANC sought to "open fresh fields for the development of a prosperous non-European bourgeois class" with the end of apartheid.[72] Its commitment to the continuation of capitalism in South Africa meant that many of the issues which brought the masses of Black South Africans to rebel—lack of housing and basic services, unemployment, landlessness, and severe exploitation at the hands of multinationals—continue today under a Black majority government.

Ashwin Desai describes how Mandela, some two months after his election as South Africa's first Black president, emphasized his government's commitment to job security, accessible health care, and affordable education. Ten years later, ANC stalwart and South African president Thabo Mbeki was singing a different tune, pushing a program promoting free market deregulation and "fiscal discipline." The new program, whose acronym was GEAR, "operated as a homegrown structural adjustment program. Markets were opened, taxes to the rich were cut, state assets were privatized, services were commodified, and social spending was reduced." Small wonder that Pamela Cox, head of the South Africa division of the World Bank, enthused: "what they [the ANC] have done to put South Africa on a right footing, is, I think, almost miraculous."[73]

Workers have an interest in taking the fight for a better society further than middle-class forces that want to limit the struggle to a set of more or less limited reforms that leave the economic system of exploitation intact. If they are not to play an auxiliary role—providing the muscle while other classes reap most of the rewards—then workers must be organized politically as a class capable of asserting themselves independently. But in doing so, workers must be able to present a social and political program of change capable of leading all the exploited and oppressed in society.

Writing a few months after the outbreak of the 1905 revolution, Lenin warned: "The outcome of the revolution depends on whether the working class will play the part of a subsidiary to the bourgeoisie, a subsidiary that is powerful in the force of its onslaught against the autocracy, but impotent politically, or whether it will play the part of leader of the people's revolution."[74]

Though feudal autocracy has long since disappeared, Lenin's formula still applies to the struggle against tyranny today. Are workers to play a "subsidiary" role or a leading role in struggles against national oppression, the fight against military dictatorship, or any other fight that brings disparate class elements together against some aspect of the status quo? Is the struggle, in other words, to end in limited reforms or in complete emancipation?

Liberals and reformists who look to limit demands to what is possible within the framework of capitalism turn this question on its head, claiming that workers' interests are narrowly economic, while the movement must be broad and encompass the interests of all social "sectors." There is nothing wrong with broad forces uniting to fight for limited demands. The problem comes when, in the name of broad unity, the moderates use the cry of "unity" to prevent anyone from taking the struggle further. In the name of broadening the fight, its aims are then narrowed, and further progress is truncated, or even abandoned.

"The Bush administration is a right-wing authoritarian regime," explained Communist Party USA national chair Sam Webb in his opening remarks to a party congress in 2005, "and broad sections of the labor movement—center forces, social democrats, Democrats, social reformists, liberals, even some Republicans—are opposing its policies and battling capitalist globalization as well. Don't we have to unite with them," he concluded, "in fighting policies of the Bush administration?"[75] The need to preserve a grand coalition such as this requires that everyone hold their tongue on gay rights, immigrant rights, workers' rights, or any other rights that might frighten away the bourgeois and conservative members of the coalition. Similarly, during the Second World War, the CP's ardent commitment to a "people's front" with the Democratic Party and Roosevelt's alliance with Stalin led it to support a wartime no-strike pledge and the internment of 120,000 people of Japanese descent—calling the latter "a necessary war measure."[76] *BusinessWeek* in 1944 lauded the CP as "the most vigorous proponents of labor-management cooperation."[77]

Revolutionaries, on the other hand, have always sought to build a workers' movement in which the working class takes the lead not only in fights for better wages and conditions, but in the fight against all forms of tyranny and oppression, from racism to women's inequality. When socialists talk about workers' power, we aren't talking simply about the impact of a well-placed strike (that is, the relative social weight that workers hold in the process of production). We're talking about the need for the working class to play an independent and leading role in the struggle if we're to turn the fight into one against the system in its entirety.

Socialism doesn't arise automatically from the class struggle. Workers can play the crucial role in a revolution, but without political organization, they can find their interests sidelined. Unless workers organize as an independent force that fights for their aims, the struggle can only go so far. And they cannot play this role unless they are organized as a class and capable of using their concerted power in the interests of *all* the exploited and oppressed.

Marx learned this during the revolutions that swept Europe in 1848. "The democratic petty bourgeois," he wrote, "far from wanting to transform the whole society in the interests of the revolutionary proletarians, only aspire to a change in social conditions which will make the existing society as tolerable and comfortable for themselves as possible." The working class therefore had to be organized into an independent political party that would march with the petty-bourgeois democrats against the old autocratic regimes, but would "oppose them in everything whereby they seek to consolidate their position in their own interests."[78]

"It is our interest and our task," Marx and Engels concluded, to make the revolution permanent, until all more or less possessing classes have been forced out of their position of dominance, the proletariat has conquered state power, and the association of proletarians, not only in one country but in all the dominant countries of the world, has advanced so far that competition among the proletarians in these countries has ceased and that at least the decisive productive forces are concentrated in the hands of the proletariat. For us the issue cannot be the alteration of private property but only its annihilation, not the smoothing over of class antagonisms but the abolition of classes, not the improvement of existing society but the foundation of a new one.[79]

Chapter Seven

The Need for Socialist Organization

Organization is necessary in any struggle, for the simple reason that no social or economic change can be achieved without some group of people coming together and demanding it. If you want better wages, you must organize along with fellow workers. If you want a government to rescind a budget cut, or grant a social reform, you must organize in the workplaces and in the streets. All struggles throughout history have involved at least a rudimentary form of organization. In that sense, there is no such thing as pure spontaneity.

Spontaneity, therefore, is a matter of degree. On the extreme end of spontaneity are struggles involving a high degree of improvisation by people without prior experience of struggle and organization. As the late British socialist Duncan Hallas wrote:

> Spontaneity is a fact. But what does it mean? Simply that groups of workers who are not active with any political or even trade union organization take action on their own behalf or in support of others. From the point of view of organizations the action is "spontaneous"; from the point of view of the workers concerned it is conscious and deliberate.

The question for socialists today is how to bridge the gap between muted anger and collective action—and between collective action and socialist consciousness. To again quote Hallas:

> Spontaneity and organization are not alternatives; they are different aspects of the process by which increasing numbers of workers can become conscious of the reality of their situation and of their

> power to change it. The growth of that process depends on a dialogue, on organized militants who listen as well as argue … and who are able to find connections between the actual consciousness of their fellows and the politics necessary to realize the aspirations buried in that consciousness.[1]

The most obvious case for organization is that the other side is organized. The ruling class has its civic and economic organizations, its research institutes, its elite universities, its think tanks and its exclusive clubs. It also has the resources of the state behind it. The working class does not have any of these advantages. It has numbers—but numbers mean nothing if they are not organized into a real force. Unions are a step forward, but as we've seen, they fight the effects of capitalism and not capitalism itself. The working class, to achieve socialism, must build an organization of socialist militants.

Marx and Engels laid out the general approach in the *Communist Manifesto*. The communists, they argued, were distinguished from other working-class parties in the following way:

> (1) In the national struggles of the proletarians of the different countries, they point out and bring to the front the common interests of the entire proletariat, independently of all nationality.
>
> (2) In the various stages of development which the struggle of the working class against the bourgeoisie has to pass through, they always and everywhere represent the interests of the movement as a whole.
>
> The Communists, therefore, are on the one hand practically, the most advanced and resolute section of the working-class parties of every country, that section which pushes forward all others; on the other hand, theoretically, they have over the great mass of the proletariat the advantage of clearly understanding the lines of march, the conditions, and the ultimate general results of the proletarian movement.[2]

This concept of organization sees socialists neither as mere participants in the struggle, nor as an elite that dictates to the masses, but as comrades in struggle who, in participating in today's movements, try to move the struggle as far as it can go, introducing to wider layers of workers the need for the socialist alternative along the way. The workers' party acts not only to disseminate socialist ideas, but is involved directly in every struggle. Moreover, it doesn't offer utopian descriptions of the socialist future, but rather gathers together and distills the most important historical lessons of past struggles, in order that those experiences can provide lessons for future struggles.

The German socialists, even before Engels' death in 1895, were beginning to diverge from this concept of organization as a result of their great electoral successes. "In 1887," writes a historian of German socialism, "Social Democracy polled 10.1 percent of the vote in the Reichstag elections; in 1890, 19.7 percent; in 1893, 23.3 percent; in 1898, 27.2 percent; and in 1903, 31.7 percent.... Is it to be wondered that Social Democracy became attached to its 'tried and true tactic?'"[3] This tremendous electoral success led its trade union and parliamentary leaders to see the party not as embracing only the "most advanced and resolute," but as appealing to all workers, radical or otherwise, and even to middle-class voters. This slow accumulation of supporters, through playing to the lowest common denominator of consciousness, was the way to win elections—not through fiery radicalism.

Marx's conception was also different from its Stalinist caricature, which saw the party not as a revolutionary part of the class, but as a bureaucratic elite standing over the class and dictating to it. This all-seeing, all-knowing monolith was an invention of Stalinist hacks.

The Russian socialist movement, in particular the Bolshevik Party, put into practice and refined what were only rudimentary guidelines in the *Manifesto.* Western anti-communists who attack Lenin and the Bolsheviks read the later bureaucratic distortions of Stalinism back into the history of the Russian revolutionary movement, presenting the Bolsheviks as a top-down, highly militarized sect. According to R. N. Carew Hunt, author of a standard Cold War assessment of communism, Lenin favored building a "small and highly disciplined" organization that would "exercise control over the revolutionary movement."[4] "Tutelage by an intellectual elite of professional revolutionaries," wrote Lenin biographer David Shub, was a hallmark of Leninism.[5] Shub claimed that Lenin's conception of "democratic centralism" was a movement organized "along lines of military hierarchy and discipline."[6] These views are repeated in Stalinist literature; the only difference is that the alleged monolithic, infallible, and dictatorial character of the Bolshevik Party is presented positively.

These assertions require historians to ignore the facts: that the party membership consisted of mostly young workers who were leading activists in their workplaces; that the internal life of the party was filled with sharp debate and disagreement; and that its decisions were made, wherever conditions permitted, with the fullest democracy. Ignored are statements by Lenin such as the following:

> The Russian Social-Democratic Labor Party is organized on dem-

> ocratic lines. This means that all the affairs of the Party are conducted, either directly, or through representatives, by all the members of the Party, all of whom without exception have equal rights; moreover, all officials, all leading bodies, and all institutions of the Party are subject to election, are responsible to their constituents, and are subject to recall.[7]

The dreaded phrase "democratic centralism" was one whose meaning should be clear to anyone in any democratically run activist organization that is attempting to implement a decision—first debate, then vote, and then act in unison to put that decision into effect.

Why is democracy in the movement necessary? Because as Lenin explained, "the success of mass action requires the conscious and voluntary participation of every individual worker" in the debate. A strike, for example, "cannot be conducted with the necessary solidarity ... unless every worker consciously and voluntarily decides for himself the question: to strike or not to strike?" Lenin insisted that "firm and intelligent" decisions, not those based on "clannishness, friendship or force of habit," could be made only on the basis of open debate and discussion.[8] But socialist organizations are not talk shops that value discussion for its own sake, as do academics. Once debate is had, a decision must be made that the collective is disciplined enough to act on. That is the "centralism" part of democratic centralism.

For the real Lenin, and not the Stalinist caricature, leadership had to be won in struggle, proven not declared. The much-maligned term "vanguard" for Lenin merely meant what Marx meant in the *Manifesto* by "the most advanced and resolute section" of the working class. Lenin argued that such an organization was necessary because there were "different degrees of consciousness and degree of activity" inside the working class. In periods of retreat, when struggle was at a low ebb, only a small minority of workers actively embraced socialism. But in periods of mass upheaval, ever-larger sections of the class moved in a socialist direction. Each fresh wave of radicalization would bring new forces to the movement, but only if there was an organization fighting alongside them to bring them along. "To forget the distinction between the vanguard and the whole of the masses gravitating towards it, to forget the vanguard's constant duty of *raising* ever wider sections to its own advanced level," Lenin wrote, "means simply to deceive oneself, to shut one's eyes to the immensity of our tasks, and to narrow down these tasks."[9] This "vanguard" was not a thing standing apart from the class, but the gathering together of anticapitalist militants into a single, fighting organization.

Such an organization isn't like a foreman on the job or a teacher in a classroom. It is a comrade in struggle, both learning from and guiding the movement. "The Communists fight for the attainment of the immediate aims, for the enforcement of the momentary interests of the working class," summarized Marx and Engels in the *Manifesto,* "but in the movement of the present, they also represent and take care of the future of that movement."[10]

A socialist revolutionary must be different from the sectarian who stands outside the struggle, criticizing its inadequacies; the extreme leftist who tries to jump so far ahead that he or she is cut off from the real movement; or the activist who is content with participating in the struggle without challenging it to accomplish more. A mass party or organization that merely participates in struggle adapts to existing conditions and cannot lead it beyond its present limits. But a sect that abstains from a struggle because it isn't radical enough is simply irrelevant. The type of organization socialists should strive to build was described perfectly by the late British socialist Duncan Hallas in 1971: "The many partial and localized struggles on wages, conditions, housing, rents, education, health and so on have to be coordinated and unified into a coherent forward movement based on a strategy for the transformation of society. In human terms, an organized layer of thousands of workers, by hand and by brain, firmly rooted amongst their fellow workers and with a shared consciousness of the necessity for socialism and the way to achieve it, has to be created."[11]

Every mass movement gives rise to debates about the way forward. The trade union officialdom, the old reformist leaders, and liberal organizations step to the fore and attempt to corral the movement, to lead it and to contain it. In such a situation, a distinction needs always to be made between the reformism of the masses being drawn into activism for the first time—ordinary people who do not yet believe they have the power to run society and therefore look to *better* rulers than the old ones—as opposed to more entrenched political forces that are consciously committed to reforming but not dismantling capitalism. In every revolutionary movement, the need for an organization of revolutionaries that can fight inside the movement to break past the constraints of reformism, and win the majority of workers to the idea that they must pose a new alternative to capitalism, becomes pressing.

The possibility that workers might be able to translate their power into more than just opposition to the way things are is not at first apparent to most of them—it becomes so only through a period of hard lessons in the course of struggle. In the process of struggle, ideas of solidarity, equality, and opposition to oppression come to the fore. But workers don't become aware of their position and power in society at the same time. Some move faster than others and are ready to take the lead.

The role of revolutionary organization is to unite the most militant workers and activists in the struggle—those who have a clearer grasp of the possibilities for revolutionary change—so as to be able to turn revolutionary potential into reality.

In periods of mass struggles, the barrier between economic and political struggle breaks down. Workers who not long before believed they had no power suddenly find themselves engaging in mass action, finding confidence and demanding respect. Every manifestation of injustice becomes a target of action. Each struggle inspires the next, and no issue or grievance is beyond action. For example, a strike wave in the summer of 1981 in Poland, during the heyday of Solidarnosc, involved a strike by airline workers demanding the right to choose their own manager, a dock strike to stop the export of food (people were starving in Poland), a protest by newspaper print shop workers against anti-Solidarnosc propaganda on the news, a strike of transport workers against corruption, a strike of workers in one town demanding that those responsible for repression against an earlier strike movement be fired, and hunger marches by thousands of women demanding food.

In a mass upsurge of struggle, an increasing number of militants begin to grasp the possibility that the movement, if it is to move forward, must seize power. Things must either go forward or backward, but can't stagnate. If these militants are not organized and united around a common campaign to win over the rest of the class to a program of revolutionary action, their sentiments, ideas, and partial insights will dissipate without real effect. Reformist leaders will retain dominance in the movement, and, in the name of unity and realism, will encourage the working class to curb its enthusiasm.

In Poland many of the leaders of Solidarnosc, such as Lech Walesa, accepted the idea of a "self-limiting revolution."[12] Though many militants were aware of the fact that Solidarnosc—a mass movement of almost 10 million workers that sprang from mass strikes—had the potential to be far more than a trade union fighting for reforms, there was no organized or coherent attempt to challenge its leaders from the left. The fact that the Polish state capitalist regime had claimed the mantle of socialism, and had appropriated phrases like "class struggle" did not help; the working class was reinventing workers' power against a ruling class that had appropriated their traditional symbols and terms of revolt.

But this experience highlights the key role a genuine socialist organization of militants could have played in Poland at the time. "Solidarnosc's 'self-limitation,'" writes Colin Barker in his account, "was a disastrous strategy.... Time and time again, the leaders of Solidarnosc found themselves urging their members not to 'go too far,' not to 'frighten the authorities.' Time and time again, they reined the movement in, rather than encouraging it forward. Their members' militancy was a 'problem' for them, rather than the key to a solution."[13]

The alternative was a revolutionary strategy aimed at seizing control of workplaces, winning over the rank and file of the armed forces, and replacing the bureaucratic state apparatus with workers' democracy. Only a strong organization united around such a program could have even posed this alternative as a possibility in Poland. Sadly, none existed.

In Chile in 1973, the revolutionary process had advanced considerably further than in Poland in 1980. Left-wing militants in the Socialist Party, sharply critical of the party's right wing and of the Communist Party that claimed Chilean socialism could come through a series of peaceful compromises, demanded that the party adhere to its commitment on paper that "only by destroying the bureaucratic and military apparatus of the bourgeois state can the socialist revolution be consolidated."[14] But these militants never organized independently or coordinated their efforts nationally, and therefore were incapable of providing an alternative leadership to Allende's Popular Unity government. As a result, their left-wing rhetoric merely convinced the working class to stick with Popular Unity, even as the latter moved further and further to the right.

Without a revolutionary party, the revolutionary moment is lost and the movement either goes into decline or is defeated. Either way, society begins to flow back into its old channels and "order" is restored once again. "Without a guiding organization, the energy of the masses would dissipate like steam not enclosed in a piston-box," wrote Trotsky. "But nevertheless what moves things is not the piston or the box, but the steam."[15]

Chapter Eight

Russia: The God That Failed?

The Russian Revolution of 1917 was a historical watershed. The overthrow of tsarism and the erection for the first time of a society turned upside down, with workers on top and bosses on the bottom, gave inspiration to workers and the oppressed the world over. It sparked revolutionary upheavals from Europe to the Middle East to Asia. For the world's national ruling classes, Russia's "red specter" cast a dark shadow, striking fear into their hearts.[1] The revolution's victory over the forces of reaction convinced millions that ordinary people could rise up and seize control of society in their own interests. Socialists the world over redoubled their efforts to emulate what Russia had done. In his 1918 speech against the war, Eugene Debs expressed the enthusiasm for the Russian Revolution, and the outbreak of revolution in Germany, that was felt by millions:

> Like a raging conflagration it leaps from shore to shore. The reign of capitalism and militarism has made of all peoples flammable material. They are ripe and ready for the change, the great change which means the rise and triumph of the workers, the end of exploitation, of war and plunder, and the emancipation of the race. Let it come! Let us all help its coming and pave the way for it by organizing the workers industrially and politically to conquer capitalism and usher in the day of the people.
>
> In Russia and Germany our valiant comrades are leading the proletarian revolution, which knows no race, no color, no sex, and no boundary lines. They are setting the heroic example for worldwide emulation....

From the crown of my head to the soles of my feet I am a Bolshevik, and proud of it.

"The Day of the People has arrived!"[2]

The revolution's isolation, degeneration, and defeat at the hands of the Stalinist bureaucracy in the 1920s presented a devastating blow to the international socialist movement. All defeats are a blow, but this one was particularly damaging. In Russia, Marxism came to be associated with an ideology that represented a complete distortion—or rather inversion—of Marxism. Socialism came to be identified not with workers' democratic control of society, but with a dictatorial, one-party state and the gulag. Working-class internationalism was replaced with "socialism in one country."

Ideologues in both the East and West, for their own reasons, agreed that Stalin was the natural heir of Lenin, and that the rise of his rule represented not the revolution's failure, but its logical culmination. The only difference was that supporters of Stalin's Russia put a plus by this conclusion, and its critics a minus. Official Marxism in Russia became not a guide to action or a theory of workers' power, but a state ideology out of which all genuine Marxist content had been wrung—an ideology justifying exploitation of, and rule over, the working class. In the West, reports of militarized regimentation of society, the cult of personality around Stalin, and forced labor camps became extremely effective tools in the hands of defenders of capitalism against socialism.

Both the Stalinist defenders of Lenin as well as anticommunist historians in the West, held to the view that Stalin was the natural heir of Lenin—the one to claim Lenin's heritage, the other to demonstrate that all revolutions lead to tyranny. Yet toward the end of his life, in 1922, Lenin wrote a testament demanding Stalin's removal from power in a desperate attempt to stop the growing state bureaucracy. A few years later, Trotsky took up the same theme, organizing a faction within the Bolshevik Party in a last-ditch effort to defend workers' power in the Soviet Union against its bureaucratic degeneration.

There was another interpretation of the reasons for the degeneration of the Russian Revolution—a Marxist one. The Russian Revolution was not a coup and its leaders were not master manipulators. The defeat of the revolution was due not to Lenin or any other Russian revolutionary's hankering for power, or because socialism goes against human nature, but because the economic conditions of Russia in isolation were too undeveloped, too backward, for the building of a socialist society. To understand what's being said here, we need to examine how the Russian Revolution was won and how it was lost.

How the revolution was won

The Bolsheviks were an activist party with a mass base among Russia's 3 million industrial workers. On the eve of the October Revolution in 1917, its membership stood at 240,000. The party was neither perfect, nor the monolith that Stalinist hacks later made it out to be, but there can be no doubt that it was a mass party, not a clique of professional revolutionaries, when it led the Russian Revolution to victory.[3]

Manchester Guardian correspondent Morgan Phillips Price, by no means a supporter of the Bolsheviks (whom he called "Maximalists"), offered this observation on the eve of the revolution: "The Maximalist fanatics, who still dream of the social revolution throughout all Europe, have, according to my observations in the provinces, recently acquired an immense, if not amorphous following." He notes with a tone of disdain,

> The majority of their followers, however, have no idea of what the Maximalist means when he talks of "all power to the councils".... The peasant, furious with the delay in the land reform, hears promises of immediate seizure of the landlord's land and goes with him. The worker hears talk about State control over the banks and goes with him.... All the recent provincial elections have given immense majorities to this wing of the revolutionary democracy.[4]

The revolution came in two installments. On February 23, 1917—International Women's Day—hundreds of thousands of Russian workers took to the streets of Russia's capital, Petrograd, inaugurating a series of mass protests and strikes that would in a matter of days bring down a monarchy that had ruled Russia for centuries.[5] Eight months later, in a second installment, armed workers—led by the Bolshevik Party—brought down the capitalist "provisional" government that had rushed in to reestablish order after the tsar's fall. In its place ruled the soviets—the democratic councils of workers, soldiers, sailors, and poor peasants—that had been hastily erected throughout Russia after the February Revolution.

The revolution combined two revolts—that of peasants in the countryside and of workers in the towns. This was because Russian economic development had combined the old with the new. In his *History of the Russian Revolution,* Trotsky quoted Marx's statement that "The country that is more developed industrially only shows, to the less developed, the image of its own future." This idea, however, "has become less applicable in proportion as capitalist evolution has embraced all countries," wrote Trotsky. "England in her day revealed the future of France, considerably less of Germany, but not in the least of Russia and not of India."[6]

Newcomers to capitalism after Britain did not simply repeat the same gradual stages English economic development went through, but combined and even skipped some. In Russia, more backward forms of economic life combined with the most modern forms, which were simply grafted on top of the old. Capitalism did not develop in late-nineteenth-century Russia gradually out of its own village handicrafts. On the contrary, with the aid of state intervention and an influx of foreign capital, modern factories were built alongside "villages of wood and straw." Peasants were "thrown into the factory cauldron snatched directly from the plow," wrote Trotsky.[7]

Russia in 1917 was a country made up overwhelmingly of peasants, scratching out a meager existence under the sway of big landowners. But it was also a country where state intervention and foreign investment had superimposed the world's most modern factories on top of Russia's old feudal structure. This peculiarity of development gave rise to a weak capitalist class, dependent on the state and foreign capital, fearful of its own shadow. One sign of its weakness was the fact that the party most identified with the liberal bourgeoisie, the Constitutional Democrats, or Kadets, wasn't formed until 1905. On the other hand, Russia's industrial working class, though numerically a minority, were tremendously concentrated in a few urban centers like Petrograd and Moscow, giving them a relative power that far exceeded their numbers.

The two wings of the Russian Social Democratic Labor Party (RSDLP)—Menshevik and Bolshevik—had very different views of Russia's revolution, which affected their approach to it. The two groups had split apart in 1903 over what initially seemed a small difference—conditions for membership in the party. The Bolsheviks wanted a stricter definition of a member that would ensure that only active participants were members, whereas the Mensheviks favored a looser, much broader concept. But bigger differences developed from there, and after the first Russian Revolution, in 1905, it was clear that the two factions had very different conceptions of what a revolution in Russia should look like.

Initially, both the Mensheviks and Bolsheviks believed that Russian economic backwardness meant the country would repeat the path taken by Western Europe, as described in Marx's statement above. There would be two distinct revolutions: one bourgeois, which would overthrow tsarism, establish Western-style democracy, and distribute land to the peasants; and later a second, working class–led revolution, which would bring about socialism. Lenin, for example, argued again and again that Russia was too economically backward to move directly to socialism.

But here the similarities ended sharply. The Mensheviks believed that the liberal Russian bourgeoisie would have to lead the revolution, in the same way that the French bourgeoisie had led the revolution in 1789.[8] The role of the socialists, in their view, was to mobilize the working class to put pressure on the bourgeoisie to fulfill this task. Consequently, they always cautioned the working class not to do anything that might frighten the capitalist class into the arms of reaction. The Bolsheviks, however, argued that the Russian capitalists were far too tied up with the landowning classes to lead a revolt against the autocracy. "The bourgeoisie as a whole is incapable of waging a determined struggle against the autocracy," Lenin argued.

> It fears to lose in this struggle its property which binds it to the existing order; it fears an all-too revolutionary action of the workers, who will not stop at the democratic revolution but will aspire to the socialist revolution. It fears a complete break with officialdom, with the bureaucracy, whose interests are bound up by a thousand ties with the interests of the propertied classes. For this reason the bourgeois struggle for liberty is notoriously timorous, inconsistent, and half-hearted.[9]

This view was amply confirmed during the revolution. After the tsar abdicated, Rodzianko, the liberal president of Russia's toothless parliament, or Duma, covered his face and cried, "My God, how horrible.... Without government ... anarchy ... blood."[10]

The practical difference between the two positions was that while the Mensheviks sought to hold back workers' militancy so as not to provoke the liberals into bolting from the role Menshevism had allotted them, the Bolsheviks criticized the liberals and sought to organize the working class independently of them. Only the working class, they argued, could spearhead the movement, uniting behind them the oppressed peasants. Incidentally, the Menshevik line became the basis, later, for the Stalinist conception that revolutions must of necessity go through two stages, the democratic and then the socialist one.

Trotsky took the Bolshevik's line of reasoning a step further. If the town leads the country, and the capitalists cannot lead "their" revolution—then workers must lead it, in alliance with the peasantry. In this his views coincided with Lenin's. But if the workers led, then they would not be able to stop at the democratic or bourgeois stage. After a successful revolution, workers would be compelled to retain power in their own hands and begin to push through socialist measures. Trotsky did not disagree with the moderate socialists who argued that Russia was not economically ripe for socialism. But Trotsky placed Russia's fate in its international context. Workers could begin the fight for socialism, but could not complete it without the revolution spreading and taking hold in other, more economically advanced countries. Trotsky viewed the revolution as a link in an international chain of struggle, not as an isolated national event. Trotsky called this theory, which he first formulated in 1905, "permanent revolution."[11] By permanent, Trotsky did not mean endless, but rather a revolution that would not stop halfway, and would proceed until all exploiting classes had been driven from power.

The First World War brought disaster to Russia. Food shortages, disease, and the slaughter of troops at the front—all these factors came to a head in 1917. On the top, the ruling circles became utterly paralyzed, the tsar and tsarina retreating into mysticism, their ministers unable to act, corruption and graft rampant. The fanatical cruelty of the ruling couple was best expressed in a letter to the tsar by the tsarina, in which she exclaimed, "Russia loves to feel the whip. That is *their* nature."[12] Trotsky described how the tsar praised as "fine fellows" a certain regiment for shooting down workers, and how he "'read with satisfaction' how they flogged with whips the bob-haired girl students, or cracked the heads of defenseless people during Jewish pogroms."[13]

As the war wore on, soldiers deserted in droves. After a short patriotic lull, workers began to go back out into the streets—renewing the fervor they had exhibited through mass strikes before the war broke out in 1914. Hundreds of thousands of workers struck and demonstrated, confronting the tsar's police and troops. Discipline in the armed forces cracked, and whole regiments joined the revolution, turning against the police who stayed loyal to the tsar. The tsar completely lost his grip on power in a matter of days. The movement was not led by any political party. It began as a spontaneous revolt against food shortages. But many of its leaders on the ground were Bolshevik militants.

The outcome of the tsar's overthrow was "dual power."[14] On the one side, workers and soldiers created the Soviet of Workers' and Soldiers' Deputies, based on one delegate for every thousand workers or soldiers. On the other side, the liberal landowners and bourgeois representatives formed—after some prodding and begging from the Menshevik leaders—the provisional government. This was in fact a counter-revolutionary government. It fully recommitted Russia to the imperialist war; it opposed workers' control in the factories, and opposed land seizures by the peasants—all the while promising at some future date, always put off, a constituent assembly that would solve Russia's problems.

The soviet had at this point far more power and prestige than the provisional government. However, the delegates of the first soviet meeting elected Mensheviks and Socialist-Revolutionary (SR) leaders who were committed to handing power to others. Though the peasantry formed its mass base, the SR Party balked at immediate land redistribution, appealing to the peasantry to wait for elections to a promised constituent assembly rather than take action into its own hands. "Those socialists who stood at the head of the soviet," wrote Trotsky, "were already looking around with alarm to see if they could find a real 'boss.' They took it for granted that the power ought to pass to the bourgeoisie."[15] Consequently, they insisted that the provisional government take power into its hands, even though the liberals who comprised it feared the revolution and expected the soviet to arrest them. As the situation unfolded, the moderate Mensheviks and SRs not only supported the provisional government, but entered it as cabinet members.

The Bolsheviks had around twenty-five thousand members at the start of the revolution, were concentrated in the biggest factories of Petrograd and other towns, and had a mass-circulation daily—*Pravda,* or "truth" in Russian—that regularly sold forty thousand copies. They were thus in no position immediately to lead a revolt against the provisional government. In these initial stages of the revolution they were still scattered and disorganized by months of intense police repression. They began with only a small minority of delegates in the Petrograd Soviet—forty out of sixteen hundred.

What accounted for this paradox? "The elections to the organs and institutions of the victorious revolution attract and challenge the infinitely broader masses than those who battled with arms in hands," wrote Trotsky.[16] In this early phase, workers did not make a distinction between the different socialist parties, and the influence of the intellectuals and of the petty officers in the army impressed their moderating stamp on consciousness. "In giving their confidence to the socialists the workers and soldiers found themselves, quite unexpectedly, expropriated politically."[17] A period of struggle was necessary to clarify where matters stood, who was for workers' power and who was not. "The country," argued Lenin from exile, "is passing from the first stage of the revolution—which, owing to the insufficient class-consciousness and organization of the proletariat, is in the hands of the bourgeoisie—to its second stage, which must place power in the hands of the proletariat and the poorest sections of the peasants."[18]

At first, Lenin's views were not embraced by other party leaders. Clinging to the old formula that Russia must first pass through a bourgeois phase, many (Stalin, for example) called for critical support for the provisional government. But the essence of party policy had in fact been to stress the leading role of the working class in the revolution. Entire party committees, including the famous industrial Vyborg district of Petrograd, had already come to the conclusion that the provisional government should be replaced by soviet power. After some hard debate—in which they were able to appeal to the rank and file of the party that had in many cases come independently to the same conclusions—Lenin and others were able to convince the party leaders of a strategy aimed at transferring all power to the soviets. Thus, in practice, Lenin adopted Trotsky's theory of permanent revolution.

It should be noted here that, even in the heat of the mass movement, the Bolsheviks made major decisions on the basis of open and democratic debate and discussion. There were countless times when Lenin was in fact a minority in the leadership and had to fight to convince the others of his views. The myth of the Bolshevik Party as a conspiratorial dictatorship derives from a misreading of the party's history. During periods of autocratic reaction, all left-wing parties in Russia were forced to operate clandestinely, and, consequently, no democracy was possible because no open meetings were possible. But whenever the class struggle created the conditions for the party to operate more openly, the party followed the principle of democratic decision-making and debate.

Lenin argued that workers' power must replace the provisional government:

> The Soviet of Workers' Deputies is an organization of the workers, the embryo of a workers' government, the representative of the interests of the entire mass of the poor sections of the population, i.e., of nine-tenths of the population, which is striving for peace, bread and freedom....
>
> He who says that the workers must support the new [provisional] government in the interests of the struggle against Tsarist reaction ... is a traitor to the workers.... For the only *guarantee* of freedom and of complete destruction of Tsarism lies in *arming the proletariat*, in strengthening, extending and developing the role, significance and power of the Soviet of Workers' Deputies.[19]

The Bolsheviks were not interested in a putsch by a minority, let alone a rising by the working class without support among the soldiers and peasantry. The task of the Bolsheviks, Lenin wrote, was to "patiently explain" to the as-yet unconvinced the need for the movement to transfer all power to the soviets, that only a soviet government would end the war, give land to the peasants, and create a full democracy in Russia. Once they secured a majority for this position in the soviets—which served as a barometer of mass feeling—the provisional government could be replaced by soviet power.

The Bolshevik line struck a chord with a growing number of workers, and thousands of them joined the party. Already by April, workers in Petrograd were demonstrating in support of Bolshevik demands. Here the Bolsheviks played a crucial role in the struggle, actually restraining a premature insurrection. By June, a majority of workers in Petrograd supported the Bolsheviks and were ready to overthrow the provisional government. The danger, as the Bolshevik leaders saw it, was that a revolt in Petrograd would be isolated and easily crushed. More time was needed to win over Moscow and other towns. In early July, Lenin and other leaders appeared at the head of an armed demonstration and, much to the chagrin of the protesters, urged calm.

After a series of desultory armed clashes with police, the protests disintegrated, and for a few weeks the Bolsheviks were driven underground. Lenin, framed on trumped-up charges that he was a German agent, and vilified by the other socialist parties, was forced to flee to Finland to avoid arrest and possible execution. Trotksy and some other Bolshevik leaders were arrested. But the movement was not crushed, and the Bolsheviks quickly bounced back. Trotsky was released, and in a new upsurge of revolutionary ferment was elected president of the Petrograd Soviet (as he had been in 1905 when he was only 25). He was also elected head of the "military-revolutionary committee," which was set up to mobilize workers' militias and troops loyal to the soviet to defend it against counterrevolutionary forces.

Then, in August, a right-wing general, Lavr Kornilov, began mobilizing a coup to smash both the soviets and the provisional government—which was headed by the right-wing Socialist-Revolutionary leader Alexander Kerensky. The ruling class had decided, in a last-ditch effort, that Kerensky could not be depended on to repress the revolution, and so he had to go. The Bolsheviks, the only left party untainted by support for or participation in the provisional government, proposed a joint struggle to all the soviet parties—even those that had supported crushing the Bolsheviks during the "July days"—aimed at stopping Kornilov. They proposed to Kerensky a united front against the coup, though not relinquishing their criticisms of the provisional government. Lenin argued that the provisional government could be dealt with more easily once the immediate threat of a coup was defeated.

With Bolshevik militants in the lead, Kornilov's conspiracy was dissolved before it ever reached Petrograd. Workers simply stopped Kornilov's troop trains and convinced his soldiers to switch sides. The Bolsheviks acquitted themselves as the best and most consistent defenders of the revolution. As a result, after August 1917, they won a majority of delegates in the soviets. Lenin, Trotsky, and a handful of other leaders argued that the time for talk had passed, and that workers now expected the Bolsheviks to organize an insurrection to disperse the provisional government and transfer all power to the soviets. Lenin came up against resistance from some Bolshevik leaders, like Kamenev and Zinoviev, who feared that the time wasn't ripe. But Lenin, Trotsky, and others were able to overcome this hesitancy and win the Bolshevik leadership to insurrection. So the party in the end played three crucial roles: first, it outlined a clear strategic policy aimed at winning a majority of workers to the idea that they should take power into their own hands. Second, it was able to tactically restrain sections of the class when it was clear that other sections were not ready to go. Third, it was able to win a majority of workers to its side by demonstrating in practice its superior leadership in the struggle, informed by a clear set of politics that corresponded to workers' own experience as the revolution unfolded.

The result was that on October 25, the Bolshevik Party and its allies organized a successful armed insurrection. The timing was meant to coincide with the opening of the Congress of Soviets, and Trotsky, who had recently been elected president of the Petrograd soviet, provided capable leadership of the uprising. Workers easily dispersed the provisional government and transferred power to the soviets. Though the subsequent civil war and isolation of the revolution eventually robbed Russian workers of their victory, the Russian Revolution shows us not only that ordinary people can change society, but that to win, we must build a network of organized, conscious revolutionaries committed to that change. "Not by compromise with the propertied classes," wrote the revolution's able chronicler John Reed (an American journalist),

> or with the other political leaders; not by conciliating the old Government mechanism, did the Bolsheviki conquer power. Nor by the organized violence of a small clique. If the masses all over Rus-

> sia had not been ready for insurrection it must have failed. The only reason for Bolshevik success lay in their accomplishing the vast and simple desires of the most profound strata of people, calling them to the work of tearing down and destroying the old, and afterward, in the smoke of falling ruins, cooperating with them to erect the framework of the new....[20]

How the revolution was lost

The Russian Revolution initiated changes unheard of even in the most advanced capitalist countries. It granted freedom to the oppressed nationalities, established workers' control in the factories, and distributed land to the peasantry. It established the right of immediate recall for all elected officials. It legalized divorce and decriminalized homosexuality. It initiated mass literacy campaigns and began producing cheap editions of great Russian literature. It opened up free nurseries for children and communal kitchens and laundries in order to free women from the drudgery of housework. Lenin and the other revolutionaries reiterated over and over again that the success of all these changes depended on the initiative of ordinary workers, struggling to reorganize society. Sadly, these first seeds of socialist construction, through no fault of the revolutionaries themselves, failed to flower into a new society.

The Russian Marxists were clear that economic conditions were ripe for socialism on a *world* scale, but an isolated Russia could not possibly survive as a workers' state. "We always staked our play," wrote Lenin, "upon an international revolution.... In one country it is impossible to accomplish such a work as a socialist revolution."[21] The Russian Revolution could not succeed ultimately unless it spread. "Without the direct governmental support of the European proletariat," Trotsky had written in 1906, "the working class of Russia will not be able to maintain itself in power."[22]

This internationalism was as much a practical as a moral imperative. In isolation, Russia did not possess the material or cultural basis for building a socialist society. Eighty percent of the population still lived off the land, and the average income per head in 1913 was, according to one calculation, somewhat below what it was for people in 1688 in England.[23] Socialism must be based upon material abundance. This is, Marx and Engels wrote, "an absolute practical premise [of communism], because without it, privation, *want* is merely made general, and with *want* the struggle for necessities would begin again, and all the old filthy business would necessarily be restored."[24]

Engels warned what might happen if the leader of an extreme party were "compelled to take over a government in an epoch when the movement is not yet ripe for the domination of the class which he represents." That leader, he argued, would be "compelled to represent not his party nor his class, but the class for whom conditions are ripe for domination.... What he *can* do contradicts all his previous actions and principles and the immediate interests of his party, and what he *ought* to do cannot be done."[25]

A revolutionary wave swept Europe in the wake of the Russian Revolution. But nowhere were workers' parties able to take power. The Russian Revolution was forced to fight a tough civil war without the support of any other revolutionary governments. In isolation, the revolutionary leaders of the new workers' government were compelled to behave in contradiction to their principles. Temporary measures of coercion necessitated by the extraordinary conditions of civil war became permanent. Leaders made a virtue of necessity, mistaking "War Communism," an enforced equality born of extreme scarcity, for the real thing.

Trotsky and other Russian revolutionaries had expected defeat, if it came, through the physical destruction of the workers' state by counterrevolutionary armies. But the Bolsheviks triumphed in the civil war. The revolution degenerated from within rather than being overthrown. The failure of the German Revolution of 1918–23 sealed the revolution's doom.[26] Instead, the revolution, besieged, blockaded, and starved, degenerated from within.

In 1918, Germany occupied the Ukraine, Russia's breadbasket. With arms and money from Western powers, the former generals of the Russian Army formed counterrevolutionary "white armies" to attack the new regime. They were aided by the initial leniency of the workers' state, which let former tsarist officers out of detention, on the written promise that they not take up arms against the revolution.[27] Japanese and U.S. troops also invaded, and Czech troops along the trans-Siberian railway also rose up in arms against the Soviet government. There were also military interventions by Britain, France, Italy, Romania, Serbia, Poland, and Canada.

The results of the civil war and blockade were catastrophic. If socialism is workers' control of production, by 1919 in Russia there were neither workers nor production. The most militant workers left the factories to fight at the front against the white armies or to join the new government. Fuel became scarce, and railroad transportation—the country's lifeblood—was reduced to a shadow of its prewar capacity. What meager resources there were went toward fighting the war. By the end of 1920, factory production had declined to 12.9 percent of its 1913 level, iron ore to 1.6 percent. There was a mass exodus of workers from the towns to the country in search of food. The number of industrial workers in 1921–22 was less than half of what it was in 1917. In three years, Petrograd lost 57.5 percent of its population, and Moscow 44.5 percent.[28] The working class, the social base of soviet power, ceased in any meaningful sense to exist as a class.

To make matters worse, the Bolsheviks were forced to requisition grain from the countryside in order to feed the troops and the towns because they had nothing to trade for it. This drove a wedge between the soviet government and the peasantry. The worker-peasant alliance continued to hold together precariously during the civil war, but when it ended, the peasantry turned against the Bolsheviks. The revolution was like a furious wooden train, tearing off pieces of itself to feed the engine—consuming itself in an effort to keep moving. Faced with these conditions, as Duncan Hallas wrote, "the Bolshevik party came to substitute itself for a decimated, exhausted working class that was itself a small fraction of the population."[29]

Increasingly, as soviet democracy atrophied, democratic control from below was replaced by control of the party, and society, by an apparatus of functionaries that drew heavily on the engineers, technicians, and bureaucrats of the old tsarist state. Lenin was forced to admit in 1922 that a thin veneer of Bolsheviks stood at the head of a vast layer of old tsarist administrators.[30] The party was forced to see itself as the trustee of workers' power, until such time as the international working class aided Russia in reviving its industry and reestablishing direct workers' rule once again. But as that possibility faded, the bureaucracy began to settle in as a new ruling caste with its own interests. It was on this foundation that the bureaucracy, led by Joseph Stalin, grew in importance. Stalin was at that time the party's general secretary—a post that in previous times wasn't powerful, but became more so as soviet democracy withered and a centralized authority grew in order to prosecute the civil war. In his analysis of the revolution's degeneration, Trotsky explained that:

> The revolution got no direct help from the West. Instead of expected prosperity of the country an ominous destitution reigned.... Moreover, the outstanding representatives of the working class either died in the civil war, or rose a few steps higher and broke away from the masses. And thus after an unexampled tension of forces, hopes and illusions, there came a long period of

> weariness, decline and sheer disappointment in the results of the revolution. The ebb of the "plebian pride" made room for a flood of pusillanimity and careerism. The new commanding caste rose to its place upon this wave.[31]

In the twelve years following Lenin's death in 1924, Stalin, the personification of the new party bureaucrat, pushed through a complete counterrevolution, obliterating all traces of 1917. The soviets ceased to be organs of democratic control and became rubber stamps. Bureaucratic managers ran the factories, not workers' committees, and workers were deprived of legal rights. Stalin promoted anti-Marxist ideas under the guise of Marxism. His theory of "socialism in one country" justified the new bureaucratic caste that ruled society. He physically liquidated the leaders of the revolution. According to his successor, Nikita Khrushchev, Stalin was responsible for the murders of 70 percent of the members and candidates of the party's central committee elected in 1934, 80 percent of whom had joined the party before 1921.[32] Trotsky was exiled, and later murdered by a Stalinist agent in Mexico in 1940.

Returning to Engels' warning at the beginning of this section, the Bolshevik leadership was "compelled to represent not [their] party nor [their] class, but the class for whom conditions are ripe for domination." That class was the bourgeoisie—the capitalists. But in Russia the revolution had economically destroyed the capitalist class. The bureaucrats became a kind of collective capitalist. If the Bolshevik Party was forced to substitute itself for the working class, the bureaucracy in turn substituted itself for the non-existent capitalist class.

What worried Stalin most was Russia's international position. How could Russia survive without heavy industry? The turning point of Stalin's counterrevolution came in 1928 with the announcement of the first Five-Year Plan, which set drastically high goals for industrial growth. The plan was accompanied by the beginning of the forced collectivization of the peasantry, aimed at squeezing maximum surplus from agricultural production. Russia's workers and peasants were dragooned into the service of breakneck industrialization, super-exploited for the sake of Russia's industrial development. Prior to this period, economic growth was accompanied by improvements in living standards. Now, wages and social spending were entirely subordinated to the siphoning of the maximum amount of surplus wealth into expanding heavy industry. Forced labor was employed on a mass scale, entire populations were uprooted, and millions died in the state terror used to carry it all through. It was as if the period of primitive accumulation—the expropriation of the peasantry, chattel slavery, and so on—prior to the takeoff of industrialization in Britain was condensed into a period of several years instead of a few centuries. "We are fifty or a hundred years behind the advanced countries," Stalin declared in 1931. "We must make good this distance in ten years. Either we do so, or we shall go under."[33] The real meaning of socialism was distorted beyond recognition, and used not as a guide to human liberation, but as an ideology to justify a program of accumulation on the backs of the Russian workers and peasants.

Russia gave us only a brief but brilliant glimpse of workers' power. Sadly, the Stalinist bureaucracy that rose on its ruin for decades gave real socialism a bad name—one it does not deserve. Rosa Luxemburg's beautiful defense of the Russian Revolution, written in 1918, reads in retrospect as the best epitaph on the significance of the Russian Revolution:

> Everything that happens in Russia is comprehensible and represents an inevitable chain of causes and effects, the starting point and end term of which are: the failure of the German proletariat and the occupation of Russia by German imperialism. It would be demanding something superhuman from Lenin and his comrades if we should expect of them that under such circumstances they should conjure forth the finest democracy, the most exemplary dictatorship of the proletariat and a flourishing socialist economy. By their determined revolutionary stand, their exemplary strength in action, and their unbreakable loyalty to international socialism, they have contributed whatever could possibly be contributed under such devilishly hard conditions....
>
> Lenin and Trotsky and their friends were the *first*, those who went ahead as an example to the proletariat of the world; they are still the *only ones* up to now who can cry with Hutten: "I have dared!"
>
> This is the essential and *enduring* in Bolshevik policy. In *this* sense theirs is the immortal historical service of having marched at the head of the international proletariat with the conquest of political power and the practical placing of the problem of the realization of socialism, and of having advanced mightily the settlement of the score between capital and labor in the entire world. In Russia, the problem could only be posed. It could not be solved in Russia. And in *this* sense, the future everywhere belongs to "Bolshevism."[34]

The myth of "state" socialism

The single worst legacy of Stalinism was to reinforce the mistaken notion that socialism can be measured by the degree of state control of the economy. Societies with strong social spending programs and some state-run industries were considered moderately socialist—like Sweden.

(I can't count how many times I have been asked, "When you say socialism, do you mean Sweden?") Societies with more complete state control of the economy—like the Stalinist Soviet Union before it fell, or Cuba today—were considered fully socialist, or "communist."

The existence of a more or less expansive social safety net may indicate a strong history of class struggle and strong unions who at some point were able to extract important concessions from the employers. But concessions wrested from a capitalist state do not render that society socialist. Nor is the degree of state ownership a measure of socialism. State-run industries under capitalism do not operate as islands of socialism, but on the same principles of profit and loss as in the private sector. "A kind of spurious socialism has arisen … that … declares *all* state ownership … to be socialistic," Frederick Engels wrote more than one hundred years ago. "Certainly, if the taking over by the state of the tobacco industry is socialistic, then Napoleon … must be numbered among the founders of socialism."[35]

Even total state ownership, Engels argued, is not socialism:

> The transformation—either into joint-stock companies and trusts, or into State-ownership—does not do away with the capitalistic nature of the productive forces. In the joint-stock companies and trusts, this is obvious. And the modern State, again, is only the organization that bourgeois society takes on in order to support the external conditions of the capitalist mode of production against the encroachments as well of the workers as of individual capitalists. The modern state, no matter what its form, is essentially a capitalist machine—the state of the capitalists, the ideal personification of the total national capital. The more it proceeds to the taking over of productive forces, the more does it actually become the national capitalist, the more citizens does it exploit. The workers remain wage-workers—proletarians.[36]

Before Stalin expelled him from Russia in 1928, Trotsky waged a fight against the rising bureaucracy. But he clung to the idea that since nationalized property in Russia had been established as a result of a workers' revolution, Russia could not be "state capitalist," that is, a nation where the state exercised the same control over industry as the capitalists in other countries. Nevertheless, he could still stay about the nationalized industries in Mexico in the 1930s that, "The Nationalization of railways and oilfields in Mexico has of course nothing in common with socialism. It is a measure of state capitalism." Trotsky noted that in Mexico, union leaders were involved in the management of these state-run industries. This had nothing to do with workers' control. The union leaders' were expected to play the role of "disciplining the working class, making it more industrious in the service of the common interests of the state, which appears on the surface to merge with the interests of the working class itself."[37] This is certainly the role unions played in Stalin's Russia.

In 1980, a workers' newspaper, *Jednosc,* published by Solidarnosc activists in Szczecin, Poland, made the same point, arguing that a distinction must be made between state ownership and social ownership, because the Polish state "apparatus" represented the "denial" and "negation" of the "world of labor."[38]

With state ownership of production, "The capitalist relation is not done away with," wrote Engels, "it is rather brought to a head."[39] Countries where most of the means of production are concentrated in the hands of a state bureaucracy, but where workers have no control over that production, have nothing to do with socialism. Workers' revolts in Eastern Europe—including the forming of workers' councils in Hungary in 1956, similar to the 1917 soviets—were the practical proof that these societies were socialist in name only.

The Cuban Revolution overthrew a corrupt regime, stood up to the colossus to the north, and implemented a series of sweeping social reforms benefiting Cuba's poor, making it one of the most remarkable revolutions in the Western Hemisphere. But Cuba's workers played hardly any role at all in its victory, nor did they exercise any control over the state in its aftermath. Fidel Castro, Ernesto "Che" Guevara, and a relatively small group of several hundred guerrillas toppled the regime of Fulgencia Batista in 1959. Facing an American embargo, they began to nationalize U.S.-owned property. Castro only retroactively declared the Cuban Revolution "socialist" some two years later, modeling Cuba's one-party state (based on Fidel's personal rule) on Russian-style state capitalist–led development. Supporters of Cuba (that is, who support the regime itself rather than its defense against the United States) claim that various reforms such as improved health care, better education, and so on, are indications of Cuba's socialist character. These were no doubt important gains of the revolution. But then again, a number of important democratic and social gains issued also from the French Revolution, and it was not socialist. If free secondary education and national health care are to be deemed socialist, then Canada must be included on the list.[40]

The claim is also made that the Cuban government is controlled from below by the people. But this is to confuse mass participation and popularity with democratic decision-making and control. Popular organizations in Cuba are transmission belts for directives from the top, rather than institutions of control from below. Bureaucratic planning is geared toward figuring out how to develop and diversify the Cuban economy, of which labor is merely another input that is exploited in the same way workers are exploited in a GM factory in Detroit. Raul Castro, Fidel's brother, described the role of unions in Cuba in the 1970s as something akin to the role of managers in a capitalist enterprise: "One of the principal functions of the trade unions under socialism is to serve as a vehicle for the orientation, directives, and goals which the revolutionary power must convey to the working masses.... The principal tasks [in which the unions should be involved] are productivity and work discipline; [and] more efficient utilization of the work day."[41] Minister of labor Jorge Risquet was careful that same year to inform Cuba's workers that, "The fact that Fidel and I have suggested that the workers should be consulted does not mean that we are going to negate the vanguard role that the Party must play.... The decision and responsibility [in the enterprise]," he insisted, "fall to the management," which must have, "and does have, all the authority to act."[42]

The same holds true for planning. A socialist society seeks to end the anarchy of the market by introducing conscious planning. But planning alone doesn't equal socialism. There are already elements of planning under capitalism. There is planning within firms, within the Pentagon, in the post office, and so on. But none of these forms of planning eliminate the anarchy of the market. Instead, they are driven by it. There is state planning in Cuba, but the plan is shaped by Cuba's survival and the negotiation of its precarious position within the world economy, of which it is a small, isolated patch. The planning isn't democratic, or fully under the planner's control. In all of these examples, the planning is designed to maximize output and profit at the expense of the worker, not to meet human need. Imagine the tremendous organization and planning involved in executing a major U.S.-led war, and you get some idea of what might be possible if all that energy were used to adequately feed, house, clothe, and educate everyone on the planet.

The question of nationalization is not unimportant, as for example when Bolivian workers and peasants demand that the country's natural gas industry be nationalized in order that the wealth it yields doesn't end up siphoned off by global capital. But so long as nationalization is based upon production and competition in a world market, it will be *capitalist* nationalization.

For Marxists, nationalization can only be a weapon in the transformation of society in a socialist direction if the working class has first placed itself in power. Is it doing the planning or is it being planned? The question of whether socialism exists therefore does not depend on this or that form of property (private ownership or nationalization), but on whether the society is in the hands of the associated producers—the working class. In fact, the aim of workers' power is to implement a series of economic and social transformations that do away with all class distinctions and create a society whereby the state—an instrument of class domination—gradually fades away. As Engels wrote, "The proletariat seizes the public power, and by means of this transforms the socialized means of production, slipping from the hands of the bourgeoisie, into public property." The economy, now under workers' control, socializes the means of production so that production and distribution can be carried out according to a rational plan that meets human need. "In proportion as anarchy in social production vanishes," Engels continued, "the political authority of the state dies out."[43] To be successful, this process requires that socialism be international. All talk of there being long-standing islands of socialism—socialist states—floating for years on a sea of capitalist competition is simply an absurdity. Socialism in one cooperative, one city, one island, or one country, is a contradiction in terms.

Chapter Nine

Imperialism, Nationalism, and War

Historian Eric Hobsbawn calculated that 187 million people died from wars in the last century—more than the total world population in 1000 A.D. and a tenth of the total world population in 1913.[1] If the U.S. government has its way, this century promises similar, if not worse, barbarism.

Given this grim picture, it is tempting to see war as something that is inherent in human nature—something we are "hard wired" to do. In this view, war comes from the fact that people naturally divide into groups—racial, ethnic, linguistic—and develop hostility to those that are "different." This concept has been reinforced by various pseudoscientific studies that compare humans to other animals—though they are careful to choose only the aggressive ones—in order to show that we relish war.

It may be true that human beings have the capacity for aggression, submission, and a host of other behavioral traits. But for every example of "aggression" in human behavior, we can also find peaceful cooperation and sharing. If human beings are naturally warlike, one wonders why it is necessary for governments to take young men at a very early age and put them through a rigorous retraining to make them capable of systematically killing other humans. The "fight or flight" instinct, after all, implies a basic capacity to engage in two opposite behaviors, depending on circumstances.

In some pre-class societies, there was little or no warfare—as among the foraging Western Shoshone in the Southwest before European contact, for example. Anthropologist R. Brian Ferguson's partially finished survey of the archeological record supports the view that systematic warfare did not emerge until around ten thousand years ago, when populations began to live in permanent settlements and develop social hierarchies.[2]

Moreover, the character of war in pre-class and pre-state societies of which we have any record was vastly different from modern warfare. There were no professional groups of fighters. Men were hunters or fighters, as conditions demanded. Often, war consisted of skirmishes that broke off as soon as anyone was killed or injured. Among Plains Indians, war parties tried to avoid combat that resulted in death, and "counting coup," touching an enemy's body with the hand or a special stick, ranked as a higher feat than killing.[3] Renegade Rhode Island colonist Roger Williams noted that the fighting between the Indian nations he observed was "farre lesse bloudy and devouring than the cruell Warres of Europe."[4] According to Captain John Underhill, a leader of a massacre on an undefended Pequot village in 1637, a group of Narragansett Indians allied with the English withdrew from the attack, complaining that the English style of warfare "slays too many men."[5]

War wasn't as prevalent in pre-class societies for the simple reason that such societies didn't produce surpluses over and above their subsistence needs. Nor could one person be enslaved by another—for the simple reason that no one could be forced to produce wealth above and beyond their own subsistence needs. This explains why in earlier forms of warfare, captives were either killed or simply adopted by the winning side, and war itself often consisted of skirmishes producing light casualties. Only with the rise of agriculture and the production of a surplus—which in turn produced the first ruling classes (the keepers of the surplus)—did warfare become a systematic practice, engaged in by specially armed subjects of a ruler in order to gain extra surplus and slaves. The rulers in turn created loyalty among their armed retainers by giving out the spoils of conquest—land, slaves, and goods.

But the struggle for the surplus didn't just produce wars between rival kingdoms. Class society also gave rise, inevitably, to violent conflict between social classes over how the surplus was used. Systematic warfare came with the emergence of the state—of special armed bodies whose purpose was both to protect the position of the minority who controlled the surplus (from the majority who produced it), as well as pillage the wealth produced by other groups.

Modern warfare has economic rather than biological roots. "In the modern world undoubtedly the most potent cause of war is economic rivalry—a purely cultural phenomenon having no biological basis whatsoever," wrote anthropologist Ashley Montagu.[6] But even the wars of conquest and plunder by Alexander the Great and the Roman Empire pale in comparison to war as it developed under capitalism.

White man's burden

The idea of peaceful competition is an invention of economics professors. War, conquest, and plunder accompanied capitalism from its inception. With the emergence of the world's first commercial powers in Europe in the fifteenth and sixteenth centuries, violence was the rule rather than the exception. As the merchant capitalists became powerful, they depended upon their "home" governments to extend their markets and sources of raw materials and goods by force. What we know as freewheeling pirates on the open seas were often employees of one state, hired to capture and plunder the booty stolen, extracted, or extorted from some part of the world by another state. The market and the state intertwined, producing a system of competing states, fighting in Europe, North America, and Asia for control of the world's trade.

In the European powers' struggle for supremacy in North America, Native American peoples were deliberately pitted against each other. European encroachment on their farmlands and hunting grounds, and the introduction of European diseases decimated their ranks, pushing them westward and forcing them to cling to survival in tiny enclaves. Massacres were common. Marx described in *Capital* how

> In 1703 those sober exponents of Protestantism, the Puritans of New England, by decrees of their assembly set a premium of 40 pounds on every Indian scalp and every captured redskin; in 1720, a premium of 100 pounds was set on every scalp; in 1744, after Massachusetts bay had proclaimed a certain tribe as rebels, the following prices were laid down: for a male scalp of 12 years and upwards, 100 pounds in new currency, for a male prisoner 105 pounds, for women and children prisoners 50 pounds, for the scalps of women and children 50 pounds.[7]

This earlier, commercial form of imperialism—which as we've seen also involved the slave trade and forced labor—gave way later to a new form of imperialism based on the rise of industrial power.

At the time Marx wrote the *Communist Manifesto*, industrial capitalism had developed only in Britain and a few European countries. But as the twentieth century approached, capitalism became a truly global system. The relatively small capitalist enterprises of the early phase of industrial capitalism gave way, in the process of competition and crisis, to monopoly—the dominance of one or a handful of giant conglomerates over a single market. With the growth of monopoly capitalism, capitalist production burst the bounds of the nation-state, and was forced to seek outlets overseas. The result was not only economic competition—which led to its opposite, monopoly—but military competition between the great powers on an international scale.

The period of the 1890s found the most powerful new industrialized states—Britain and France, and soon the United States, Germany, and Japan—scrambling to divide the world between themselves into colonies or "spheres of influence." The new imperialism was marked off from its predecessors by the sheer scale of the conquest. In 1876, for example, Africans controlled almost 90 percent of African territory. By 1900, Europeans controlled 90 percent of African territory. Indeed, the entire surface of the globe was conquered and shared out between a tiny number of powers.[8]

The great powers sought colonies and semi-colonies in order to secure sources of raw materials (produced with cheap, sometimes forced, labor) and investments, as well as to keep out competing empires. In southern Africa, Black Africans were forced off their land and compelled to work as cheap laborers in gold and diamond mines, making a handful of men like Cecil Rhodes and J. B. Robinson extremely rich. (Knowing this, I wince every time I turn on the radio and hear a bouncy advertisement for J. B. Robinson jewelry.) When gold was discovered in Matabeleland in the 1880s, Lobengula, chief of the Matabele people, refused to accept a treaty he had been tricked into signing that gave Rhodes and his associates the right to mine for gold anywhere they wanted. Rhodes, who was already rich from mining diamonds, organized an army and invaded Matabeleland, massacring thousands using the Maxim gun. Each of the 672 soldiers in Rhodes' army was promised six thousand acres of land and twenty gold claims.[9] This is how Britain brought "enlightened" rule to Africa. The massacre prompted the poet Hillaire Belloc to write: "Whatever happens we have got / The Maxim gun and they have not."[10]

The case of the Belgian Congo is the most horrific example of how the effort to extract maximum profit could lead to mass murder. King Leopold of Belgium formed a society called the International Association of the Congo, whose "noble aim" was to render "lasting and disinterested services to the cause of progress."[11] The association's lasting service was, in reality, to provide a humanitarian cover for naked plunder.

Leopold established a system to force Africans in the Congo River Basin to bring in ivory and rubber. Historians estimate that Leopold's "humanitarian" enterprise led to the deaths of roughly 6 to 10 million people between 1885 and 1908. This genocidal "mistreatment" of Africans was extremely profitable. The Anglo-Belgian India Rubber and Exploration Company made a profit of more than 700 percent in the Congo.[12]

The impact of British rule in India was no less atrocious. India on the eve of its conquest by the British in the 1750s was economically as wealthy as Europe. But forced labor, the wrecking of India's textile industry with cheap British manufactures, and the destruction of India's traditional irrigation and granary systems all combined to wreck India's economy for many decades. Tens of millions of people died of starvation in a series of devastating famines. In Britain, criticism of the stinginess of its famine relief in India was brushed aside on social Darwinist grounds: "Every benevolent attempt made to mitigate the effects of famine and defective sanitation," finance minister Evelyn Baring assured his colleagues, only "serves but to enhance the evils resulting from overpopulation."[13] Aside from the construction of railroads—which in any case the British set up only in order to transport troops and move India's wealth out of the country—India was for a long period underdeveloped by British imperialism. "If the history of British rule in India," concluded historian Mike Davis, "were to be condensed to a single fact, it is this: there was no increase in India's per-capita income from 1757 to 1947."[14]

The eagle and its talons

There is a peculiar myth told in this country that the United States is neither an empire, nor imperialist. We are, so the tale goes, a freedom-loving nation that goes to war only for noble causes. "America the benevolent," wrote historian Sidney Lens,

> does not exist and never has existed. The United States has pilfered large territories from helpless or near-helpless peoples; it has forced its will on scores of nations, against their wishes and against their interests; it has violated hundreds of treaties and understandings; it has committed war crimes as shocking as most; it has wielded a military stick and a dollar carrot to forge an imperialist empire such as man has never known before; it has intervened ruthlessly in the internal life of dozens of nations to prevent them from choosing the leaders they did want or from overthrowing, by revolution, ones they didn't.[15]

The United States emerged as a world power in the late 1800s, and quickly became the biggest economic power in the world. But it emerged as a power after the scramble for colonies was mostly completed. As a result of this, the United States found it congenial to develop a more informal empire. Where it was unable to establish its own exclusive sphere, for example in China, Washington advanced the "open door" policy in order to push its way in. But in its own "backyard," the Caribbean and the Pacific, the United States established a "closed door" policy, using its military power to establish absolute hegemony. When the United States went to war with Spain in 1898, it claimed that it was motivated by a desire to free Spanish colonies—Cuba, Puerto Rico, and the Philippines, from Spanish tyranny. As payment for this benevolent service, the United States made colonies or protectorates out of all of them.

Politicians in Washington were not above justifying conquest on racist grounds, either. President William McKinley explained to a group of Methodist Church leaders in 1899 that granting the Filipinos "self-government" would undoubtedly create "anarchy and misrule." Therefore, the only choice for the United States was to "take them all and to educate the Filipinos, and uplift and civilize and Christianize them."[16] But first the United States had to send seventy thousand troops to the Philippines to crush the independence movement there, which had first developed in opposition to Spanish rule, but had since turned against the Americans. One historian describes how by 1901 the war had degenerated into a mass slaughter. After Filipino nationalist guerrillas attacked a town in Samar under U.S. occupation and killed fifty-four U.S. soldiers, the American military instigated a reign of terror on the island:

> General ["Howlin' Jake"] Smith, fresh from his "victories" in northern Luzon and Panay, was chosen to lead the American mission of revenge. Smith's order to his men embarking upon the Samar campaign could not have been more explicit: "Kill and burn, kill and burn, the more you kill and the more you burn the more you please me." … When asked to define the age limit for killing, Smith gave his infamous reply: "Everything over ten." Smith ordered Samar to be turned into a "howling wilderness" so that "even the birds could not live there." … The now-familiar pattern of operations began once again. All inhabitants of the island (pop. 266,000) were ordered to present themselves to detention camps in several of the larger coastal towns. Those who did not (or those who did not make it their business to learn the existence of the order), and were found outside the detention camp perimeter, would be shot, "and no questions asked." Few reporters covered the carnage; one who did noted: "During my stay in Samar the only prisoners that were

> made … were taken by Waller's command; and I heard this act criticized by the highest officers as a mistake.... The truth is, the struggle in Samar is one of extermination."[17]

In the end, the U.S. Army's murderous scorched-earth policy wiped out upwards of a million Filipinos.[18]

The barbarism of the United States in the Philippines prompted the great satirist Mark Twain to become a staunch opponent of imperialism. "I left these shores … a red-hot imperialist. I wanted the American eagle to go screaming into the Pacific," Twain told a *New York Herald* reporter in 1900. However, he explained, "I have seen that we do not intend to free, but to subjugate the people of the Philippines. We have gone there to conquer, not to redeem." He concluded, "I am an anti-imperialist. I am opposed to having the eagle put its talons on any other land."[19]

Even where the United States shunned formal colonies, its practices were almost identical. In the Caribbean, the United States made a practice of demanding that countries hand over control of their customs houses to U.S. officials and banks, in order to ensure repayment of loans. When a country refused, the United States invaded. U.S. Marines occupied Haiti and stayed there from 1915 to 1934, for example. They imposed a new constitution that opened up Haiti to foreign land ownership and handed the country's customs houses and banking system over to the National City Bank of New York, and crushed all resistance.[20]

Woodrow Wilson in 1907 clarified how, for the United States, the "open door" policy was a strategy to maximize U.S. dominance:

> Since trade ignores national boundaries, and the manufacturer insists on having the world as a market, the flag of his nation must follow him, and the doors of the nations which are closed against him must be battered down. Concessions obtained by financiers must be safeguarded by ministers of state, even if the sovereignty of unwilling nations be outraged in the process.[21]

Imperialist rivalry and war

As the earth became completely carved up into "spheres of influence" between the great powers, competition between them intensified. A "balance of power" was maintained by each state arming itself to the teeth. But the balance was continually in danger of being upset by the emergence of a new power eager for a slice of the imperial pie.

Lenin, writing at the time of the First World War, described this new period of capitalism as *imperialism*—in a nutshell, capitalism in its monopoly stage, the world market dominated by giant capitalist trusts, backed up by powerful states fighting to carve up the world amongst themselves. He called monopoly capitalism "the economic essence of imperialism," noting its main features as "monopolies, oligarchy, the striving for domination and not for freedom, the exploitation of an increasing number of small or weak nations by a handful of the richest or most powerful nations."[22]

Lenin's analysis, written in 1916 in the midst of the slaughter of the First World War, pointed to the fact that imperialism was not a policy, but a new stage in the development of capitalism that grew out of earlier conditions. Just as "free" competition gave way to monopoly, so "free trade" gave way to trade wars and armed conflict. The logic of imperialism was grounded in international economic competition between states, leading to war.

There were people at the time, like German socialist Karl Kautsky, who argued that the creation of a world market and economic interdependence between nations would make war obsolete, creating a new system of "ultra-imperialism."[23] Unfortunately, the fact that there is economic interdependence does not lead to peaceful relations between states, much less their disappearance. Two tendencies always have to be kept in mind, as Lenin noted, in capitalism's development: on the one hand, "the awakening of national life ... and the creation of nation states" and, on the other hand, "the development and growing frequency of international intercourse" and "the breakdown of national barriers."[24] These two contradictory tendencies—toward interdependence on the one hand, and toward consolidation of national states on the other—have been constant features of capitalism throughout its history. The balance between the two tendencies, and the way the contradiction has expressed itself, has shifted. But the contradiction remains, even today, at the heart of world capitalism.

In addition to its role in maintaining class rule, capitalists needed a centralized state as a means of creating a single, unified market that could facilitate commerce. But the state is also crucial in providing necessary infrastructure, and sometimes the pooling of capital resources needed for national capitalists to operate and compete effectively. As capitalism burst the bounds of the nation-state, the coercive military function of the state took on a new dimension—that of protecting (and projecting) the interests of the capitalists of one country over those of another. The role of the state increased, the size of the state bureaucracy increased, and the size of its coercive apparatus increased.

"The development of world capitalism leads," wrote Russian revolutionary Nikolai Bukharin,

> on the one hand, to an internationalization of economic life and, on the other, to the leveling of economic differences—and to an infinitely greater degree, the same process of economic development intensifies the tendency to "nationalize" capitalist interests, to form narrow "national" groups armed to the teeth and ready to hurl themselves at one another any moment.[25]

It is true that, as Trotsky wrote during the First World War, "The natural tendency of our economic system ... is to seek to break through the state boundaries. The whole globe, the land and the sea, the surface as well as the interior, has become one economic workshop, the different parts of which are inseparably connected with each other."[26] But this process, rather than leading to peaceful competition, leads to a struggle for dominance:

> The way the governments propose to solve this problem of imperialism is not through the intelligent, organized cooperation of all of humanity's producers, but through the exploitation of the world's economic system by the capitalist class of the victorious country; which country is by this War to be transformed from a great power into a world power.[27]

Two devastating world wars that consumed millions of lives underscored the truth of Trotsky's observation. The whole history of world conflict up to the present day consists of the continual rejigging of power relations between a handful of states and their allies. The economic relations between different states continually change (think of the recent rise of China and India), compelling new trade and diplomatic intrigues, as "upstarts" try to assert their power and the established powers try to hang on, or expand, what power they have. Ultimately, force decides who is to be top dog. But since the economic balance of forces keeps changing, new conflicts always emerge and the game begins anew.

Today, we no longer have a world divided between many contending colonial powers, as in the early twentieth century. A series of anticolonial movements and revolutions, combined with the declining economic value of the colonies, put an end to this era in the years following the Second World War. The United States emerged as the world's dominant power, both economically and militarily. Instead of a world divided between several centers of world power, imperial rivalry took the form of a Cold War between two superpowers, the United States and the Soviet Union. Each had enough nuclear weapons to destroy the world several times over, in a balance of terror appropriately called MAD—mutually assured destruction. Much of the conflict of the Cold War took the form not of direct military conflict between Russia and the United States, but of smaller conflicts on the system's periphery, such as the Korean and Vietnam Wars. Russia was never economically strong enough to challenge U.S. hegemony over major parts of the globe. Ideologically, though, the United States used the Russian threat as an excuse for whatever interventions it undertook, such as when it destabilized and overthrew nationalist regimes it opposed. Fighting communism was used as the excuse to overthrow the Mossadegh government in Iran in 1953, the Arbenz government in Guatemala in 1954, the Allende government in Chile in 1973, and many others.[28]

The end of the Cold War did not mean the end of imperialism or military conflict, but it has changed the playing field. The United States emerged as the sole superpower, more than twice the size of its nearest economic rival and several times bigger militarily. The United States alone accounts for half the world's military spending.[29] It is the only state with a truly global military reach, boasting 725 military bases around the globe, not including the United States.[30] The logic of imperialist rivalry compels America's rulers to continually demonstrate and reinforce this dominance, lest its relative position in the world pecking order slips or any potential challengers detect any weakening.

After the fall of the Soviet Union, the United States cast around for a new rationale for its role as global hegemon. It found it in the "war on terror." The Bush administration saw in the September 11, 2001, tragedy a unique window of opportunity—a modern-day Pearl Harbor—that created ideal conditions for advancing its agenda. Some months after September 11, Secretary of State Condoleezza Rice described the attacks as an "enormous opportunity," and that the United States "must move to take advantage of these new opportunities."[31]

The invasion of Afghanistan was first and foremost a warm-up for the invasion of Iraq, and was secondarily about establishing a strategic military presence in Central Asia. Overthrowing the Taliban and going after al Qaeda was merely a pretext. Likewise, the invasion and occupation of Iraq had nothing to do with the character of the Iraqi regime. The United States has always supported "friendly" dictators—and will continue to do so. The U.S. invasion of Iraq in 2003, in the extremely accurate pre-invasion prediction of Jay Bookman of the *Atlanta Journal-Constitution*, was "not really about Iraq. It is not about weapons of mass destruction, or terrorism, or Saddam, or U.N. resolutions." Rather, the war was intended "to mark the official emergence of the United States as a full-fledged global empire, seizing sole responsibility and authority as planetary policeman." They never had an "exit strategy," argued Bookman, not out of incompetence, but because the United States was interested in creating "permanent military bases in that country from which to dominate the Middle East, including neighboring Iran."[32]

It is tempting to see the movement of American imperialism into overdrive after September 11 as the product of temporary insanity. Some of the pronouncements of the Bush administration would have come off as almost Monty Pythonesque if it weren't for the terrible bloodletting they justified. "The generals in Iraq must understand clearly there will be consequences for their behavior," Bush smugly warned on the eve of the U.S. invasion. "Should they choose ... to behave in a way that endangers the lives of their own citizens, as well as citizens in the neighborhood, there will be a consequence. They will be held to account."[33] In reading this, I was reminded of the *requierimiento*, an official document sixteenth-century conquistadors were meant to read out loud to their victims (in Spanish, a language those about to be attacked could not understand) before they slaughtered them. The document insisted that its listeners accept the Church and the Spanish Crown, warning:

> But if you do not do this, and maliciously make delay in it ... we shall powerfully enter into your country, and shall make war against you in all ways and manners that we can, and shall subject you to the yoke and obedience of the Church and of their highnesses. We shall take you, and your wives, and your children, and shall make slaves of them, and as such shall sell and dispose of them as their highnesses may command; and we shall take away your goods, and shall do you all the mischief and damage that we can, as to vassals who do not obey.... And we protest that the deaths and losses which shall accrue from this are your fault, and not that of their highnesses, or ours, nor of these cavaliers who come with us.[34]

The text may be arcane but its twisted logic strikes me as utterly modern. Obey the United States, and if you refuse, you will be to blame for the destruction we visit on you. Only now a twist is added: Since we are here to give you "freedom," you have no reason to resist. "We're here to give you your fucking freedom," a U.S. Marine shouted at a crowd of Iraqis protesting the occupation in Baghdad. "Now back off."[35]

The insanity thesis ignores the essential continuity in U.S. foreign policy. The disagreements between different administrations and parties in Washington have not been over *whether* the United States should militarily and economically dominate the world, but *how* (unilaterally or with subordinate allies?). Democrat Bill Clinton, it should be recalled, ratcheted up the military budget by $112 billion, rehabilitated Reagan's "Star Wars" missile defense program, and sent troops into other countries more times than all four previous presidents combined. He enforced sanctions against Iraq that resulted in a million deaths. Indeed, the Clinton administration made the case for intervening in "failed states" to impose "regime change," setting the table for what was to come.[36]

Three of the chief goals of U.S. imperialism today, according to Chalmers Johnson, are: to "maintain absolute military preponderance over the rest of the world, a task that includes imperial policing to ensure that no part of the empire slips the leash"; "attempting to control as many sources of petroleum as possible, both to service America's insatiable demand for fossil fuels and to use it as a bargaining chip with even more oil-dependent regions"; and "providing work and income for the military-industrial complex (as, for example, in the exorbitant profits Halliburton has extracted for building and operating Camps Bondsteel and Monteith)."[37] This comprehensive framework has the advantage of explaining not only why the United States invaded Iraq (oil), but why it meddles in Africa, Asia, and every other corner of the globe.

The United States has been an imperialist power now for more than a century, cloaking its predatory aims with claims to be spreading democracy, removing tyrants, fighting communism, bringing humanitarian help, and now defending the "homeland" against terrorism. The most significant innovation after September 11 was the brazenness with which pundits proclaimed America's God-given right to police the world. It is now fashionable to accept that the United States is an empire that has the right and duty to be, in the words of international relations professor and former army colonel Andrew Bacevich, "the world's sole military superpower until the end of time."[38]

That does not mean that everything has gone Washington's way. The defeat in Vietnam was a clear reminder that the beast is not invulnerable. The way in which the occupation of Iraq, which was meant to be a cakewalk, turned into a quagmire, thanks primarily to the stiff resistance Iraqis put up to the destruction of their country, is another reminder. And though the United States will for years continue to be top dog, its relative economic and military power is bound to decline.

The "national interest"

Politicians from both sides of the aisle are fond of making pronouncements about "national interests," or what's good or bad for "America" and its "national security." It is a time-honored practice to present the interests of the dominant class as those of the nation as a whole. An appeal to nationalism justifies all sorts of nefarious practices, from government surveillance and repression to building up large military arsenals and bombing other countries.

The idea of the nation has some basis in reality—everyone on the planet belongs to some nationality and lives in a territory ruled over by a state. But everyone also belongs to a social class, and national policy serves the interests of the dominant one. "Beware of people who make a sacred idol of the State," writes international studies professor Benedict Anderson, "and beware of those who talk a lot about 'our splendid ancestors.' Your pocket is about to be picked."[39]

Whenever phrases like "national interests" are thrown around to defend some government action—whether it is a spending cut or a declaration of war—it is necessary to ask, in Lenin's words, "who stands to gain?" "It is not important," wrote Lenin,

> *who* directly advocates a particular policy, since under the present noble system of capitalism, any money-bag can always "hire," buy or enlist any number of lawyers, writers and even parliamentary deputies, professors, parsons and the like to defend any views. We live in an age of commerce, when the bourgeoisie have no scruples about trading in honor or conscience.[40]

In every war the United States has fought, the country's rulers have claimed it was fought in the "national interest." Yet in each case the beneficiaries were a minority at the top. Every extension of empire benefited not the majority, whose conditions of life always had more in common with the majority of the people being conquered, but bankers, industrialists, military contractors, and so on. This truth, in wartime, can be a dangerous one for those expressing it. "Wars throughout history have been waged for conquest and plunder," Debs told a crowd in 1918. "The master class has always declared the wars; the subject class has always fought the battles."[41] For that speech, Debs was imprisoned at age sixty-two.

Globalization: the new frontier-less frontier?

Capitalism has always been a global system. But the term "globalization," as used by politicians and the media, seems to mean something more.

What are they referring to? Globalization is "shorthand for an aggressive program," first developed in the late 1970s, "that involves government deregulation of industry, privatization of government services and liberalization of barriers to international finance and trade."[42] These policies, pushed by international financial and trade institutions like the World Trade Organization, the International Monetary Fund, and the World Bank over the last twenty-five years, are designed to pry open national markets to American and European capitalist interests. As an ideology, globalization has been used to justify the necessity of domestic austerity measures, job cuts, and social service cuts. "Each national ruling class and government can wash their hands of responsibility, saying essentially, 'Globalization made me do it,'" wrote labor journalist Lee Sustar.[43]

Some writers see globalization as more than neoliberal economic policies—instead, it is a new stage of world economic development. Capitalist production, trade, and investment are so footloose, the argument goes, that national states have become irrelevant. "This emerging new stage in world capitalism," writes one left-wing economist, "points to a supersession through transnational integration of 'national' economies. Fundamentally, there has been a progressive dismantling of autonomous ... national production systems and their reactivation as constituent elements of an integral world production system."[44]

The changes over the past three decades are certainly impressive. State capitalism has disappeared in Russia and Eastern Europe, as part of a steady worldwide trend away from state-led economic development. World trade, foreign investment, and international financial transactions have increased astronomically over the past few decades. Foreign direct investment increased between 1982 and 2000 from $57 billion to $1.3 trillion, and the value of world exports "more than doubled in 1982–90, from $2.1 billion to $4.4 billion, and then had surpassed $7 billion by 2000."[45] Some 63,000 transnational corporations with about 690,000 foreign affiliates dominate world trade and production.[46] In 1998, the total foreign sales of these corporations exceeded total world exports by $4.3 billion.[47] Production systems are now so globally integrated that a single product is made in several countries using raw materials from several other countries.

These facts have led some to revive the arguments made by Karl Kautsky in 1914 that economic integration signals the end of imperialism, that is, of competition between states for world domination. "The United States does not, and indeed no nation-state can today, form the center of an imperialist project," argue Michael Hardt and Antonio

Negri in their influential tome, *Empire*. "Imperialism is over. No nation will be world leader in the way modern European states were."[48]

The Hardt and Negri thesis is especially strange given the scale and number of military interventions by the United States in recent decades, from Panama (1989) to the Balkans in the mid-1990s, Iraq in 1990 and 2003, and Afghanistan in 2001. If anything, the U.S. empire is far more dominant in the world today than any European power was in the era of classical imperialism. Moreover, it is committed to maintaining, in the words of neoconservative Paul Wolfowitz in a draft policy statement written in 1992, "the mechanisms for deterring potential competitors from even aspiring to a larger regional or global role."[49]

International economic institutions that are meant to reflect capitalism's global integration are actually controlled by a handful of nations. The IMF and the World Bank are not located in Washington, D.C., by coincidence. The United States established these institutions after the Second World War, and they, along with the World Trade Organization, have been largely under its control. IMF "structural adjustment policies"—under which loans are advanced to poor countries on condition that they privatize, cut public spending, and open up their economy to foreign investment—are examples not of stateless globalization, but of economic imperialism.

The argument that corporations are internationally footloose is exaggerated. Big corporations like General Motors and Monsanto may have a global reach, but they still rely on their "home" state to provide the proper infrastructure—transportation, communication systems, and so on—necessary to make their businesses run profitably. In addition, multinationals in the United States receive enormous amounts of government help in the form of direct subsidies, tax breaks, government-funded university research and development, and a host of other forms of corporate welfare. To cite a few examples: Wal-Mart, the world's largest retailer, with more than thirty-five hundred stores nationwide and eighteen hundred overseas, has received state and local subsidies amounting to $1 billion, according to a 2004 report.[50] A 1996 *Boston Globe* study on government handouts to corporations concluded,

> The $150 billion for corporate subsidies and tax benefits eclipses the annual budget deficit of $130 billion. It's more than the $145 billion paid out annually for the core programs of the social welfare state: Aid to Families with Dependent Children (AFDC), student aid, housing, food and nutrition, and all direct public assistance (excluding Social Security and medical care).[51]

A stateless corporation is at a disadvantage compared to one backed by an economically and militarily powerful state that can provide various services to give it an edge over its rivals. The United States Export-Import Bank, for example, spends $1 billion a year to promote the sale of U.S. products overseas, mostly as subsidies to Fortune 500 companies.[52] The member countries of the Organization of Economic Cooperation and Development (OECD)—that is, the world's richest countries—impose high tariffs on food imports and give generous subsidies to domestic agricultural interests. It is questionable whether agriculture could stay afloat without these supports.[53] Foreign aid is notoriously employed to pry open foreign markets for the donor country's products.[54] "There are many companies with worldwide operations," writes one analyst. "Some even have multinational boards and executive teams. But, almost without exception, the world's most successful companies remain clearly identified with their countries of origin."[55]

Corporations also depend on other states when they operate overseas, requiring domestic and foreign governments to maintain a "good business climate." They sometimes have recourse to police and other armed support in order to keep the class struggle in check, and they depend on borders to manipulate the flow of migrant labor. Cheap immigrant labor has always been an effective tool for dividing workers and driving down their wages.

When "peaceful" financial manipulation fails, the threat—and use—of violence, remains. Conservative columnist Thomas Friedman formulated the relationship between the "free market" and armed force most famously: "The hidden hand of the market will never work without a hidden fist."[56] So long as there is no international (or supranational) state, backed by its own armed forces, that represents the world capitalist class, capitalists will need the armed forces of their own national territory.

Capitalism is even more integrated, more interdependent, than ever. But the fundamental contradiction between the anarchic world market and competing nation-states remains. The Russian Marxist Nikolai Bukharin's thoughts on the matter are still very relevant today. It doesn't follow from the internationalization of economic life, he argued,

> that social progress has already reached a stage where "national" states can coexist harmoniously. For the process of the internationalization of economic life is by no means identical with the process of the internationalization of capital interests.... Only those who do not see the contradictions in capitalist development, who good-naturedly assume ... anarchic internationalization to

> be organized internationalization—can hope for the possibility of reconciling the "national" capitalist groups in the "higher unity" of peaceful capitalism.
>
> The process of the internationalization of economic life can and does sharpen, to a high degree, the conflict of interests among the various "national" groups of the bourgeoisie. Indeed, the growth of international commodity exchange is by no means connected with the growth of "solidarity" between the exchanging groups. On the contrary, it can be accompanied by the growth of the most desperate competition, by a life and death struggle.[57]

The end of war

War isn't hard-wired into our brains, but it is "hard-wired" into capitalism. Its continued existence is bound up with the existence of capitalism itself. War cannot be abolished unless the class interests upon which it rests are abolished. But most solutions for ending war assume mistakenly that war can be gotten rid of without getting rid of the system which breeds it. "Politics must continue; war cannot," explains war historian John Keegan. "That is not to say that the role of the warrior is over. The world community needs, more than it has ever done, skillful and disciplined warriors who are ready to put themselves at the service of its authority. Such warriors must properly be seen as the protectors of civilization, not its enemies."[58]

But it is not possible to separate war and politics. Lenin was fond of quoting the nineteenth-century theorist of war, Karl Von Clausewitz: "War is a mere continuation of policy by other means."[59] Keegan's idea of ending war, perhaps unconsciously, is for the world's dominant powers—for they control the "world community"—to come together and militarily impose peace. His answer to imperialist war is the answer every aspiring power strives for: a peace based on its own dominance, a "Pax Romana, or a "Pax Britannica," or a "Pax Americana." Implicitly, though he states otherwise, he accepts the fact that war and politics are inseparable.

The same confusion surrounds the belief that the United Nations can be an instrument of peaceful conflict resolution. Also established after the Second World War, the UN's only decision-making body with enforcement power, the Security Council, is dominated by five permanent members—the United States, Russia, Britain, France, and China. Each member has veto power over council decisions, ensuring that U.S. interests can never be threatened. It is not an international parliament, but a committee of the most powerful states. When they all agree, the council acts; when they disagree, the big states simply ignore it. John Bolton, U.S. ambassador to the UN as of 2006, gave the clearest description of the organization's international role: "There is no United Nations. There is an international community that occasionally can be led by the only real power left in the world, and that is the United States, when it suits our interest, and when we can get others to go along.... When the United States leads, the United Nations will follow. When it suits our interest to do so, we will do so. When it does not suit our interests we will not."[60]

Marx likened the international capitalist class to warring brothers, ready to join forces against threats from below, but also in competition with each other, and therefore able to form only temporary agreements and alliances. One state may possess the power to impose some kind of peace based on its own ability to wield superior force—like a mafia don whose gangs have cleaned out all competitors and created the conditions for "peaceful" commerce in a particular city. This is the peace of the victor; a peace that lasts only until a rival gang emerges to oust the old boss.

Though socialists look to a world without war, no socialist can condemn all wars. Wars of conquest and imperial rivalry are reactionary, but wars are also waged by the oppressed against their subjection. A million mostly working-class men died in the battle of the Somme (during the First World War) for the sake of profits for the British, French, and German empires. That war was reactionary to the core, even though each side in the dispute claimed to be defending itself against the other. The Civil War in the United States—a bloody affair—was fought to destroy the institution of slavery. That war was progressive and justified.

We live in a world of abundance in which there is no longer any justification for war. Given a different social order, one based upon planned production and distribution for human need, it would be possible to provide everyone with a healthy existence without recourse to exploitation of one by another, or of warfare.

But unlike pacifists, who believe that simply an appeal to reason or moral suasion can convince those who rule today to act differently, Marxists understand that war is built into the very fabric of capitalism, and that it can only be abolished when the weapons of the world's ruling classes are wrested from their hands. We want the end of war, but we also understand that those who hold power in the world will not relinquish it peacefully. Marxists understand that the violence of the oppressor cannot be equated with the violence of the oppressed. As Trotksy explained in his defense of the use of violence by the Russian working class against the counterrevolution in 1919:

> When a murderer raises his knife over a child, may one kill the murderer to save the child? Will not thereby the principle of the "sacredness of human life" be infringed? May one kill the murderer to save oneself? Is an insurrection of oppressed slaves against their masters permissible?…
>
> Does life cease to be sacred when it is a question of people talking another language, or does Kautsky consider that mass murders organized on principles of strategy and tactics are not murders at all? Truly it is difficult to put forward in our age a principle more hypocritical and more stupid. As long as human labor power and, consequently, life itself, remain articles of sale and purchase, of exploitation and robbery, the principle of the "sacredness of human life" remains a shameful lie, uttered with the object of keeping the oppressed slaves in their chains…. To make the individual sacred we must destroy the social order which crucifies him.[61]

The war in Vietnam ended in a victory for the independence movement in Vietnam because of a combination of mass protests at home, armed resistance to the U.S. occupation in Vietnam proper, and the disintegration of the U.S. Army as soldiers increasingly refused to fight in an unjust war. During the first Christmas of the First World War German and British soldiers, disobeying their officers, laid down their weapons and fraternized in "no man's land."[62] The Russian Revolution of 1917 forced Russia out of the First World War and sparked revolts of workers in Germany and other countries, including mass fraternization between soldiers of opposing countries. This kind of international struggle and solidarity is the key to ending war.

Internationalism

The *Communist Manifesto* ends with the resounding phrase, "workers of the world, unite." This was not simply a moral appeal. Capitalism has created a world working class in the hundreds of millions upon whose labor the profits of the world's multinationals derive. Workers face the same essential conditions the world over. Whether their pay is high or low, all workers are exploited. They therefore have a common interest that spans national borders, in spite of their national differences.

Some argue that the plunder of one nation by another precludes working-class solidarity, because the workers in the plundering nation benefit from the plunder. The steady decline of living standards for American workers, the growing gap between rich and poor, and the diversion of social spending toward military spending and corporate welfare makes this argument today seem out of touch with reality.

Workers in Europe and the United States, so the argument goes, are better paid because they are somehow benefiting from the comparatively lower pay of workers in Mexico. It is true that an autoworker in the United States and an autoworker in Mexico working at the same level of productivity receive different wages, but they are both exploited, and by the same masters. Indeed, in many cases, well-paid workers are as exploited—in terms of how much surplus work they perform for the bosses—as low-paid workers, if not more. The lowest pay is usually associated with industries that are the most "labor intensive," that is, where the rate of exploitation is lowest because less labor-saving machinery is employed. The inequality of wages worldwide acts to the detriment of the world working class because it permits capitalists to pit lower-paid workers against better-paid. A rise in the standard of living for any section of the working class, on the other hand, cannot but benefit all.

Capitalism's economic crises are also increasingly global in scope. That means that struggle also takes on an increasingly international character. In the mid-1840s, when industrial capitalism was limited to Britain and parts of mainland Europe, a series of revolutions spread across Europe. They were bourgeois revolutions, and they ended in defeat, but in each country the working class emerged for the first time as a social force to be reckoned with.

Again, in 1917, the Russian Revolution sparked international revolution. Coming on the heels of world war and economic hardship, it set off a world conflagration. German workers rose up and overthrew the Kaiser, setting up workers' councils similar to the Russian soviets. There were soviets in Hungary and Finland before the revolution was crushed. Workers in Italy formed factory councils, and in 1920 came to the brink of revolution before they were undercut by moderate socialists. "The whole of Europe," fretted British prime minister Lloyd George, "is filled with the spirit of revolution."[63] The war and the Russian Revolution also set off anticolonial revolts in India, Ireland, and elsewhere. Victor Serge described the atmosphere of both bourgeois panic and revolutionary hope in 1918:

> The newspapers of the period are astonishing. Each day, in large type with headlines across the page, they carry last-minute dispatches, vague rumors picked up in Stockholm by anxious ears: riots in Paris, riots in Lyon, revolution in Belgium, revolution in Constantinople, victory of the Soviets in Bulgaria, rioting in Copenhagen. In fact, the whole of Europe is in movement; clandes-

> tine or open Soviets are appearing everywhere, even in the Allied armies; everything is possible, everything. On 15 October, Vorovsky telegraphs Zinoviev from Stockholm: *Revolution builds up in France* (so runs the headline of his dispatch in the news-papers); "a workers' popular movement began two days ago, and is spreading energetically in Paris.... The workers are demanding the immediate release of all political prisoners.... A Soviet of Allied soldiers has made contact at the front with the Soviet of German soldiers."[64]

The division of the world into national states means that struggles in each country have a certain tempo and dynamic that is not identical in timing or character. Revolution starts in one or a few states and then spreads. But as the experience of the Russian Revolution shows, any revolution that remains in isolation cannot survive. Engels understood this as early as 1847, in a question-and-answer piece he wrote that was scrapped for the *Communist Manifesto:* "Will it be possible for this revolution to take place in one country alone? No. By creating the world market, big industry has already brought all the peoples of the Earth ... into such close relation with one another that none is independent of what happens to the others."[65]

The call for workers to unite across national boundaries, then, is not merely a moral appeal. The material condition for socialism—abundance—exists on a world scale, but not within the confines of national borders. This is true because economic development is extremely uneven, with enormous wealth and productive power concentrated in some regions far more than others. Any country that attempts to fall back on its own resources quickly finds that its production system is too lopsided and incomplete to pull itself up by its own bootstraps. Having been shaped in connection with the world economy, one country finds it doesn't produce enough agricultural products and must import them, another, not enough machinery and spare parts. The problem, moreover, is most acute for countries that were dependent colonies in the past, because their economies were distorted by the needs of the country that exploited them, which usually meant turning them into sources of cheap labor and raw materials, and retarding their industrial development. Cuba, for example, remained dependent on sugar exports for 80 percent of its capital needs for decades. First dependent on the United States, it later depended on Russia for substantial support. But even then, it has never been able to create a fully diversified industrialized economy. This is the reason why the Marxist movement always argued—until Stalinism distorted and inverted the message—that there cannot be isolated pockets of socialist development.

Chapter Ten

Marxism and Oppression

The right to self-determination

The ruling classes of every country play upon nationalist sentiments to solidify their rule. National chauvinism is a corrosive ideology that poisons workers' minds and turns them against their natural allies—workers of other countries. One of the goals of socialists is to challenge attempts to set workers of one nation against those of another, or to elevate in workers' minds "their" nation or culture over those of another. Socialists aim to break down national divisions and foster solidarity between workers of different countries based on their common class interests. This is, incidentally, not an argument for the obliteration or homogenization of cultures (music, language, food, customs), but against the elevation of any one culture over another, or the suppression of any nation or culture by another. Genuine internationalism, however, requires full equality between nations.

It follows from this that Marxism does not lump all nationalisms together. In a phrase, we make a distinction between the nationalism of the oppressor and the nationalism of the oppressed. The distinction can sometimes be confusing, because all nations in wartime claim that they are the aggrieved party, defending themselves against aggression. Some examples are in order. When the thirteen colonies fought for independence from the British Empire, it was a case of an oppressed nation fighting an oppressor nation. However, when the United States wrenched away half of Mexico in the 1847 war, it was a war of conquest. Every overseas military intervention conducted by the United States since then has placed it in the position of the British Empire when it fought the Boston Minutemen.

The irony of American imperialism is that when it oppresses other nations, it cloaks its actions in the garb of 1776. It was a complete inversion of reality, for example, for Bush the younger to call the Iraqi resistance "terrorists" and the occupying U.S. Army "liberators."[1] But the British used the same jargon during the American Revolution. In his failed 1777 military campaign in northern New England and Canada, General John Burgoyne claimed that he was fighting an "unnatural Rebellion" whose aim was to establish "the compleated system of Tyranny."[2] Burgoyne quickly moved from appeals to threats, promising "devastation, famine and every concomitant horror that a reluctant but indispensable prosecution of military duty must occasion."[3]

National equality can only be established if oppressed nations have the right to self-determination—not to be colonized, annexed, occupied, or otherwise denied their own sovereignty. "If we were to forget about [self-determination] or were afraid to put it forward for fear of impinging on the national prejudices of our compatriots of Great-Russian origin," wrote the Russian Marxist Plekhanov, "the battle-cry of world Social-Democracy, 'Workers of all countries, unite!' would be a shameful lie on our lips."[4]

Karl Marx made a similar argument in relation to Britain's oppression of its first colony, Ireland. "It is a precondition of the emancipation of the English working class," Marx argued, "to transform the present forced union (i.e. the enslavement of Ireland) into equal and free confederation if possible, into complete separation if need be."[5] Working-class liberation in England was impossible, Marx contended, without Irish liberation. Marx applied the same methodology to the question of slavery in the American South, arguing that working-class emancipation could not be accomplished without destroying slavery. "Labor in a white skin cannot emancipate itself where it is branded in a Black skin," he argued in *Capital*.[6]

In the era of imperialism, the questions of national oppression and national liberation became of pressing general importance to the socialist movement worldwide. Everywhere, workers in the oppressor nations were being encouraged to support colonial oppression by "their own" governments. Lenin argued that working-class internationalism was impossible unless workers in the oppressor countries—the dominant nations that forcibly held colonies all over the world—were broken from any allegiance to their own ruling class. That meant socialists in countries that oppressed other nations had to support the oppressed nation's right to be free and independent. Only then could there be unity between workers of both nations on the basis of equality. "Can a nation be free," he asked, "if it oppresses other nations? It cannot."[7]

But Lenin made a sharp distinction between the Marxist position for self-determination, and the concern that the statesmen for the great powers mouthed about the rights of nations—a concern that never extended to the nations they themselves ruled over. When President Woodrow Wilson touted the self-determination of nations in his 1918 "Fourteen Points" speech, for example, the United States was three years into a brutal Marine Corps occupation of Haiti that had handed that country's customs house and banking system over to the National City Bank of New York.[8]

Lenin compared the right of self-determination to the right of divorce. Marxists support the right of women to dissolve a marriage not because all marriages should break up, he argued, but because equality of the sexes cannot exist where women are legally bound to their husbands.[9] Lenin's point wasn't that marriage is better than being single. But, all other things being equal, the more national differences and animosities break down, the better. The increasing interdependence of nations, as well as the breakdown of national boundaries between peoples, is a good thing—so long as it is based on voluntary association—because it increases the international solidarity of the working class. But socialists adamantly oppose any forced unity. For example, in the United States, socialists oppose efforts to make English the nation's official language, or to prevent people from being able to speak or teach their children in their native tongue. Socialists stand strongly in favor of the right of people to be provided with instruction in their own language. On the other hand, we are not in favor of the breakup of students into separate schools on the basis of sex, language, nationality, race, ethnicity, or religion. The free mingling of peoples of all languages and nationalities, and the breakdown of national exclusiveness—that is, anything that tends to separate and divide workers and their families from each other—is progressive. Capitalism works hard to keep people of different races and nationalities divided, because it is then easier to pit them against each other. Our job is to combat that separation, rather than reinforce it.

To be consistent internationalists, socialists must oppose all efforts by the United States to impose its will on other countries and peoples—whether in Iraq, Puerto Rico, Afghanistan, or Venezuela. Puerto Ricans must have the right to separate from the United States and form an independent nation. Venezuelans have the right to be free of U.S. meddling in their affairs, and Iraqis have a right to resist occupation.

This does not mean a positive support for nationalism in its own right. For in these national struggles, there are different class interests involved. Every national struggle involves different classes, and each class strives, beyond national independence, for very different things. The wealthy classes in the oppressed nation try to limit the scope of the national struggle, to elevate *nation* over the class interests of workers, and to stifle the aspirations of the most oppressed for complete liberation, lest their struggles threaten the rule of the rich. Indeed, in some cases, fear of mass mobilization from below has rendered bourgeois nationalists half-hearted and vacillating in the fight for independence. They also have their own national aspirations as a ruling class that involve oppression of other groups—for example, Indonesia's bloody seizure of East Timor after it achieved independence, or the conquest of the West at the expense of Native Americans by the newly-independent United States.

Lenin argued that,

> The bourgeois nationalism of *any* oppressed nation has a general democratic content that is directed *against* oppression, and it is this content that we *unconditionally* support. At the same time we strictly distinguish it from the tendency towards national exclusiveness; [for example,] we fight against the tendency of the Polish bourgeois to oppress the Jews.[10]

Lenin argued that while socialists in the oppressed country must wholeheartedly support the national struggle against imperialism, the working class should retain its own independent organization. Form alliances, he argued, but do not merge with the nationalists. "A resolute struggle must be waged," he wrote in 1920, "against the attempt to clothe the revolutionary liberation movements in the backward countries, which are not genuinely communist, in communist colors."[11] The rise of Stalinism led precisely to this tendency Lenin warned against—to paint what were essentially nationalist movements in "communist colors." A number of national liberations movements in the last century—from China to Cuba to various African nations—were led by middle-class nationalist forces, rather than the working class. They drew inspiration from the Russian model of state development, and thus proclaimed their national revolutions "socialist." These movements, though genuinely fighting for national liberation, were not led by the working class, nor did they put the working class in power.

Roots of women's inequality

All societies require both production *and* reproduction—the propagation of the species. We've already seen how the state of the productive forces shapes the production relations in a given society. While the essential biological aspects of reproduction, until recently, have not changed, the same cannot be said of the institution that encompasses reproduction—the family. Much in the same way that modern economists project capitalist relations into the past, so too do defenders of the nuclear family project an unchanging unit—consisting of a man, a woman, a few children, and a dog—into the past. This nuclear family, they argue, constitutes the "natural" order of things. The truth is that the family is an institution, not a biological fact, and it has changed historically from one mode of production to the next. As a result the status of women in society has also changed considerably.

The popular idea is that relations between the sexes are shaped by the unchanging nature of men as providers and women as nurturers—thus it has been and thus it always will be. Yet this view of a woman's role is not supported by the historical evidence. In many pre-class societies, women engaged in productive work beyond child rearing and housecleaning. In these societies, there was a strong sexual division of labor. Men tended to do the jobs that took them further afield: hunting, for example. Women, as child-bearers, tended to do the work that kept them nearer to the home base: gathering roots and berries, preparing hides and clothes, and cooking. Later, in the first horticultural societies, women moved naturally from gathering to planting and harvesting. In both cases, with the exception of very cold climates where hunting was the primary source of food, women's role as gatherers and agriculturalists was more important for the survival of the group than men's hunting.

Both because women's work was central to the survival of the band, and also because relations of economic coercion did not yet exist, doing different things from men did not mean being oppressed by men. On the contrary, in many reported cases, women exercised ultimate decision-making power over questions such as the choice of war chief and whether or not to go to war, or when to break off a marriage. These facts blow out of the water the most childish and least supported argument as to why women are oppressed—because men are stronger. According to this argument, children should have also always been oppressed by adults. Yet, as we've seen in a previous chapter, children were raised in relative freedom in these societies. What this questionable theory boils down to is that men oppress women because they can, which isn't an explanation of anything.

In many pre-class societies, sexual relations were treated more freely, often without the jealousy, possessiveness, and objectification that is associated with sexual relations today. In most matrilocal or matrilineal societies—where descent is reckoned through the female rather than the male—women and men were free to engage in unrestricted sexual activity before marriage without any fear of stigma. Women were able to combine both reproductive and productive work because such societies did not make much of a distinction between them. The ethnographer Bronislav Malinowski studied the Trobriand Islanders of northwest Melanesia in 1929. In this matrilineal tribal society, "women have a considerable share in tribal life, even to the taking of a leading part in economic, ceremonial, and magical activities—a fact which deeply influences all the customs of erotic life as well as the institution of marriage."[12] Malinowski noticed that children were raised without adult coercion, something that appeared to the Trobrianders to be "unnatural and immoral."[13] Children were allowed to explore their sexual curiosity without fear or shame: "There is no interference by older persons," he wrote, "in the sexual life of children."[14]

With the rise of class society, women's status changed. As gatherers, women played a key role in the discovery and development of plant domestication, and in many horticultural societies, such as the Iroquois in upstate New York, women's status remained high. Men hunted and did the heavy work of clearing fields for planting, but women planted and tended the crops. The invention of the heavy plough and the domestication of animals changed that. Men became the primary agricultural laborers, and because of their traditional role as hunters, were also in charge of animal domestication. Men, in other words, dominated in the sphere of production, and became therefore the owners of society's surplus wealth. Or at least some men, for the rise of class society and the state, as Engels pointed out, did not only represent the "world historic defeat of the female sex," it also represented the economic subordination of the majority of men to a tiny minority of wealthy men.[15]

With the development of agriculture and animal domestication came private property. The family as a patriarchal setup in which descent was reckoned through the male head of the household developed as a way to ensure that a father passed his wealth to his male offspring. In the new monogamous family, men expected strict chastity from women, but not from themselves. Engels wrote that, "The man seized the reins in the house too, the woman was degraded, enthralled, became the slave of the man's lust, a mere instrument for breeding children."[16]

The sexual division of labor thus only took on an oppressive dimension with the rise of class society, when a handful of men became the controllers of the agricultural surplus. Women—and most men unlucky enough to be slaves or serfs—became subordinated to a new ruling class. In the patriarchal household, women were expected to rear children as well as engage in various kinds of labor for the family's survival (sowing, milking, etc.). But capitalist development creates technological changes that render the sexual division of labor more or less obsolete, and creates, as we shall see, the conditions for women's full emancipation.

Capitalism and the family

With capitalism came the complete separation of the realm of production from reproduction. Work and home became totally separate spheres. In the families of the wealthy and of the middle classes, men were still the patriarchs of the family, and women were expected to be polite ornaments. But initially, capitalism wrecked family relations for workers. The development of markets for consumer goods rendered obsolete women's work in the home, like spinning and weaving. In the early phases of industrialization, factory owners coveted the nimble fingers of children and women, and hours were impossibly long. The result was that family life almost ceased to exist. Marx and Engels saw the entry of women into the workforce, however horrific its implementation and effects on the working-class family, as an important starting point for women's freedom, because it created the conditions necessary for women to assert themselves as the equals of men.

But even capitalists at some point realized that for a steady supply of labor they needed some way for workers to reproduce themselves—they needed workers to be able to have families. Socialized reproduction—the creation of public kitchens, child care centers, and so on—were not considered options, in part because the ruling class was not willing to foot the bill even if anyone at that stage had demanded it.

Under real pressure from below, laws were passed restricting the labor of children and women. In the Victorian era, the middle-class ideology of the nuclear family, of the man at work supporting the wife at home who cleaned and took care of the kids, was born. In exchange for some relief from the horrors of endless factory labor, working-class women became subordinate to men, and were almost solely responsible for rearing children in the home. Men were expected to make a wage that could support a family. The invasion of the market into virtually every sphere of life also transformed sex into a commodity, reinforcing the idea of women as sexual objects to be "possessed" by men.

But women were never completely shut out of the public sphere. The demands of capitalism for cheap and plentiful labor acted as too strong a pull, as did women's interest in leading lives beyond the cramped confines of the home. Whereas only 5.6 percent of married women were counted in the workforce in 1900, by 2002, 56.1 percent of mothers with children were in the labor force—and 70 percent of childbearing-age women.[17] This change has not by itself freed women by any means. Instead, it has imposed a double burden on women, who are expected to cook, clean, and raise children, as well as work outside the home. "Thus, although women play a productive role in advanced capitalism," writes Sharon Smith, "this alone hasn't translated into equality with men as it did in pre-class societies."[18]

Today, there is an "uncomfortable mismatch between cultural norms and images and the ways in which people are actually living their lives."[19] The "ideal" family portrayed in old television shows like *Leave It to Beaver* were never very close to the truth, even in the 1950s. They are even less true today, though this fantasy family is still the ideal of the Christian right. In fact, over half the workforce in the United States is made up of women. Many families are headed by single parents. Rather than being a haven in a heartless world, in many cases the family acts as a breeding ground for frustration and violence, focusing the frustrations that workers feel outside the home. While relations between men and women have changed a lot over the past few decades, women's status is still one of inequality with men. "Women have gained the freedom both to have children and to pursue careers," writes author Arlene Skolnick, "but society and institutions have not adapted to a world where women are in the workplace to stay."[20]

Women are still paid less than men, and they still bear the brunt of childrearing and housework. Women are portrayed in various media as physical objects of sexual desire rather than as full human beings. Sexual abuse, from verbal harassment to more severe forms of domestic violence and rape, is commonplace. Women's reproductive rights are circumscribed—one product of the backlash of the past few decades against women—through restricted access to health care and abortion, especially for working-class women.

Why are women still oppressed? This question is usually answered in two unsatisfactory ways: male biology (men are stronger) or male psychology (men *need* to dominate women), or a combination of the two. According to this view, held often by both conservatives *and* many feminists, women's oppression isn't going to disappear as long as there are men around.

But today, modern technology has rendered any physical or biological differences between women and men largely irrelevant. Women's oppression persists because of the way in which capitalism benefits from women's unpaid labor in the home. Under capitalism, the tasks of raising the next generation of workers falls to the private family, rather than being taken on by society as a whole. This explains why woman's entry into the workforce, the public sphere, has not resulted in her liberation. Society still expects her to play her allotted role in the home, and provisions (wages, good health care, child care, and so on) don't exist to allow her to step out of that role.

Women's liberation from oppression, therefore, is inseparably bound up with the fight to socialize the process of childrearing and other household tasks that are now left entirely up to the members of families. Today, it means fighting for equal pay, free and available health care and access to abortion, and more daycare centers. It also requires a fight against sexist ideas held by men—and also internalized by women themselves. Such a fight is possible because these changes would benefit working-class men as well as women.

Sexist ideas can and do break down, however, as the women's movement definitively showed. Attitudes about everything from a woman's proper role in society to interracial relationships have shifted dramatically since the 1960s. The film *Salt of the Earth*, about a strike of copper miners in Arizona in the 1950s, is brilliant in showing how struggle can challenge and break down sexist ideas. A legal injunction against men picketing during the strike prompts the women to insist that they take over the picket lines. The men violently reject this idea, but in the end relent because it's their only chance of success. In the process, gender roles are completely reversed. The women go to the picket line every day and the men take care of the kids. The experience gives women confidence to speak in public, and to assert themselves with their husbands.

The solution to women's inferior status cannot be solved, though, simply by getting men to share more housework. In some households, men do share the housework, and that is a good thing. But this doesn't change the fact that the family is privatized, or that men are typically paid more than women in the workforce, which creates an economic incentive for women, rather than men, to take time off to take care of children and elderly relatives. Those who can afford it deal with the problem of juggling work and family by hiring maids and servants. In working-class families, equal sharing of housework "would mean ... that working-class men would share the burden for the reproduction of labor power along with working-class women—to the continued benefit of the capitalist class."[21] The willingness of men to share housework is a product of struggles such as those of the women's movement in the 1960s, and reflect the way in which struggle can break down old ideas about what is natural and what is not. These changes are important because they improve our chances for a successful struggle to achieve more far-reaching changes.

As with other forms of oppression, women's oppression cuts across class lines, a fact which has led some feminists to claim that women and men do not share any common interests. Liberal feminism pursues a strategy of improving the lot of middle-class women within the confines of capitalism, whereas separatists look for the complete separation of women from men as the only solution to their oppression. The former strategy is limited, the second unrealistic, and neither will end women's unequal status in society. "However apparently radical the demands of the feminists," wrote the Russian revolutionary Alexandra Kollontai of the bourgeois women's movement, "one must not lose sight of the fact that the feminists cannot, on account of their class position, fight for that fundamental transformation of the contemporary economic and social structure of society without which the liberation of women cannot be complete."[22]

Working-class women, on the other hand, require a more thorough social transformation, one that takes into account the family burden that they primarily bear. Capitalism isn't willing to carry the cost of socializing the functions now borne by the family. In the long run, we must create a society in which the means of production *and* reproduction are socialized, where sex is no longer debased as a commodity that can be bought and sold, and where women have full control of their own bodies, including the right to abortion. Communal laundries, kitchens, and child-care centers would free women from the double burden of work and housework, and provide them with the means to become fully free and equal members of society. As a founding leader of the German socialist movement, August Bebel, argued, "The goal ... is not merely the realization of equal rights of woman with man within present society, as is aimed at by bourgeois women's emancipationists. It lies beyond—the removal of all impediments that make man dependent on man; and, consequently, one sex upon the other."[23]

Heroic attempts were made in Russia to build a new society of freedom after the revolution. Homosexuality was decriminalized, and abortion was also legalized. Laws denying recognition of children born out of wedlock were wiped away. The Bolshevik government established communal laundries, kindergartens, nurseries, and kitchens. Special efforts were made to provide literacy and education, especially to women. "Not a single bourgeois republic," said Lenin, "had done in decades so much as a hundredth part of what we did [for women] in our first year in power."[24] Lenin believed that it was impossible to talk of real communism until women had been completely emancipated. But the material resources did not exist in Russia to create an alternative to the old family and free woman from her status as a domestic slave. "You cannot abolish the family," wrote Trotsky, "you have to replace it. The actual liberation of women is unrealizable on a basis of 'generalized want.' Experience soon proved this austere truth which Marx had formulated eighty years before."[25] The Russian Revolution could pose a solution to women's oppression, but it could not solve it.

Origins of racism

Racism—the singling out of one group for oppression, on the basis of observable physical characteristics—has a long history. Prior to the rise of Nazism, biological theories about the superiority of "the white race" were widespread, along with various other arguments used to justify colonial conquest and violence. But more recent best-sellers like *The Bell Curve*, which purport to show innate racial differences in intelligence, reveal the extent to which such ideas have made a comeback among conservatives.[26]

Clear evidence to the contrary never got in the way of this kind of spurious pseudoscience. Arguments like those in the *Bell Curve* are used to justify cuts in funding for social programs and affirmative action, not to serve the truth. Racists were pleased by studies of Black draftees during the Second World War that found they had lower IQs than white draftees. But as genetic biologist Thedosius Dobzhansky points out, the average IQ of Northern African-American draftees "was higher, not lower, than that of white draftees from southern states."[27] Not surprisingly, this evidence was not offered as proof that whites were genetically inferior to Blacks.

Racism is not innate—it is a historical invention. Indeed, the concept of race itself is a historical invention rather than scientific fact. There is no genetic foundation for singling out groups of people according to some superficial physical characteristic and treating that group as a separate race. Nevertheless, race as a social concept is very real, and has a very real impact on people. "Blacks in America," writes anthropologist Ashley Montagu,

> have … been deprived, oppressed, discriminated against, impoverished, ghettoized, and generally excluded from the brotherhood of man. Hence it should not be surprising that there have been and continue to be significant differences in the achievements of Blacks and whites as "measured" by tests which have been arbitrarily standardized on middle-class Whites.[28]

In the New World, the planter class adopted slavery because labor was scarce. Indians and white indentured servants were either not plentiful enough or not cheap enough. According to Caribbean historian Eric Williams, the reason for the enslavement of Black Africans was "economic, not racial." The African slave's so-called "subhuman" characteristics "were only the later rationalizations to justify a simple economic fact." Therefore, argues Williams, "Slavery was not born of racism; rather, racism was the consequence of slavery."[29]

In the South, during slavery and after, racism was fostered among poor whites to prevent them from seeing that they shared with Blacks the same exploiters—the white planter class. "The slaveholders," wrote Black abolitionist Frederick Douglass, "by encouraging the enmity of the poor, laboring white man against the Blacks, succeeded in making the said white man almost as much of a slave as the Black himself.… Both are plundered by the same plunderer."[30]

The ideology of white supremacy justified not only continental conquest (over Indians and Mexicans) and slavery, but also overseas expansion in the Pacific and the Caribbean. With the rise of imperialism and colonialism came attempts to put a scientific gloss on racist ideas. Social Darwinism—the idea that there is a genetic hierarchy of humans, with white conquerors at the top—became widespread. In the struggle for markets and colonies, "survival of the fittest" operated—and put the "fittest," i.e., whites, at the top. "Slavery disappeared," writes Lance Selfa, "but racism remained as a means to justify the enslavement of millions of people by the United States, various European powers, and later Japan."[31]

In his discussion of England's oppression of Ireland, Marx got to the root of why capitalism fosters and depends on racism to this very day:

> In *all the big industrial centers in England*, there is a profound antagonism between the Irish proletarian and the English proletarian. The average English worker hates the Irish worker as a competitor who lowers wages and the standard of life. He feels national and religious antipathies for him.
>
> He regards him somewhat like the poor whites in the southern states of North America regarded black slaves. This antagonism among the proletarians of England is artificially nourished and kept up by the bourgeoisie. It knows that this scission is the *true secret of maintaining its power.*[32]

The same logic is at work under capitalism today. One has only to think of the deliberate racism fostered against Mexican immigrants. If native-born workers can be made to believe that immigrant workers threaten their jobs; if white workers can be made to hate or resent Blacks; or if Americans can be made to think that Arabs and Muslims are the enemy, it makes it more difficult for workers and the oppressed to unite against their common enemy. Racist and xenophobic ideas do not benefit workers and the poor, whatever their race, sex, or ethnicity. But they do benefit the exploiters—by making sections of the exploited believe they have common interests with their exploiters because they share the same language or skin color. For example, certain industries view illegal immigrant labor as ideal because illegal immigrants cannot organize unions and live in constant fear of deportation, so it's easy to pay them next to nothing. The solution is not to restrict immigration, but to organize immigrant workers alongside native-born workers to fight the common enemy.

Historically, unions have been weakest in the South. This has kept wages lower than in the rest of the country. But the reason unions have been weak in the South is purely and simply because of racism. The antagonism of whites toward Blacks has been the secret by which employers in the South have kept workers from organizing successfully. The fight against racism, therefore, cannot be separated from the class struggle as a whole. As the old labor slogan tells us, an injury to one is an injury to all. The special oppression faced by one part of the working class drags down the rest. Conversely, the elimination of that oppression, the liberation of the oppressed, is the condition for lifting up all.

Can Black and white unite?

After losing the Civil War, the old Southern planter class aimed at "getting things back as near to slavery as possible."[33] But they were temporarily stymied during the period of Radical Reconstruction. Blacks were granted the right to vote. In some cities, laws restricting the rights of Black people were thrown out. Biracial public education was established where there had never before been any public education. Fourteen Blacks were elected to Congress from the South. These changes also benefited poor whites, who had had no public education and few rights under slavery. The importance of this period is that it showed how quickly racist ideas could break down in periods of rapid change. But by the 1870s, the Northern capitalists joined the Southern planter class in being eager to put an end to Radical Reconstruction. They feared the possibility that a population of poor whites and Blacks, "if combined for any political purpose, would sweep away all opposition the intelligent class might make," as the *New York Tribune* opined in 1871.[34]

The Southern ruling class successfully defeated Reconstruction by using racism, Klan terror, and fraud. The biggest threat to their rule came with the populist movement in the 1890s. A national movement of farmers and sharecroppers who were losing their farms to bankers and speculators, the populists vowed to "raise less corn and more hell."[35] Populism's most radical wing was in the South. The Georgia populist Tom Watson said of the government, "there is no remedy for it but destruction."[36]

The movement began to break down the divisions between Blacks and whites. The Southern Alliance, a multi-state league of populist farmers, claimed 3 million members—1.3 million of them Black—in1890. Watson appealed to Black and white tenant farmers, saying: "You are made to hate each other because upon that hatred is rested the keystone of the arch of financial despotism that enslaves you both." When a leading Black populist was threatened with lynching, two thousand white farmers responded to Tom Watson's appeal for help to defend him.

Fearing that populism was a threat to their class rule, the planters resurrected a campaign of violence and intimidation. The cry of "Black domination" was raised to convince poor whites that racial supremacy was in their interests. But the movement kept growing. It collapsed in 1896 when the populist People's Party decided to back Democratic presidential candidate William Jennings Bryan, based on the argument that he was a lesser evil to Republican McKinley. Bryan adopted the rhetoric of populism, but he was no populist. His job was to kill the People's Party in a smothering Democratic Party embrace.

With the collapse of the movement in the South, the Southern ruling class used a variety of devices like poll taxes, literacy tests, and property qualifications, to disenfranchise Blacks. Poor whites did not benefit from the defeat of populism. On the contrary, in the process of disenfranchising Blacks, the Southern planters also disenfranchised poor whites. In Louisiana the Black vote declined by 90 percent. The white vote also declined, by 60 percent. This pattern was repeated throughout the South.[37] One Southern newspaper aptly described the move to impose white supremacy as "the struggle of the white people of North Carolina to rid themselves of the danger of the rule of Negroes and the lower class whites."[38]

The populist movement gives us a glimpse of what enormous changes are possible if the oppressed and exploited unite against their common enemy. But it also explains why the ruling class depends upon racism to keep workers divided. The use of Black strikebreakers in the past, for example, was a classic tactic that the employers used to divide workers and weaken their organizing efforts. During and immediately after the First World War, for instance, employers saw in Black workers migrating north "the effective means of staving off or preventing the movement toward organization ... which is now spreading among the foreign worker," explained the manager of a Pittsburgh factory.[39] The steel corporations quite consciously and deliberately used Black strikebreakers to defeat the 1919 steel strike.

There have been high points of class struggle where Black and white workers united to fight their common exploiters. Appeals to racism by lumber mill operators failed to break the unity of thirteen hundred Black and white workers who struck a Louisiana lumber company in 1913; in the end, only violent repression worked. Prior to the strike, Industrial Workers of the World leader Big Bill Haywood had succeeded in convincing the Black and white workers of the Southern Lumber Workers union to affiliate to the IWW. In defiance of Jim Crow laws, Black and white workers also agreed to meet in the same hall. "Let the Negroes come together with us," announced the assembled white union members, "and if any arrests are made, all of us will go to jail, white and colored together."[40] In the upsurge of industrial unionism in the 1930s, Black and white unity was commonly forged in struggle. But it didn't come about automatically. It had to be encouraged and fought for. Ferdinand C. Smith, a Black member of the Communist Party and a founding member of the Congress of Industrial Organization's National Maritime Union, was acutely aware of how the employers attempted to use racial animosity to break down labor solidarity. "If the companies show preference for men of one race now, it is only for the time being. Once they get us divided, they will attack one race just as viciously as another. They know that race equality in a trade union is necessary to successful trade unionism—and successful trade unionism is one thing they fear most."[41]

There have also been periods of intense racism where Blacks felt so cornered that separation seemed the only option. But while racism sometimes impels Blacks to organize separately against their oppression, African Americans cannot end racism through their efforts alone. This is not only because Blacks constitute a minority of society; it is also because what is referred to as "the Black community" is divided by competing class interests. An appeal based on nationalist terms cannot address this division. "As a political current, Black nationalism is extremely heterogeneous, including advocates of Black capitalism, cultural nationalism, reformist politicians, and revolutionaries who oppose the system," notes Ahmed Shawki.

> What *all* varieties of Black separatism share is inconsistency and vacillation. This is necessarily built into *all* varieties of Black separatism, because neither the analysis nor strategy locate the one agent capable of transforming capitalist society—the working class. So while a separatist strategy can often tap the alienation felt by Blacks, it cannot provide a solution to the problems that face the mass of Black workers. At times, Black nationalist ideas can be radical in their critique of capitalism as the [Black] Panthers were. But they can also be much more conservative and pro-capitalist, stressing the need for "racial unity" as the basis for Black capitalism.[42]

The Civil Rights and Black Power movements posed a serious challenge to racism in the United States. The struggle was carried in the main by mostly poor and working-class African Americans, though it had the support and participation of many whites, too. These struggles did not end racial oppression, however. The Civil Rights movement lifted up the Black middle class and small Black bourgeoisie far more than it did the majority of poor and working-class Blacks. Today, African Americans still face double the unemployment rate of whites. Though they constitute 12 percent of the population, Blacks are half of those in prison. And decades after *Brown v. Board of Education*, cities and schools are still heavily segregated in the North and South.

The end of racial oppression can only come when the system that fosters and depends on it—capitalism—is ended. That requires a body blow delivered by a united working class. Only a conscious, organized battle against racism can foster that kind of unity. Lance Selfa, in an essay on the origins of racism, sums up the matter well:

> First, racism is not part of some unchanging human nature. It was literally invented. And so it can be torn down. Second, despite the overwhelming ideological hold of white supremacy, people always resisted it—from the slaves themselves to white antiracists.
>
> Understanding racism in this way informs the strategy that we use to combat racism. Antiracist education is essential, but it is not enough. Because it treats racism only as a question of "bad ideas" it does not address the underlying material conditions that give rise to the acceptance of racism among large sections of workers. Thoroughly undermining the hold of racism on large sections of workers requires three conditions: first, a broader class fightback that unites workers across racial lines; second, attacking the conditions (bad jobs, housing, education, etc.) that give rise to the appeal of racism among large sections of workers; and third, the conscious intervention of antiracists to oppose racism in all its manifestations and to win support for interracial class solidarity.[43]

Class and oppression

Marx and Engels argued that the foundation of society is its relations of production, and its corresponding class relations. But society is not reducible to these relations. On their basis arise the legal and political superstructure and corresponding forms of beliefs, morals, and consciousness—as well as family relations. There are also intermediate strata between the two main classes—what is usually referred to loosely as the middle class, that contains disparate elements from well-paid professionals and small businesspeople to managers. Marxism puts together an analysis of all these elements, showing them in their various connections, but without losing sight of the role that social production plays as the core element.

Engels explained that ideas about morality, of good and bad, for example, were not immutable ethical principles that stand above history:

> We maintain on the contrary that all moral theories have been hitherto the product, in the last analysis, of the economic conditions of society obtaining at the time. And as society has hitherto moved in class antagonisms, morality has always been class morality; it has either justified the domination and the interests of the ruling class, or ever since the oppressed class became powerful

> enough, it has represented its indignation against this domination and the future interests of the oppressed.... A really human morality which stands above class antagonisms and above any recollection of them becomes possible only at a stage of society which has not only overcome class antagonisms but has even forgotten them in practical life.[44]

Marxism is sometimes presented as concerning itself solely with economic questions. As ZNet's Michael Albert summarized it in an Internet debate, "Marxism … tends to exaggerate the centrality of economics and gives insufficient attention to gender, race, [politics] and the environment."[45] Exaggerated or not, the emphasis on economic relations did not prevent Marxists from dealing with questions of race and gender, or anything else. On the contrary, it provided a powerful tool to unlock answers to issues that have more commonly been presented as having nothing at all to do with economics and more with innate "human nature," "bad ideas," or both.

Marxism seeks not to separate exploitation and oppression, but to show how they are connected, and how the solution to one cannot be separated from the solution to the other. "No nation can be free," Marx wrote, "if it oppresses other nations."[46] To the argument that it was woman's "natural calling" to be a home-based "wife and mother," August Bebel, a leading German socialist wrote, "There can be no emancipation of humanity without the social independence and equality of the sexes."[47]

It is not Marxism, but its critics, who tend to put the working class over on one side, and the oppressed over on the other. But this is an artificial separation. Workers are men, women, gay, straight, Black, white, brown, speaking many different languages, comprising many nationalities, and speaking many languages. If the working class is to successfully challenge capitalism, it must surmount these divisions. If the working class is to devise a strategy to overcome them, it must discover the root sources of division and inequality.

Socialism is not only a theory of the liberation of the working class. It is a theory of the liberation of the working class as the foundation for the liberation of all of humanity—and not only from class exploitation, but all forms of oppression. As Lenin writes in his book *What is To Be Done?,* "Working-class consciousness cannot be genuine political consciousness unless the workers are trained to respond to *all* cases of tyranny, oppression, violence, and abuse, no matter *what class* is affected…. The [socialist's] ideal should not be the trade-union secretary, but *the tribune of the people*, who is able to react to every manifestation of tyranny and oppression, no matter where it appears, no matter what stratum or class of the people it affects."[48]

The working class can only lead a popular revolution if it is capable of fighting not only for its immediate economic interests, but for the interests of all those who are oppressed by capitalism. The Russian socialists, for example, organized against anti-Jewish pogroms and stood against Russia's enslavement of Poland, the Ukraine, and other nations.

It would be strange if this were not the case. A revolution that destroyed economic exploitation, but failed to destroy the institutions and ideologies of oppression that historically have buttressed that exploitation, would be a strange bird. And indeed, throughout history, all revolutionary movements consist in more than simply workers seizing control of production. Revolutions are, in Lenin's words, "festivals of the oppressed and exploited," in which all those in society who have been beaten down in various ways rise up and challenge everything that has held them down and stultified their lives and personalities. "At no other time are the masses of the people in a position to come forward so actively as creators of a new social order as at a time of revolution. At such times the people are capable of performing miracles, if judged by the narrow, philistine scale of gradual progress."[49]

Contrary to the critics, Marxism has always argued, first, that class and oppression cannot be separated—the latter is conditioned by the former. Second, that oppression itself cannot be overcome unless the system, which thrives on oppression, capitalism, is overthrown. Finally, therefore, the working class must be at the center of the struggle against oppression for it to be eliminated.

But oppression is not limited to workers. By definition, sexism, national oppression, or racism affect people of all classes in the oppressed group. But each class experiences oppression differently. Restrictions on abortion disproportionately impact working class and poor women. A wealthy woman will always be able to get the best medical care, including discreet and medically sound abortions. The intense racism in the United States means that even a very rich Black man can get pulled over for driving a fancy car ("driving while Black"); but the justice system is far harsher on working class and poor Blacks. As the O.J. Simpson trial showed, money takes the edge off racism. In truth, a Black auto-parts worker in Ohio has more in common with his fellow white workers than he does with an Oprah Winfrey or a Bill Cosby; a hotel maid more in common with the men she works with than the rich woman whose room she cleans.

The oppressed must fight to free themselves, but in each struggle of the oppressed, the working class has an interest in carrying the fight the furthest, that is, beyond the limits its middle-class leaders wish to place on it. "None so fitted to break the chains as they who wear them, none so well equipped to decide what is a fetter," wrote the Irish socialist James Connolly. "But whosoever carries the outworks of the citadel of oppression, the working class alone can raze it to the ground."[50]

Chapter Eleven

Capitalism and the Environment

From acid rain to the depletion of the ozone layer, from soil depletion to reckless deforestation, from the poisoning of rivers and seas by chemicals to the contamination of the earth by nuclear waste—the evidence of environmental degradation is everywhere. Global warming—caused primarily by the exponential increase over the last few centuries in carbon dioxide emissions—threatens the inundation of coastal cities and towns, promises longer droughts and more severe storms, and increases the probability of bacterial blights and viral epidemics. The very advances made in production that have brought us the possibility of a world without want are also wrecking the environmental basis for our own survival as a species on the planet.

What causes this environmental destruction? Most people who are concerned with environmental issues agree with two main, overlapping arguments: Too many people are chasing too few resources, and unchecked industrial growth is fouling the environment. The only way to reverse the trend—so the argument usually goes—is to reduce consumption, curtail production, and limit population growth.

These arguments have their origin in the theories of the nineteenth-century British economist Thomas Robert Malthus. "Population, when unchecked, increases in a geometrical ratio," he proposed. "Subsistence increases only in an arithmetical ratio."[1] Malthus transferred an observable fact of the non-human animal kingdom to human society, without offering a shred of evidence. He used this theory to contend that it was no use trying to ameliorate the conditions of the poor. "The implications of this line of thought," said Engels, "are that since it is precisely the poor who are the surplus, nothing should be done for them except to make their dying of starvation as easy as possible."[2]

Malthusian explanations for poverty and environmental degradation continue to thrive. It is not social relations that explain inequality, hunger, and environmental crisis, but too many people. This has become everyday common sense, an apparently self-evident truth that requires no proof. The publication of Anne and Paul Ehrlich's 1968 book *The Population Bomb* heralded the beginning of an almost continuous alarm on the part of environmentalists over rampant unchecked population growth. In the authors' 1990 sequel, *The Population Explosion,* the alarm became hysteria: "In the six seconds it takes you to read this sentence," they warn, "eighteen more people will be added. Each hour there are 11,000 more mouths to feed; each year, more than 95 million. Yet the world has hundreds of billions *fewer* tons of topsoil and hundreds of trillions *fewer* gallons of groundwater with which to grow food crops than it had in 1968."[3] Without the reduction of population, of resource consumption, and of energy use, they argue, "civilization will collapse."[4] After making this cataclysmic prediction, they offer a list of individualistic solutions analogous to trying to collapse a stone wall with a pea shooter: encourage parents to have fewer kids, eat less beef and "more vegetables," wear sweaters and turn down the thermostat, drive a fuel-efficient car, and donate "some of your leisure time to tree planting."[5]

Garret Hardin, a professor of human ecology in California, draws reactionary conclusions from similar dire predictions: "To survive, rich nations must refuse immigration to people who are poor because their governments are unable or unwilling to stop population growth."[6] He calmly asserts that, "Freedom to breed is intolerable."[7] Hardin compares the earth to a lifeboat. You can guess who he wants to throw off—and he's not on the list.

Marxists certainly agree that environmental damage is a serious problem, one that threatens to wreck the environmental basis for our own survival on earth if unchecked. But this crisis is not the result of overpopulation or industrial growth per se, but rather the way in which capitalism organizes production. In fact, capitalism creates for the first time the potential to eliminate poverty and hunger once and for all. Moreover, we now have the scientific knowledge to produce abundance in a way that won't destroy the environment.

Let's look first at the idea that there are limited resources. In 1981, Lester Brown, a well-known ecologist and president of the Worldwatch

Institute, wrote a book that argued the world would run out of oil in 1996.[8] Yet throughout the period from 1981 to 1996, estimated oil reserves actually increased—in spite of the fact that oil production and consumption grew considerably. It is obviously true that there's a finite amount of oil under the ground, and there are varying estimates about when it might run out. At *some point* in the future the world will run out of oil—and there is a raging debate about whether oil production has peaked yet. Long before oil runs dry, though, the cost of extracting oil will make its retrieval unprofitable. Other energy sources will be used before that time comes. There are other, far less polluting technologies, such as water and hydrogen fuel systems, as well as technologies that harness the sun, sea, and wind. What prevents them from replacing oil today is simply that oil and coal are cheap to get out of the ground and are extremely profitable. Energy companies are not interested in the massive retooling and investment a shift in energy sources will require—not to mention the amount of capital they have sunk into oil exploration, extraction, and refining that they will be forced to write off. Existing forms of alternative energy, moreover, are at this point not nearly sufficient to meet present needs. What is needed is massive investment in research and development to develop viable alternatives to oil, on a scale that can only be coordinated by the state.

What about the idea that there's not enough food to feed the planet's growing population? Some 852 million people in the world go hungry, and some 6 million children die from hunger-related causes every year. But it isn't because there isn't enough to feed them. Food production, far from falling behind the population, outstrips it year after year. The United Nations Food and Agricultural Organization estimates that world food output per head "has increased steadily over the past 30 years with an average annual growth rate reaching 1.2 percent during the past decade. Both developing and developed countries shared in this expansion, with per capita production growing at higher rates in the developing countries vis-à-vis the developed countries."[9] Enough grain is produced worldwide to feed everyone on the planet.[10] When we throw in other foodstuffs, there is enough to feed double the number of people living in the world today.[11] People go hungry not because of shortages of food, but because they can't afford to buy it. To argue otherwise, as neo-Malthusians do, is merely to provide a convenient cover for a system that throws away food to keep prices up rather than feed starving people.

In 1844, Engels, in a scathing criticism of Malthus' "vile, infamous theory," noted, "every adult produces more than he can himself consume."[12] This obvious truth is an ironclad refutation of Malthus. Since every worker can produce "far more than he needs," the "community ought therefore to be glad to furnish him with everything that he needs."[13]

It turns out, in any case, that dire predictions of endless population growth are mistaken. The world rate of population growth slowed to 1.2 percent in 2002, down from a peak of 2.2 percent forty years earlier.[14] In Russia, Japan, Germany, and Italy, populations are projected to fall between 5 percent (Germany) and 23 percent (Russia). China's population is also expected to decline by 2030.[15] Depending on the region, some of the decline is attributable to declining birth rates; but the ravaging effect of AIDS in Africa is another factor.[16]

Under capitalism, overpopulation is not a measure of scarcity in relation to human need, any more than capitalist overproduction signifies production over and above the needs of the majority. The irony of capitalism is that it produces a surplus population (unemployment) as a byproduct of tremendous productive growth. Human productivity has leaped far beyond anything Engels could have imagined. It isn't scarcity that produces hunger and unemployment, but overabundance. Capitalism has its own laws of population, in which surplus population is created as a result of the advance of social productivity, not because of any absolute shortage of the means of subsistence. "Surplus population or labor power is invariably tied up with surplus wealth," wrote Engels.[17] Capitalist overpopulation is never overpopulation in relation to available subsistence, but in relation to available employment. As capitalist industry develops, it takes larger and larger amounts of capital to employ smaller and smaller amounts of labor, and market fluctuations in profitability periodically throw workers onto the streets.

But this doesn't fully answer the other question: Aren't all the potential benefits of mass production undermined by pollution and environmental degradation of the planet? We may be able to feed everyone now, but at what cost to our long-term prospects for survival, given deforestation, soil depletion, and destruction of the ozone layer? These are real problems, but they are problems of capitalism that can be solved by socializing the means of production.

The same scientific knowledge that is used to produce things in ways that recklessly pollute the earth could, under different circumstances, be used to create a more harmonious balance between human beings and their environment. The scientific know-how exists, for example, to dramatically reduce greenhouse gases, acid rain, and prevent rampant deforestation. Intelligent use of available arable land and the planned distribution of goods and services could sustain large populations without wrecking our ability to produce food in the future. It is simply not profitable for capitalism to do so. The unplanned, anarchic character of the free market, and the scramble for immediate profits, mean capitalists give no thought or care to the after-effects, or unintended consequences, of the production process.

"What cared the Spanish planters in Cuba," wrote Engels, "who burned down forests on the slopes of the mountains and obtained from the ashes sufficient fertilizer for one generation of very highly profitable coffee trees—what cared they that the heavy tropical rainfall afterwards washed away the unprotected upper statum of the soil, leaving behind only bare rock!"[18] Haiti was one of the lushest islands in the Carribean, and at one time the world's most profitable slave colony. Today, much of it is also "barren rock."

Capitalism represents, on the one hand, a tremendous advance in production, in the ability of human beings to understand nature's laws and use them to enhance our own productive powers. Yet there is a problem. "Let us not ... flatter ourselves overmuch," Engels wrote, "on account of our human victories over nature. For each such victory nature takes its revenge on us. Each victory, it is true, in the first place brings about the results we expected, but in the second and third places it has quite different, unforeseen effects which only too often cancel the first."[19]

This problem is a product of our incomplete understanding of the workings of nature and the effects of our actions upon them. The phenomenon becomes more acute under capitalism, argued Engels, where only "the social effects of human actions in the fields of production and exchange that are actually intended" are examined, and even here the "intended" effects are motivated solely by "the profit to be made on selling."[20] We could cite many examples since Engels' day demonstrating the reckless disregard for the environment by shortsighted capitalists. But his words are extremely relevant today:

> Thus at every step we are reminded that we by no means rule over nature like a conqueror over a foreign people, like someone standing outside nature—but that we, with flesh, blood and brain, belong to nature, and exist in its midst, and that all our mastery of it consists in the fact that we have the advantage over all other creatures of being able to learn its laws and apply them correctly.[21]

In order to create a long-term, sustainable environment for human life on the planet, far more is required than individuals deciding to drive fuel-efficient cars or taking time out to plant trees—arguably a waste of human energy given the scale of the crisis. What is required is nothing short of a revolutionary reconstitution of society—"a complete revolution in our hitherto existing mode of production, and simultaneously a revolution in our whole contemporary social order," as Engels concluded.[22] The point is not to leave nature alone, but to transform human social relations so that production (and the technology accompanying it) develops in a planned manner. Human need—and, by extension, the care of the natural environment upon which human needs depend—must be central to that planning. Only by the overcoming of capitalism's contradiction between production and distribution, between social planning and market blindness, and between classes, can all the scientific knowledge that we have acquired be used in a completely conscious and rational way:

> With the fusion of the interests now opposed to each other there disappears the contradiction between excess population here and excess wealth there; there disappears the miraculous fact (more miraculous than all the miracles of all the religions put together) that a nation has to starve from sheer wealth and plenty; and there disappears the crazy assertion that the earth lacks the power to feed men.[23]

How natural are natural disasters?

Marxists are sometimes rebuked for blaming everything on capitalism. Yet often, if a chain of events is traced back carefully, capitalism *is* to blame. A trucker driving after midnight and veering into oncoming traffic may be considered an accident, until you discover that he worked for a non-union company that paid him nine dollars an hour to drive sixty hours a week.

But surely there are terrible natural events that have nothing to do with capitalism, right? Certainly, if a giant meteor strikes the earth, no one in his or her right mind would blame it on capitalism, any more than human agency can explain the demise of the dinosaurs. Nevertheless, there are ways in which capitalism shapes the impact of naturally occurring events. Hurricane Katrina, which struck the Gulf Coast in 2005, is a clear case in point. The disaster was anything but "natural." First, global warming is causing more frequent and severe storms. Second, the mangrove swamps around the gulf that once acted as a break on tidal surges have been wiped out by development. Third, the levees protecting New Orleans were poorly constructed and maintained. And fourth, there was simply no adequate evacuation plan for millions of the city's mostly Black poor population. All of this meant that a Category Five storm had an impact far beyond its wind speeds.

Take another example: the wildfires that rage practically every year in the Western states. The five-year wildfire average from 1996 to 2000 was the highest in forty years. The media often blame these fires on the forces of nature: hot, dry conditions and several years of drought. To the extent that human beings play any role, it's as individual scapegoats—someone carelessly discarded a lit cigarette or left an unattended campfire burning. While some fires may begin as a result of negligence—though, as the case of the overworked trucker shows, even this may have a social explanation—lightning starts most fires. Before we let the officials pass the blame onto these hapless individuals or lightning, let's look at whether there aren't human-made conditions that have contributed to the problem. According to a study by the Bluewater Network, global warming—the raising of the earth's temperature as a result of greenhouse gases—is causing the dry drought conditions that make for more devastating wildfires.[24]

The story doesn't end there. Decades of rapacious logging have played their part. According to the World Wildlife Fund, "In their natural state, many Western forests are comprised of large, old, fire-resistant trees spaced about 20–30 feet apart. But today, after a century of logging, livestock grazing, road building and indiscriminate fire suppression, Western forests are primed for intense fires."[25]

In the past, before European conquest, Indians used controlled burning to reduce the underbrush and smaller, less fire-resistant trees. This practice, which encouraged the size and spacing of trees referred to in the World Wildlife Fund report, made not only for better traveling and hunting, but also reduced the danger of catastrophic fires. As whites pushed the Indians off their land, existing forests, fallow fields, and new forests that sprang up in clear-cut areas were allowed to grow into tangled forest thickets. The term "firestorm" was coined in the 1870s after a series of devastating fires began ravaging the Midwest. Sixty firestorms ripped through the region between 1870 and 1918, killing thousands of people.[26]

The clear-cutting of today's timber industry also leaves dried wood scattered around, often close to populated areas. Moreover, the deliberate suppression of fires around more populated areas only made fires more devastating once they broke out. As the Wildlife Fund report concludes, "Fire suppression has disrupted the natural cycle of fire that cleanses the forest floor of young trees and other flammable plants which fuel catastrophic fires.... Bottom line—the body of scientific evidence shows that forests that are roaded, clear-cut, grazed and subjected to indiscriminate fire suppression are more prone to catastrophic, damaging fire."[27]

Add to this budget cuts that slashed the number, as well as the training, of firefighters, and we have a disaster waiting to happen. Everywhere we turn, the priorities of capitalism—profit at any human, social, or natural cost—help create, or at the very least, exacerbate, the "natural" disasters we face.

Live simply?

One of the most popular reactions to society's problems, and one popular among some environmentalists, is to withdraw, to create a small oasis of "correct living" through vegetarian coops, anarchist collectives, and the like. Sometimes, the same people who seek to create these spaces of alternative living also get involved in public protests, seeing no contradiction in doing both—fighting the powers that be for something better, but also creating a "lifestyle" alternative. The idea is that we should all "live simply" by not consuming too much and not buying things that are wasteful or harmful.

But mass collective action and changing one's personal consumption habits are very different approaches to changing the world. This isn't an argument against anyone deciding to make personal changes that suit them. People should have the right to eat and live as they please. But can such choices have any significant impact on society?

What motivates people to decide to change their lifestyle is their genuine alarm at the emptiness of consumer capitalism. But this choice is a luxury, affordable only to the middle class, who are brought up in relative comfort, believing that their lives are governed by choices about career, lifestyle, education, and so on. These options are simply out of reach to the vast majority of the world's population. For this majority, the question is not what lifestyle to choose, but figuring out how to get by. Three and a half billion people—more than half the world's population—live on less than two dollars a day.[28] Even in the United States, the richest country in the world, the U.S. Census Bureau counts 37 million poor people[29]—and a more reasonable measure of poverty would put this figure significantly higher.[30] Many more live on the edge of poverty, one paycheck away from disaster. Even better-paid workers are mired in debt and are overworked. The main choices in their lives—and in the lives of most working-class people—are work or starve, work or lose your home, get a better-paying job or forget about education for your kids, and so on.

A factory worker in Los Angeles may prefer to take a bus to work rather than drive his or her car. Unfortunately, the public transportation system in Los Angeles is so bad that taking the bus often isn't really an option.

Collective problems require collective solutions. The worst environmental problems—like the depletion of the ozone layer and global warming—can't possibly be solved by individual consumer choices. You may choose not to drive a car. But what impact will this have when power plants burn coal and the national transportation system consists of fleets of diesel trucks spewing filth into the air? Someone may eat organic food free of pesticides and chemical fertilizers. But organic food is out of the price range of the majority of people.

The struggle in Bolivia in 2000 against privatization of the water system is a good example of why collective action, rather than individual lifestyle, is the key to real change. Millions of Bolivian workers, peasants, and poor people took to the streets and forced the government to back down on its plans to hand the country's water systems over to the American-owned Bechtel Corporation. The movement was fuelled by an understanding that Bechtel would have massively increased the cost of water for Bolivians. Routing the government's plans not only achieved what individual consumer choices never could have—after all, you can't decide not to consume water—but mass struggle raised the possibility of collective solutions to capitalism.

The danger of focusing on individual choices is that it can end up blaming the victim—the people who are most hurt by the system, whereas the root of the problem is the way production is organized, not what people choose or don't choose to buy. As the English writer William Morris put it so eloquently:

> It is profit which draws men into enormous unmanageable aggregations called towns, for instance; profit which crowds them up when they are there, into quarters without gardens or open spaces; profit which won't take the most ordinary precautions against wrapping a whole district in a cloud of sulphurous smoke; which turns beautiful rivers into filthy sewers; which condemns all but

> the rich to live in houses idiotically cramped and confined at the best, and at the worst, in houses for whose wretchedness there is no name.[31]

Only when the world's united producers collectively seize the means of production can we establish the conditions in which corporate profiteering and degradation of our planet can be reversed. If production were planned rationally, for example, we would build urban and national mass public transit systems to reduce carbon pollution, traffic, and urban congestion.

Chapter Twelve

But What about...? Arguments against Socialism

We've already dealt, throughout this book, with many objections to Marxism and socialism. In this chapter, I'll take on some other common objections.

Capitalism is more efficient than socialism

A typical argument against socialism is that capitalism is far more efficient and less bureaucratic than socialism. A look at the health care system in the United States completely destroys the argument that private is less bureaucratic than public. The private, for-profit health care industry in the United States generates a massive bureaucracy whose sole purpose is to perform the paperwork involved in ensuring that revenues and profits flow to the "right" people.

A 2004 study by Harvard Medical School researchers and Public Citizen found that the health care bureaucracy cost the United States $399.4 billion that year, and that a national health insurance system could save at least $286 billion annually on paperwork. That would be enough money to provide health care for all of the 43 million uninsured people in the United States, as well as full prescription drug coverage for everyone in the country.[1]

The study found that bureaucracy accounts for 31 percent of U.S. health care spending, whereas in Canada, where the national health care system still hangs on, bureaucracy accounts for only 16.7 percent of health care spending. Canada's system also manages to provide more health services per dollar spent. A separate study conducted by Boston University found that "about 50 percent of health care spending is eaten up by waste, excessive prices and fraud."[2] But then again, health care in the United States isn't about helping people—it's about a tiny number of capitalists making a large amount of money.

A nationally funded and planned health care system in the United States would deliver more service for less cost. Imagine how much more efficient in delivering quality care a national health care system would be if it were run by nurses, doctors, and other medical workers, rather than health care bureaucrats?

What do we make of the related argument that society is too large and complex for there to be efficient planning? Capitalism is already a planned society. There is, first of all, planning within enterprises. Massive global corporations that employ tens of thousands of people engage in systematic planning to figure out how to allocate labor and resources within their enterprises. The Pentagon engages in large-scale planning to conduct its overseas military operations and wars. As capitalism ages, collective, socialized organization becomes more and more prevalent.

But that planning takes place inside a world economy that is unplanned and anarchic. A company can plan how much it will produce one year, but it cannot plan who will buy what it produces. By definition markets are not planned. This simple fact accounts for economic shocks—not to mention the fact that the market fails to "efficiently" deliver anything to the hundreds of millions of people who cannot pay. The increasing social character of production under capitalism comes into conflict with capitalism's private appropriation of wealth by a minority of owners, and with the anarchy of the market, and periodic economic crises are its most glaring expression. From the standpoint of human need, capitalism is not only inefficient, it is downright criminal.

Efficiency is a relative thing. Life would be far better for the majority if we crudely and inefficiently planned how to allocate goods and resources on the basis of human need, rather than efficiently organizing them to intensify exploitation, wipe out competitors, or annihilate nations. A society in which "abundance becomes the source of distress and want" cannot by any reasonable measure be considered efficient except in the most narrow, constricted sense.[3]

Aren't people naturally competitive?

A further argument against the possibility of socialism is that human beings are naturally competitive. There are plenty of examples of spontaneous acts of sharing and cooperation in our present society that contradict this one-sided picture—for example, when people pitch in during a disaster. Moreover, even as it encourages individualist thinking and competition, capitalism is also a breeding ground of cooperation. Mass production and distribution would be impossible without it. In every workplace, hundreds and sometimes thousands of people must labor cooperatively to turn out a product. This socialized, cooperative aspect of capitalism is a partial negation of market competition, and it provides the basis for workers' own sense of themselves as a collective class whose interests compel them to take collective action.

The biggest problem with the "everyone is competitive" argument is that in a society based upon abundance, people won't need to fight over resources. "In the socialist society, when there is plenty and abundance for all," wrote American Trotskyist James Cannon,

> what will be the point in keeping account of each one's share, any more than in the distribution of food at a well-supplied family table? You don't keep books as to who eats how many pancakes for breakfast or how many pieces of bread for dinner. Nobody grabs when the table is laden. If you have a guest, you don't seize the first piece of meat for yourself, you pass the plate and ask him to help himself first.[4]

The point is that, under socialism, society's surplus wealth would be collectively used to enhance the welfare of all rather than that of a small group. Why would I steal what was freely available? Such a society may seem too utopian. But as Cannon said: "What's absurd is to think that this madhouse is permanent and for all time."[5]

"Hang on," say the naysayers: "Without competition, creativity and invention would stagnate. There would be no incentive to work hard, to achieve." The implication of this, one of the oldest arguments against socialism, is that capitalist market competition is the best and only guarantee of hard work.

Marx and Engels dealt with the question in the *Communist Manifesto*. "It has been objected," they write, "that upon the abolition of private property all work will cease, and universal laziness will overtake us." Their answer is as simple as it is devastating: "According to this, bourgeois society ought long ago to have gone to the dogs through sheer idleness; for those of its members who work, acquire nothing, and those who acquire anything do not work."[6]

The majority of people do not work for their own benefit, but for the benefit of others. Their only incentive is that without work they cannot survive. Yet there are plenty of examples of people putting in hours of hard work for no financial gain. Anyone involved in high school or community theater can attest to the satisfaction that comes from pouring hours after school or work into making a theatrical production come to life. I myself met many ordinary people in Mississippi and Louisiana in the wake of Hurricane Katrina who came from all over the country to bring supplies and distribute food to the storm's victims. I met a student from a Nashville divinity school who spent hours in the polluted floodwaters of New Orleans helping stranded Katrina victims onto dry land from rescue boats. Those boats had been donated or commandeered by concerned citizens.

Nor can the argument be leveled that socialism takes incentive away because it doesn't allow for personal possessions. It is only property used to exploit others that socialism prohibits. Socialism will allow for people to have more, not less, of the things that enhance their lives. And the incentive to invent better technology will remain, even without the profit motive, because such inventions will reduce work hours and enhance everyone's quality of life.

And while it is true that capitalist competition acts as a spur to increase production, it is also extremely wasteful. One need only think of the multi-billion-dollar advertising industry or the military-industrial complex to see how much labor is expended upon essentially worthless enterprises. Imagine what hundreds of billions of dollars now spent on weapons of mass destruction or on advertisements aimed at convincing us to buy one brand of sugary water over another could do to fix crumbling schools, provide universal health care, and clean up environmental degradation.

Moreover, because capitalist enterprises depend upon increasing profits and market share, they must continually sell their products in ever-greater quantities. There is therefore a built-in incentive on the part of capitalists to produce things of poor quality that do not last. This is called planned obsolescence. Think of the college textbook industry, where the same one-hundred-dollar book is reissued (with a higher price tag, of course) that has nothing more than a new introduction and several rearranged chapters, or the new housing developments that use the cheapest building materials to construct flimsy homes that won't last.

The health care business is probably the most distressing example of what happens when we "let the market decide." Health care for profit means delivering the least amount of health care service possible and selling the service for as much as possible. HMOs deny people access to important medical procedures because they want to maximize their profits. Insurance companies refuse coverage to those who need it the most—the chronically ill with "preexisting conditions"—because it isn't profitable. Richard Scott, president of the now notorious Columbia/HCA hospital chain, compares health care to fast food: "Do we have an obligation to provide health care for everybody? Where do we draw the line? Is any fast-food restaurant obligated to feed everybody who shows up?"[7]

Capitalism wastes human life above all. It spends billions of dollars to warehouse people in overcrowded prisons. It provides sub-par education to millions of poor students, sending a message that their lives will amount to nothing. Capitalism negates the most important incentive—the incentive to feed, clothe, and house everyone, and to provide all with meaningful work. Are people homeless in America because there is a shortage of homes? And if that is the case, is there a shortage of homes because we don't have the concrete, the wood, and the steel to produce them? Or perhaps we don't have the workers who can build them? The labor and the materials are there, but there is no incentive to build low-cost housing for the homeless, simply because it is not profitable to do so.

Do the ends justify the means?

In one of our many fruitless arguments, I remember my father attacking Marxism for believing that "the ends justify the means." By this, he meant that Marxists have no moral scruples and will stop at nothing to achieve their goals. Ironically, this is the same person who once told me, with a straight face, that the United States had to drop the atomic bomb on Hiroshima and Nagasaki "to save lives."

In fact, every ruling class in the world operates on the assumption that the ends justify the means. In every war, these rulers risk the lives of millions of ordinary soldiers in the pursuit of their goals. The U.S. government stands poised to use the world's most terrible weapons of mass destruction if it deems their use necessary. Asked by a reporter in 1995 if U.S.-imposed economic sanctions against Iraq that had killed half a million Iraqi children were "worth it," Madeleine Albright, then the U.S. ambassador to the UN, responded that "the price, we think, is worth it."[8] The end justified the means.

"The ruling class," wrote Russian revolutionary Leon Trotsky in his book *Their Morals and Ours*, "forces its ends upon society and habituates it to considering all those means which contradict its ends as immoral. That is the chief function of official morality."[9]

It is therefore "immoral" to kill in peacetime but a sacred duty to kill in wartime. It is impermissible for strikers to use force to stop a scab crossing a picket line but perfectly acceptable for a police officer to use force to break up that same picket line.

Lying and deception are defended by CIA and military leaders as indispensable means to confuse and disorient other governments, while children are told that lying and cheating is immoral. The 1936 Flint Sit-down strikers could not have won a victory over the auto bosses if they had not employed deception, creating a diversion that led law enforcement officials and company goons to the wrong plant, while workers occupied another plant.

The real question for socialists is this: What justifies the ends? In the American Civil War, for example, both sides engaged in similar acts of violence. But one side was fighting to defend slavery and the other to end it. In Russia, the soldiers who turned on their officers and joined the working-class struggle to overthrow tsarism were justified, whereas the officers who defended the tsar by shooting at workers were not. As Trotsky wrote: "Armies in combat are always more or less symmetrical; were there nothing in common in their methods, they could not inflict blows upon each other."[10]

If all lying and violence are considered out of bounds, then of course humanity must renounce revolution and accept things as they are. In practice, not even struggles committed to nonviolence can refrain from it in the face of the violence committed against them. During the Civil Rights movement, for example, all of the Black Student Nonviolent Coordinating Committee (SNCC) activists in the Deep South, facing the daily threat of deadly white violence, were armed.[11] The Deacons of Defense, an armed self-defense group, protected many nonviolent protests from the Klan and racist police.[12]

Nevertheless, we cannot for a minute forget that not only the aims, but also the methods, that ordinary people use in fighting for their freedom are fundamentally different from the methods of the ruling class. Workers' power depends on collective rather than individual action, democratic debate and action rather than mutual deceit. While it may be tactically necessary to lie to the bosses during a strike, mass movements must not lie to themselves.

Ends and means are dialectically interrelated. The violence of a revolution, though necessary to break the will of the dominant classes, does not prefigure the future society that it aims to establish—i.e., one that is free of all coercion. Nevertheless, as the failure of the Russian Revolution shows, the means must be subordinated to the ends. If a workers' state, in its desperate isolation, requires too much coercion to maintain its rule, then the means can overwhelm and smother the ends.

"A means can only be justified by its end," concluded Trotsky. "But the end in turn needs to be justified."[13] For Marxists,

> the end is justified if it leads to increasing the power of humanity over nature and to the abolition of the power of one person over another. Permissible and obligatory are those and only those means, we answer, which unite the revolutionary proletariat, fill their hearts with irreconcilable hostility to oppression … imbue them with consciousness of their own historic mission, raise their courage and spirit of self-sacrifice in the struggle. Precisely from this, it flows that not all means are permissible. When we say that the end justifies the means, then for us, the conclusion follows that the great revolutionary end spurns those base means and ways which set one part of the working class against other parts; or attempt to make the masses happy without their participation; or lower the faith of the masses in themselves and their organization, replacing it by worship for the "leaders."[14]

Aren't we all middle class?

The Marxist conception of class is not widely accepted in the United States. Our textbooks offer up deliberately fuzzy terms that blur and cover up extreme class and wealth inequality. Terms such as "the American people," the "average American," and "middle class" are far more common than any mention of "workers" or "the working class." The historian James W. Loewen examined twelve U.S. high school textbooks and found that

> six of them contain no index listing at all for "social class," "social stratification," "class structure," "income distribution," "inequality," or any conceivably related topic. Not one book lists "upper class," "working class," or "lower class." Two of the textbooks list "middle class," but only to assure students that America is a middle-class country.… Talking about the middle class is hardly equivalent to discussing social stratification, however; in fact, as Gregory Mantsios has pointed out, "such references appear to be acceptable precisely because they mute class differences."[15]

The use of the term "middle class" conveniently lumps together everyone who is neither extremely poor nor extremely rich. Even a 1999 book titled *The Coming Class War in America* can argue that the middle class in the United States is 60 percent of the population, a neat trick accomplished by simply taking the 60 percent of the population whose income lies between the 40 percent that fall below or above them, and slapping the label "middle class" on it.[16] One could just as easily divide incomes into six categories and say there are six classes in the United States: lowest, low, lower-middle, middle, upper-middle, and wealthy. There's no end to the creative but arbitrary subdivisions we could come up with, but they wouldn't help us much, because they don't get beyond the surface.

Income doesn't necessarily tell us about a person's place in the economic system—for example, whether someone *worked* for their wealth or not. Even the concept of "haves" versus "have-nots," or "rich" versus "poor," while an improvement, is still only a descriptive devices that tells us nothing about why some have and others have not. Calibrating class by income can be very misleading. For example, a small business owner who exploits ten employees might in a given year have a smaller income than a skilled carpenter. If we were to determine class by income, the carpenter would be "above" the business person, completely obscuring the fact that the carpenter's labor is exploited for the profit of the builder, whereas the business person is in fact a small-scale *exploiter.*

Classes are defined by their relationship to the production process in any given society; in particular, the production and control of the *surplus* are key. What this means is that a skilled auto mechanic who works for Firestone might make a great deal more money than a strawberry picker—but both are part of the working class because both perform surplus labor for capitalists. By this definition, workers are a majority of society. The ruling class "could easily be seated in Yankee stadium, which holds 57,000 people."[17] The middle class, more accurately defined as supervisory staff, high-paid professionals, small business people, and farmers, constitutes at most 25 percent of the working population.[18]

The shrinking working class?

Some analysts claim we have entered a "post-industrial" society in which automation is shrinking, if not eliminating, the working class. As a result, workers no longer have the power that Marx attributed to them. "Capital has succeeded," writes French radical author André Gorz, "in reducing workers' power in the production process."[19]

This analysis is based on the mistaken idea that workers' power depends on the absolute size of the working class. But workers exhibit a concentrated power far beyond what numbers alone would suggest. Surely this is one of the important lessons of the Russian Revolution, where the industrial working class was less than 2 percent of the total population, but had its hands on the economic jugular of Russian capitalism. The same logic applies even more so today. The U.S. manufacturing working class is six times larger than Russia's in 1917, and it is far more productive.

Undeniably, there has been a relative shift in employment in the United States and other advanced industrial countries since the late 1960s—from industry to the service sector. About a third (32.7 percent) of workers were employed in manufacturing, mining, and construction in 1963, whereas just over a fifth, or 20.8 percent, were employed in this sector thirty years later.[20] One author estimates that the United States lost "3.5 to 4 million jobs between 1978 and 1982, or one out of every four jobs in large manufacturing facilities."[21] The manufacturing workforce in the United States stood at 22.5 million in 1979, and had dropped to 18.1 million by 2002. But that isn't the whole picture. While economic restructuring was shrinking the size of the manufacturing workforce in the United States, industrial growth was increasing it dramatically in countries like Brazil, Mexico, and South Korea. In South Korea, for example, the size of the manufacturing workforce increased from 1.2 million in 1969 to 4.7 million in 1994.[22] Even in the older manufacturing centers, the absolute number of industrial workers increased slightly until the mid-1990s. "In the industrial (OECD) nations of the North as a whole there were 115 million people employed in 'industry' in 1994 compared with 112 million in 1973."[23] The numbers have declined since then.

The point, however, is that the relative decline in the number of industrial workers is really just another indicator of the increase in labor productivity, a fact that strengthens rather than weakens the potential power of workers at the point of production. In the United States, manufacturing output increased by 44 percent between 1992 and 2002, at the same time that manufacturing employment declined by 7 percent, representing a 55 percent increase in productivity.[24] Though industrial workers' relative numbers have decreased due to productivity increases, their social weight has increased. Moreover, capitalist production has become so integrated that a single strike by a few thousand workers at a strategically critical factory can shut down an entire industry.

Finally, it would be a mistake to think that only industrial workers are part of the working class. The majority of white collar and public sector workers are also part of the working class. Along with the relative decline in manufacturing jobs, service industry jobs have mushroomed: cashiers, nurses, orderlies, janitors, truck drivers, warehouse workers, waiters, sales workers, social workers, and schoolteachers. These are people who work for a wage—in many cases, a wage that is lower than that of a factory worker—and who have little or no control over their work. They are subject to the same logic of exploitation, and share the same interests, as workers in factories, mines, building sites, and fields.

The working class is still the majority, though its structure has changed. Economics professor Michael Zweig estimates that the class of wage workers in the United States constitutes about 62 percent of the population—a low estimate because he excludes schoolteachers.[25] Teachers' strikes are practical proof that, no matter how much society attempts to instill middle-class professionalism in teachers, their working conditions force them to behave just like other workers.

As the mass protests of millions of immigrant workers showed in the spring of 2006, the working class is a sleeping giant whose awakening will once again remind us all of its awesome potential.

Can ordinary people run society?

A common argument against socialism is that the majority, the working class, is incapable of ruling collectively. We need educated, intelligent experts to run such a complex system. The legendary stupidity of George W. Bush, whose rich parents and crony friends bought him passing grades and much more, or the incompetence of Federal Emergency Management Agency bureaucrats during Hurricane Katrina in 2005, are both strong arguments against this view. "I think we are welcomed," said Bush, when asked about Vice President Dick Cheney's predictions that U.S. troops would be greeted with thanks by Iraqis. "But it was not a peaceful welcome."[26] When Brazilian president Luiz Inácio Lula da Silva showed him a map of Brazil, Bush exclaimed, "Wow! Brazil is big."[27]

There are many other examples that could be cited of presidents, industrialists, and bureaucrats with limited, if nonexistent, abilities. "Howard Hughes was another mediocrity," wrote Paul Foot.

> He started life as a playboy and ended it as a lunatic. He had no ability at all. Yet through a mixture of luck and the ability to read a balance sheet, Hughes became the boss of a gigantic financial and industrial empire. He was able, almost alone, to nominate the President of the United States, Richard Nixon, who also had no

> ability, knowledge or skill of any kind. Howard Hughes designed an aeroplane which crashed and directed a film which was a monumental failure. He couldn't do anything which mattered. Yet *he* made the decisions. The list is endless. Successful capitalists, almost to a man, are not people with any natural ability. Yet they decide what the experts do.[28]

Most people at the very top of society, the multimillionaires and billionaires, play no direct function in society's running—they merely collect the rewards of ownership. The ruling class today has become entirely parasitic, siphoning wealth but serving no useful social function. As early as 1881, Frederick Engels wrote that the capitalists do little but cash in dividend checks. "The social function of the capitalist here has been transferred to servants paid by wages; but he continues to pocket, in his dividends, the pay for those functions though he has ceased to perform them."[29]

"We [can] manage very well without the interference of the capitalist class in the great industries of the country," Engels concluded. "Stand back! Give the working class the chance of a turn."[30]

Bankers and investors don't make steel. It hardly takes intellectual brilliance for someone who inherits a million dollars to double it. Society could do away with the ruling class and suffer no more than when an appendix is removed from a human body. But do workers possess the capacity to rule? Won't they still depend on experts? Often it is workers' own hard-won, firsthand knowledge that engineers and managers use to figure out how to improve production, that is, to squeeze as much out of workers as possible. Not to deny the genius of a Newton or an Einstein, but "if science is understood in the fundamental sense of *knowledge of nature,"* writes Clifford Connor in his *People's History of Science,* "it should not be surprising to find that it originated with the people closest to nature: hunter-gatherers, peasant farmers, sailors, miners, blacksmiths, folk healers, and others forced by the conditions of their lives to wrest the means of their survival from an encounter with nature on a daily basis."[31]

Given the opportunity, everyone is capable of learning the scientific, administrative, and mathematical skills necessary to play a direct role in running society, just as in pre-class society knowledge of terrain, plants, and animals, or of tool-making, was shared by the group, and not treated as the monopoly of a minority.

Experts and scientists would still be needed for a time even under socialism, until the education system was improved so that the majority received education that today is only reserved for the privileged few. For a time, workers would have to exercise democratic control over the bookkeepers, managers, and engineers. But with society's vast resources diverted toward education, the distinctions between mental and manual work would break down, and the majority would be capable of doing many different kinds of jobs, from manual work to scientific work to administrative work. If workers, through their own directly elected representatives, were to seize control of production, no doubt mistakes would be made. But they would be the mistakes of the collective rather than the blind workings of the market—and could quickly be remedied by experience.

For example, if the workers of Chicago ran the city, instead of corporate bigwigs and their corrupt political hirelings, they would immediately begin solving the city's most pressing problems. The homeless would be quickly housed in unused homes, excess hotel space, and the requisitioned second and third homes of the rich. Meanwhile, unemployed construction workers would be organized to begin building houses. The ill-gotten gains of the city's patricians and their hangers-on would be seized and used to feed the hungry, improve dilapidated schools, provide better park services, update and extend transportation, and create real after-school programs for *all*. The run-down, destroyed ghettos of the West Side would become beautiful neighborhoods by redirecting the millions in parking-ticket money siphoned off to crony mafia friends, as well as funds earmarked for boondoggle stadiums. Real jobs (and real job training) would be made available to the thousands of young unemployed African Americans, Latinos, and poor whites who have been left to languish in the streets or in prison, where their great human potential is wasted.

On a national level, billions earmarked for the utter waste of weapons of mass destruction would be diverted into projects that benefit the mass of the population. The solution to homelessness is simple—build homes for the homeless.

But in our society nothing is done if it isn't profitable. In a society run by the collective producers, these problems can be solved because social need, rather than the market, will determine how decisions are made.

Isn't socialism about conformity?

Socialism will make us all like lemmings. This idea, "delicately stoked by the press and television of a capitalist society which is increasingly stamping sameness and conformity on its working people,"[32] was aided by images and stories of people in the so-called communist regimes. We saw people wearing identical clothing, schoolchildren mouthing slogans by rote to the great leader, work and leisure time regimented to the hour, row upon row of drearily identical buildings, the absence of any public debate, and so on.

But the system of totalitarian conformity that Stalin and Mao imposed in the Soviet Union and China respectively had nothing to do with socialism. Rather, it was part of a policy designed to regiment and dragoon the population, as the military does its soldiers, into making the maximum exertion for the purposes of building up industrial and military strength. This swift, blitzkrieg-style industrialization required strict labor discipline. Along with that went an ideology emphasizing national unity, and strict conformity to the dictates of the party bureaucracy, centered around a deified leader—the infamous cult of personality. "Thank you, Comrade Stalin, for our happy childhood," Russian students were required to say in class.[33] One Chinese official sang this "hymn of praise" to Chairman Mao at the 1955 National People's Congress: "The sun shines only in the day, the moon shines only at night. Only Chairman Mao is the sun that never sets."[34]

The irony of the Cold War is that the United States exhibited its own brand of stifling conformity, particularly in the 1950s. The climate of fear surrounding the anticommunist witch hunts, and the sterile clichés offered up by film, television, and advertising of suburban family life, sent a clear message that uniformity was paramount. Never mind that these images didn't really conform to reality. A 1957 novel expresses some of the frustration felt at the sameness of mass-produced suburban tract housing:

> In any one of these new neighborhoods, be it in Hartford or Philadelphia, you can be certain all other houses will be precisely like yours, inhabited by people whose age, income, number of children, problems, habits, conversation, dress, possessions and perhaps even blood type are also precisely like yours.[35]

Mass-market capitalism imposes conformity on the majority. This is true both at work and outside work. At work, we are expected to follow strict rules about our time and behavior; we are expected to follow a dress code. We churn out the same product, day in and day out, with no let-up, and we have very little control over the process. Outside of work, we are "mass consumers," coaxed, exhorted, and seduced into showing up in our millions to buy exactly the same product, whether it is an Egg McMuffin (each one indistinguishable from the other) or a toaster oven. Only the wealthy have the money and leisure to have palaces built by craftsmen, send their kids to the best schools, and take vacations in private jets.

But it does not have to be this way. The alternative is not between two different brands of conformity. Real equality is not about the leveling of personality or experience, but the creation of an equality of condition; not an equality of scarcity, but of abundance. Socialism means providing basic necessities for billions of people who lack them today, but it means much more than that. In a socialist society, the productive power of society is harnessed to serve everyone's needs. The collective provides the foundation of a flowering of creative expression and individual achievement. Think of it this way: In ancient Athens, the work of a few hundred thousand slaves provided about fifty thousand citizens with the freedom to meet, debate, and make decisions democratically. It allowed the flowering of great philosophy, theater, and art. Imagine now a society where the productive powers of society are so advanced that able-bodied people need only work a few hours every day to provide what is needed by society as a whole. In such a society—a socialist society—everyone will have the leisure time to pursue all sorts of dreams that today are out of reach to all but a minority. As Trotsky wrote:

> Spiritual creativeness demands freedom. The very purpose of communism is to subject nature to technique and technique to plan, and compel the raw material to give unstintingly everything to man that he needs. Far more than that, its highest goal is to free finally and once and for all the creative forces of mankind from all pressure, limitation and humiliating dependence. Personal relations, science and art will not know any externally imposed "plan," nor even any shadow of compulsion. To what degree spiritual creativeness shall be individual or collective will depend entirely upon its creators.[36]

Chapter Thirteen

Can It Happen Here?

Socialism, it has often been argued, has never taken hold in the United States because of certain peculiarities that distinguish this country from the rest of the world. Various arguments are offered to back up this claim of "American exceptionalism": Americans are too individualistic, the United States is too egalitarian (or, everyone is middle class), workers can easily become their own boss, divisions between workers are too strong, and finally, workers are too prosperous to want another kind of society. Each of these reasons for the weakness of the socialist tradition in the United States is either false, historically obsolete, or surmountable.

Be all that you can be?

A uniquely fluid class system that allows for significant upward mobility is "the promise that lies at the heart of the American dream," according to a *New York Times* study on class in the United States.[1] The ability of the poor and the working class to climb the social ladder has always been exaggerated. But in the early phases of industrial development it had a certain amount of validity. The abundance of cheap land in the West for a time offered workers the opportunity to "retire" from wage labor and become farmers. Each new wave of immigrants would start at the bottom, but might dream of improving their lot by moving up and out of the working class. This provided a safety valve preventing the formation of what Engels called a "permanent proletariat."[2]

Once westward expansion had completed its course by the end of the 1890s, however, the safety valve was closed.

But the "dream" never disappeared. Being your own boss—starting up a small business where there aren't any foremen or managers bossing you around—continues to be seen as a way out of the working class. The dream is a backhanded acknowledgement of the alienating, tedious, and unrewarding quality of wage labor. But the dream also has an ideological purpose—to promote the idea that individuals can make something of themselves, not through collective struggle, but by dint of individual spunk and hard work. Conversely, it reinforces the idea that those who are stuck in the working class or in poverty deserve it because they haven't tried hard enough to get out.

How realistic is it for most workers to become their own boss? There are lots of small businesses in the United States, but they are responsible for only a small part of total employment and total wealth. In the United States, there are 3,551 larger firms that employ twenty-five hundred or more workers, accounting for 37 percent of the total workforce and 43 percent of the total payroll. On the other hand, the 3.75 million businesses that employ 9 or fewer workers account for only 11 percent of employment and a paltry 8.7 percent of total payroll.[3]

The problem with the dream of owning your own business is that it is a precarious existence that often ends in bankruptcy. Only half of newly created small businesses are still in business after four years. Indeed, every year about as many small businesses close as are created. In 2004, for example, 580,900 new small businesses opened, but 576,200 closed—34,317 of these ended in bankruptcy.[4]

For millions of people, the dream of ownership means pouring your life savings into a business venture that requires endless work and the constant threat of failure to show for it. The small minority that are lucky enough to grow into real businesses end up surviving by exploiting other workers—profiting from the difference between labor's output and labor's pay. That is, by becoming their own boss, they also became someone else's boss.

According to the *New York Times* study, income mobility in the United States has been on the decline for the last three decades. In the past, notes one Michigan economist cited in the study, "people would say, 'Don't worry about inequality. The offspring of the poor have chances as good as the chances of the offspring of the rich.' Well, that's not true. It's not respectable in scholarly circles anymore to make that argument."[5] According to Sharon Smith, "This is … the first generation of young workers in U.S. history that faces a substantially lower standard of living than their parents."[6]

While there are certainly some people who move out of the working class, and some middle-class people who become capitalists, the movement also works in the other direction, toward downward mobility. Whether we use the more superficial measure of income, or whether we use the more accurate measure of class mobility, the overall picture doesn't change much from year to year; income distribution today is as unequal as it was on the eve of the Great Depression.[7]

The ultimate argument against the dream of upward mobility for the majority is the fact that the economy is a social pyramid; lots of room at the bottom, very little room at the top. Workers in the United States, just like workers everywhere else, can only advance through joint struggle with their class, not by trying to climb out of that class.

Playing on divisions

Another obstacle to workers' unity in the United States, Engels noted, was the way in which native-born workers were pitted against immigrants, established immigrants pitted against newly arriving immigrants, and white workers pitted against Black workers. Native-born workers "assumed an aristocratic posture," leaving the "badly paid occupations to the immigrants."[8] The immigrants, moreover, were divided by nationality and language. "And your bourgeoisie," wrote Engels to a fellow socialist in the United States, "knows much better even than the Austrian Government how to play off one nationality against the other: Jews, Italians, Bohemians, etc., against Germans and Irish, and each one against the other.... In such a country, continually renewed waves of advance, followed by equally certain setbacks, are inevitable."[9]

These divisions, however, were never absolute barriers to class unity. We have already spoken of the populist movement, which demonstrated impressive class solidarity across racial barriers in the Jim Crow Deep South. The United Mine Workers, from its formation in 1890, organized Black and white coalminers in the South, often in the same locals. Half of the UMW members in Alabama were Black, many of the union's officers were Black, and the state's largest local was integrated.[10] The 1912 Lawrence strike—which brought together twenty-five thousand textile workers made up of twenty-eight different nationalities and who spoke forty-five different dialects—is another example.[11] Historian Phillip Foner wrote of Lawrence:

> The spontaneous outburst quickly gave way to a methodical strike organization rarely paralleled in the annals of the American labor movement.... A general strike committee of 56 members was set up. The 14 largest nationality groups were each allowed to elect four members. (Later, another nationality was given representation thus increasing the membership to 60.) Of the principal nationalities taking part in the strike, only the Germans were not represented on the committee.... The strike committee was the executive board of the strikers, charged with complete authority to conduct the strike, and subject only to the popular mandate of the strikers themselves. All mills on strike and their component parts, all crafts and phases of work, were represented. The committee spoke for all workers.[12]

A history of class struggle

The U.S. working class has a long and rich tradition of struggle. But it has followed a boom and bust pattern: extended periods of surface calm interrupted by huge explosions. The eruption of pent-up anger appears on the surface to come from nowhere, but it has its roots in the preceding period of employer attacks on the working class and its organizations. The attacks, which often involve intense violence directed against strikers and their families, have usually been successful in weakening or destroying unions and crippling the left. The result has been periodic breaks in the organizational and political continuity of the movement. Each new wave of struggle has not necessarily had the benefit of learning from the experiences of previous waves. This herky-jerky history prompted Trotsky to observe, "The American workers are very combative—as we have seen during the strikes. They have had the most rebellious strikes in the world. What the American worker misses is a spirit of generalization, or analysis, of his class position in society as a whole."[13]

An example of the break in continuity is the fact that until the mass protests of immigrant workers on May Day, 2006, most American workers were only vaguely aware of May Day's significance as a holiday marking the international solidarity of the world working class. Fewer still know that the first May Day in the world was marked in 1886 by a strike of two hundred thousand U.S. workers demanding the eight-hour day. The memory of the working class can only be embodied in organizations that are capable of carrying on the tradition. In the United States, that memory has been continually lost, and then relearned.

Yet having said this, it is important to point out that in every upturn of mass struggle, tens of thousands of workers have embraced socialist ideas and organization. The Socialist Party, for example, peaked at 150,000 members in 1915. Eugene Debs got almost a million votes in his 1912 presidential run. Tens of thousands of workers went through the school of the IWW, and at its height in 1938, the Communist Party (CP) boasted 80,000 members and twice as many close collaborators. In 1969, at the height of radical ferment, FBI director J. Edgar Hoover warned President Nixon that "a recent poll indicates that approximately 25% of the black population has great respect for the Black Panther Party, including 43% of blacks under twenty-one years of age."[14]

The American ruling-class tradition is one in which it uses every means at its disposal to divide and weaken the working-class movement—and to try and crush it when it rises up. It is distinct from other ruling classes not in nature, but in degree. The racism it has employed, for example, has historically surpassed that of every other advanced industrial society, with the exception of apartheid-era South Africa. Moreover, the political system it presides over is based on the rule of nearly identical capitalist parties, in which one party masquerades as an ally of workers and the oppressed in order to absorb the movements. And the scale of violence it is willing to use to smash workers' resistance is the most extreme in the industrialized world. These are the real obstacles workers have faced. Yet these obstacles would not be placed in front of workers by the bosses unless the possibility of class unity was a real threat.

Workers can choose two different responses to the bosses' attempts to divide them. They can accept those divisions, and see lower-paid, more oppressed workers as their competitors. Or they can learn from their own hard experience that the best way to defend themselves is to unite and raise the conditions of all. Obviously, American capitalism would not have survived to this day without succeeding in dividing workers. But every example of real solidarity reminds us of the potential for things to be different. As Philip Foner recounted:

> "We are commencing to see a few things," declared a Davenport, Iowa, local of the United Brotherhood of Electrical Workers after the employers had taken advantage of the union's discrimination policy to use Negro workers as strikebreakers. "The prejudice we have held against color is beginning to vanish. A man may be white, black, brown, red or yellow, if he is a toiler he is one of us and part of us, for if his scale of living is lower than ours, our own is not secure, for 'no chain is securer than the weakest link in it.'"[15]

1930s—the aborted possibility

The 1930s were a time when the working class had a real opportunity to fulfill its revolutionary potential.[16] The statistics show the scale of the upheaval. Strikes tripled to 1,856 between 1933 and 1934, and peaked in 1937 at 4,470. Union membership rose from 2.6 million in 1934 to 7.3 million in 1938. In 1930, only 50,000 Black workers were in unions. By 1940, half a million were unionized. In 1937, 193,000 workers engaged in 247 sit-down strikes in the aftermath of the Flint strike, and before the year's end half a million workers had engaged it the sit-down tactic. Out of this upheaval came the formation of the mass industrial unions and the Congress of Industrial Organizations (CIO).

Communist Party militants played a leading role in many struggles, attracting to their ranks many of the best working-class rebels. The party took on racism head-on—organizing Black sharecroppers in the South, and picketing stores, demanding the hiring of Black workers in New York City. It organized a campaign for justice for the "Scottsboro Boys" (nine young Black men framed for rape in Alabama) that united Blacks and whites in marches and meetings across the country. As a result, thousands of Blacks joined the party, increasing its African-American membership in 1938 to about 9 percent of its total membership. It was able to demonstrate, in a society racked by racism and lynching, not only that Black and white workers could unite in the struggle for common demands, but that white workers could be won to the fight against racism.[17]

But if the CP showed that American workers weren't at all averse to socialism, it also was the single greatest obstacle to building a left challenge to the Democratic Party. The problem is that by the 1930s the CP had ceased to be a genuine revolutionary party. At the height of the struggle in the 1930s, the CP was in its "Popular Front" phase—having been ordered along with other Western Communist Parties to make uncritical alliances with bourgeois parties as part of Stalin's agreement with the Allies against Hitler. In the United States, this meant instructing members to give their full backing to Roosevelt and the Democratic Party. The party that had denounced Roosevelt as "an inspirer of fascism" in 1935 was singing his praises just a year later. Though the Communist Party's members had played a leading role in the sit-down strikes, the party's leadership agreed to throw a wet towel on the struggle. A December 1937 article in the CP's paper, the *Daily Worker*, declared "unequivocally and emphatically that the Communists and the Communist Party had never in the past and do not now in any shape, manner or form advocate or support unauthorized and wildcat action and regard such strikes as gravely injurious ... to the cause of cooperative action between labor and middle-class groups."[18]

Instead of building a party of workers committed to genuine socialism, the CP helped steer workers away from that alternative, and into the arms of the Democratic Party. When thousands of workers expressed support for a labor party alternative to the Democrats, the CP and the union bureaucracy created fake local labor parties whose purpose was to siphon workers' votes toward Roosevelt's reelection.

Bought off? The race is to the bottom, not to the top

In the period after the Second World War, world capitalism entered an unprecedented boom. For a layer of workers, it seemed that 1930s-style poverty was a thing of the past. Workers could now expect that their children's lives would improve, and their children's after that. Radical ideas seemed unnecessary. Labor unions partnered up with the employers, trading economic benefits for their members in exchange for class peace. The Cold War anticommunist witch hunts, carried through by employers, the state, and the union bureaucracy, purged thousands of socialists and militants from the trade unions and other institutions, severing the connection between the radical traditions of the 1930s and later generations of workers. The tragedy is that the CP contributed to this process. To ingratiate itself with Roosevelt, it applauded repression against other radicals in the labor movement. When it was attacked and vilified by the state and in the unions, it failed to mount any defense. Party activists denied they were members, and some even participated in the red-baiting.

The postwar prosperity prompted a new battery of pundits to herald the end of socialism and the triumph of capitalism, giving rise to new arguments about how workers were too contented to want change. The claim was exaggerated, though it contained a grain of truth. But there were contradictions. The Civil Rights movement, and later the fight for Black power in the North, was a stark reminder that the "American Dream" never applied to African Americans. These social movements provided the impetus for the anti–Vietnam War movement, the women's movement, and the stirrings of a new labor movement.

The endless prosperity came to an end in the late 1960s, shattering the postwar honeymoon. As crisis began to hit the U.S. economy, and as the social movements peaked, workers began to stir, bucking against both employers and a sclerotic labor bureaucracy that had become proud of its partnership with capital and looked on picket lines with unease. The number of wildcat strikes doubled from one thousand to two thousand through the 1960s. A strike wave in 1970 included a strike by forty thousand miners demanding disability benefits, and postal workers, though legally prohibited from striking, organized a successful two-week national walkout. In the Detroit auto plants, Black workers organized the Dodge Revolutionary Union Movement and other similar organizations to fight racism and demand rights for Black workers. Socialist ideas became attractive again to a layer of students and young working-class activists. There was a real possibility at this point to begin the process of rebuilding a militant, socialist current rooted in the working class.[19] But there was a problem. The bulk of the radicalized activists were attracted to Maoist and Stalinist politics that turned their back on the working class as "bought off," looking instead to third world national liberation movements for inspiration. Some left organizations did make a turn to the working class, but in the mid-1970s economic recession hit and, instead of provoking more working-class rebellion, heralded the beginning of a retreat.

The balance of class forces shifted decisively toward the employers beginning in the late 1970s. Unions, wages, and the social safety net were ravaged while corporations fed at the state trough, courtesy of the working-class taxpayer. As wages and unionization rates declined, there was a tremendous shift of wealth from the poorest to the richest—shown most dramatically by the 728 to 1 ratio of average CEO compensation to average wages in the United States.[20] This economic offensive was backed up by a right-wing ideological assault that pinned the blame for poverty on the poor themselves. The 1980s became known as the "looting decade."

The collapse of what passed for socialism seemed another dagger in the heart of the left, already battered and demoralized by the Reagan era. After the fall of the Berlin Wall, writes Ahmed Shawki,

> Western politicians and the mainstream press were celebrating the miracles of the market system and proclaiming the victory of capitalism over communism. The introduction to the 1989 edition of the annual *Economic Report of the President* proclaimed, "The tide of history, which some skeptics saw as ebbing inevitably away from Western ideals ... flows in our direction."[21]

But the excitement of capitalists and their spokespeople could not conceal the fact that their gain turned out to be a great loss for most people. Continues Shawki, "The much-heralded promises of Western politicians and business leaders at the time of the collapse of the Eastern Bloc in 1989 have given way to the stark realities of a global capitalist system."[22] The stark reality was that in the United States and the rest of the world, inequality grew to staggering proportions while a handful of people became very rich.

Indeed, the period since 1989 has been one that Sharon Smith describes as "the employers' offensive unhinged"—with record profits accompanying a growing race to the bottom for the working class.[23] Anyone who can argue today that the working class is "bought off" simply does not know what happened to the working class at the end of the last century and the beginning of this one. Income inequality, child poverty, and a widespread lack of access to health care are more pronounced in the United States than in all other advanced countries. The minimum wage in 2005 was below what it was fifty years ago. According to one report, "The wealthiest 20% of households in 1973 accounted for 44 percent of total U.S. income, according to the Census Bureau. Their share jumped to 50 percent in 2002, while everyone else's fell. For the bottom fifth, the share dropped to 3.5 percent from 4.2 percent."[24]

The very ferocity of the ruling-class attack was bound to provoke a response. As Shawki notes, the "class inequality and social polarization [that] have accelerated over the decade of the 1990s ... form the underpinnings to a new radicalization."[25] Yet that radicalization, emerging from a long period of defeat for the working class and the left, was at first slow in coming. As Shawki relates,

> While the collapse of Stalinism opened up the possibility of rebuilding a genuinely revolutionary socialist movement internationally, it also produced enormous demoralization and confusion within the existing left.... Thus, in many countries, the immediate beneficiaries of the end of Stalinism were the defenders of capitalism.[26]

A strike by Teamsters in 1997 was one of many false starts in the return of working-class combativity, gaining popular support but failing to spark further class struggle. Then came the "Battle in Seattle" in 1999, the mass antiwar protest of February 15, 2003, in cities across the country, involving hundreds of thousands of people, and then the mass immigrant rights upsurge in Spring 2006. In Los Angeles alone, a million people—mostly low-paid workers, many of them undocumented, formerly invisible—poured into the streets on two separate occasions in March and May to demand their rights. These were the stirrings of the most downtrodden sections of the working class that has for years not been able to see or feel its own power.

The argument of today's pundits is not that the United States is different, but that the rest of the world is now as exceptional, that is, as closed to a socialist alternative, as the United States. In this depressing view, the United States provides the dystopian model—low wages, poor benefits, and inadequate social services—that the rest of the world is bound to follow. This may be a model that capitalists salivate over, but for the majority it is a model to resist. And they are resisting, from Paris to Buenos Aires, from Los Angeles to La Paz. The single biggest obstacle to the development, or the redevelopment, of genuine socialist currents in the United States and elsewhere—Stalinism—is gone; and the claims of capitalism's great triumph look like a cruel joke. In these conditions, genuine socialist ideas can once again spread and take hold.

Chapter Fourteen

Imagine... The Future Socialist Society

"We know what you're against. What are you *for*?" is a question often asked of socialists. Socialism can be summed up simply. These words by Eugene Debs are clear and elegant:

> The earth for all the people! That is the demand.
>
> The machinery of production and distribution for all the people! That is the demand.
>
> The collective ownership and control of industry and its democratic management in the interests of all the people! That is the demand.
>
> The elimination of rent, interest and profit and the production of wealth to satisfy the wants of all the people! That is the demand.
>
> The end of ... class rule, of master and slave, of ignorance and vice, of poverty and shame, of cruelty and crime.... That is the demand.[1]

Socialism cannot come from "ready-made utopias," but must be created by workers themselves. That doesn't mean, however, that we have no idea what a future socialist society would be like or how it might develop.

The initial basis for socialism is the working-class solidarity that is forged in struggle prior to workers coming to power. In these struggles, racist, sexist, and xenophobic ideas begin to break down. The mass struggles that are necessary to bring down the old order are also necessary to begin the process of creating a different human being. But this is only the starting point. Socialism will be created by people emerging from a system that stunted and suppressed their human potential. Only over a long transition period will a new generation of people be raised who are free from these old constraints.

"What we have to deal with here," wrote Marx, "is a communist society, not as it has *developed* on its own foundations, but, on the contrary, just as it *emerges* from capitalist society; which is thus in every respect, economically, morally, and intellectually, still stamped with the birthmarks of the old society from whose womb it emerges."[2]

Hence we cannot immediately leap straight into a completely communist society. There must be a transition period in which the old is dissolved, broken apart, and reshaped, and new social relations and habits of intercourse gradually emerge. "Between capitalist and communist society there lies the period of the revolutionary transformation of the one into the other," wrote Marx. "Corresponding to this is also a political transition period in which the state can be nothing but *the revolutionary dictatorship of the proletariat.*"[3] So the first premise of socialism is that workers are in control and are therefore in a position of power from which they can start to reshape society.

The aim of socialism is to do away with all class distinctions and create a society whereby the state—an instrument of class domination—gradually fades away. As Engels wrote, "The proletariat seizes the public power, and by means of this transforms the socialized means of production, slipping from the hands of the bourgeoisie, into public property."[4]

Having gained power, the working class then uses that power, first to ensure that the old order cannot gain a foothold again. Though this new workers' state represents the interests of the majority, it must still use coercion, where necessary, to suppress those who would use violence to attempt to restore the old exploitive relations in society. Second, the new workers' state must begin implementing a series of reforms that, step by step, abolish profit and the market and replace it with conscious, democratic planning.

"The proletariat will use its political supremacy to wrest, by degree, all capital from the bourgeoisie," Marx and Engels wrote in the *Manifesto*,

> to centralize all instruments of production in the hands of the state, i.e., of the proletariat organized as the ruling class; and to increase the total productive forces as rapidly as possible.
>
> Of course, in the beginning, this cannot be effected except by means of despotic inroads on the rights of property, and on the conditions of bourgeois production; by means of measures, there-

> fore, which appear economically insufficient and untenable, but which, in the course of the movement, outstrip themselves, necessitate further inroads upon the old social order, and are unavoidable as a means of entirely revolutionizing the mode of production.[5]

Some of these measures might include: introducing a progressive income tax against the rich; establishing free education at all levels; abolishing advertising and all other wasteful and costly diversions, with the use of these funds going toward health, education, and artistic needs; instituting free abortion on demand and free childcare provisions; confiscating all empty houses and mansions of capitalist developers and the rich in order to house the poor and homeless; immediately reducing the workday and providing jobs for the unemployed; creating a community police force on a rotating, elected basis.

The market and money cannot be done away with at one stroke. But the workers' state can nationalize the banks and place them under workers' control, and redirect funds into much-needed state projects, like building a better public transportation system. Money can be transformed from a means of profit-making into a means of accounting for what is produced and how it is distributed. The associated producers, organized into a democratic system of councils, can reorganize production and distribution according to a rational plan that meets human need.

Although inequality cannot be abolished all at once, a number of measures could be implemented to uproot it. Special organizations could be created to wipe out prejudice in the education system, and various affirmative action programs could be stepped up on a qualitatively more intensive level to provide opportunities for education and equal participation in society for all, regardless of race, nationality, sex, or language. Education could be provided in all languages, and could be designed to allow individuals to switch jobs, moving from intellectual to manual work with ease. At first, workers may need to exercise joint control over technicians, engineers, and planners, some (but not all) of whom may still hanker for the privileges they received under capitalism. But the extensive reorganization of education and the production process would give everyone the opportunity to pursue a variety of jobs, gradually weakening the barrier between mental and manual labor, and providing an environment in which the full potential of every individual was given the means to develop.

Committees of workers and technicians would begin to reengineer production so that everything was produced to last, and with the best materials. Productivity has advanced to the point that the workday could be reduced to three or four hours. In a socialist society, improvements in labor productivity would be a means to shorten the workday to a minimum in order to free people up as much as possible to devote their energies to other pursuits, including participating in the running of society. Moreover, since workers would own and control the labor process as well as its results, work would no longer have the sense of emptiness it possesses today. Instead of workers dreaming of Fridays and working only in order to receive a paycheck, work would be a source of fulfillment. The mad intensity of work today, whose pace is a mental health issue for millions, will be humanized in a society where workers control the nature and pace of work collectively.

When the resistance of the old ruling classes is gone, so too is the need for the state. With the abolition of class distinctions comes what Engels called "the withering away of the state." Since the state is an instrument for the enforcement of class oppression, the dissolution of class divisions renders the state obsolete. The coercive apparatus of state repression disappears, leaving only purely administrative tasks such as the postal service, transportation, or maintaining the power grid.

What replaces the state is the free association of people—communism. Society is administered according to a plan, but there is no need for organized coercion, because everyone gives what they can and takes what they need. Society might freely choose or pick volunteers to handle small-scale threats of violence, for example from deranged individuals, or to defuse drunken brawls. But because society is not divided into classes, this coercion would be incidental rather than systematic, and could be handled without the need for "special bodies" of armed people.

Only in such a consciously and democratically planned and administered society can the potentialities slumbering in the millions of people now oppressed and stunted by capitalism have a chance to flourish. In this higher phase of communist society, wrote Marx,

> after the enslaving subordination of the individual to the division of labor, and therewith also the antithesis between mental and physical labor, has vanished; after labor has become not only a means of life but life's prime want; after the productive forces have also increased with the all-around development of the individual, and all the springs of co-operative wealth flow more abundantly—only then can the narrow horizon of bourgeois right be crossed in its entirety and society inscribe on its banners: From each according to his ability, to each according to his needs![6]

Conclusion

The Point Is to Change It

There are three conditions that make socialism imperative for humanity: the abundance that makes class inequality unnecessary, the class solidarity that makes it possible, and the threat of social and environmental ruin that awaits us if we fail to achieve it.

The resources are there in abundance. The 1994 UN Human Development Report estimated that just 12 percent of military spending in the developing countries (not including the far larger military budgets of the United States and other more developed countries) could provide health care for the 1 billion people who lack access to it; eliminate severe malnutrition in the 192 million children that suffer from it; and provide safe drinking water for all.[1] The assets of the two hundred richest people in the world (more than $1 trillion in 1999) were more than the combined income of 41 percent of the world's population. A yearly contribution of 1 percent of their wealth could provide universal access to primary education for all, according to the 1999 Human Development Report.[2]

We stand on either a threshold or a precipice. Either we move forward to socialism, or the world faces unimaginable barbarism that could come in many forms: nuclear holocaust, environmental disasters, the return of 1930s-style depression. Capitalism condemns itself as a system, in the prophetic words of Marx, because in the midst of the riches labor creates, the capitalist class cannot even assure the survival of humanity, let alone the survival of the poor.

> And here it becomes evident, that the bourgeoisie is unfit any longer to be the ruling class in society, and to impose its condi-

> tions of existence upon society.... It is unfit to rule because it is incompetent to assure an existence to its slave within his slavery, because it cannot help letting him sink into such a state, that it has to feed him, instead of being fed by him. Society can no longer live under this bourgeoisie, in other words, its existence is no longer compatible with society.[3]

The alternative is socialism. Shorn of the baggage it never asked to carry, it is an attractive idea. It is not a dream concocted in the head of a utopian thinker: It was born in the collective action of workers themselves. Eugene Debs first toyed with the idea of going into Democratic Party politics before he became a socialist. But his experience as a trade union organizer changed him. As leader of the newly formed American Railway Union, Debs led a strike of workers at the Pullman Sleeping Car Company in 1894. The strike spread throughout the nation, becoming a national boycott of Pullman cars involving 150,000 workers. The government stepped in on behalf of the employers and declared the strike illegal because it was obstructing delivery of the U.S. Mail (the government was deliberately attaching mail trains to Pullman cars so they would have this excuse). The government sent in federal troops, and the strike was broken—twenty-five strikers were killed, and Debs was imprisoned for six months. Debs learned that the government—its army, its courts—serves the employers. He learned that they will go to any lengths to try and stop workers from organizing and fighting for what is right. "In the gleam of every bayonet and the flash of every rifle the class struggle was revealed," he later explained. "This was my first practical lesson in socialism, though wholly unaware that it was called by that name."[4]

In every struggle, there are many people who go through the kinds of experiences that Debs went through. Whether they fall back into obscurity, returning to the dull routines of daily life, or become active socialists depends on the existence of groups of socialists in every workplace and school that can relate to their experiences and transform their unconscious strivings for socialism into a conscious commitment to its achievement.

The hydra of social revolution

Given half a chance, genuine cooperativeness among workers flourishes, even in dire situations. Larry Bradshaw and Lorrie Beth Slonsky, two medical workers trapped in New Orleans during Hurricane Katrina, expected the media to project heroic images of troops and police, but the official relief effort they experienced was atrociously inadequate:

> What you will not see, but what we witnessed, were the real heroes and sheroes of the hurricane relief effort: the working class of New Orleans.
>
> The maintenance workers who used a forklift to carry the sick and disabled. The engineers who rigged, nurtured and kept the generators running. The electricians who improvised thick extension cords stretching over blocks to share the little electricity we had in order to free cars stuck on rooftop parking lots. Nurses who took over for mechanical ventilators and spent many hours on end manually forcing air into the lungs of unconscious patients to keep them alive. Doormen who rescued folks stuck in elevators. Refinery workers who broke into boat yards, "stealing" boats to rescue their neighbors clinging to their roofs in flood waters. Mechanics who helped hotwire any car that could be found to ferry people out of the city. And the food service workers who scoured the commercial kitchens, improvising communal meals for hundreds of those stranded.[5]

The real looters were not the people helping themselves to food and goods to survive a disaster, but the government and their corporate friends who have set the whole system up as a massive looting operation in which the haves take from the have-nots.

Larry and Lorrie Beth helped organize a group of several hundred stranded survivors. Their first camp was broken up by police at gunpoint, and when they tried to cross a bridge into neighboring Gretna, they were turned back by a line of cops firing shotguns over their heads. But the group held together and in doing so taught us something about what ordinary people are capable of:

> Our little encampment began to blossom. Someone stole a water delivery truck and brought it up to us. Let's hear it for looting! A mile or so down the freeway, an Army truck lost a couple of pallets of C-rations on a tight turn. We ferried the food back to our camp in shopping carts.
>
> Now—secure with these two necessities, food and water—cooperation, community and creativity flowered. We organized a clean-up and hung garbage bags from the rebar poles. We made beds from wood pallets and cardboard. We designated a storm drain as the bathroom, and the kids built an elaborate enclosure for privacy out of plastic, broken umbrellas and other scraps. We even organized a food-recycling system where individuals could swap out parts of C-rations (applesauce for babies and candies for kids!).
>
> This was something we saw repeatedly in the aftermath of Katrina. When individuals had to fight to find food or water, it meant looking out for yourself. You had to do whatever it took to

> find water for your kids or food for your parents. But when these basic needs were met, people began to look out for each other, working together and constructing a community.[6]

Reading their account of the heroism of ordinary workers and poor people in New Orleans, I was reminded of the statement the Spanish anarchist revolutionary Buenaventura Durruti made to Canadian journalist Pierre Van Paasen in 1936, during the Spanish Civil War. Durruti fought with the Spanish workers against the danger of Franco's fascist counterrevolution. "You will be sitting on a pile of ruins if you are victorious," Van Paasen told the Spanish revolutionary. He replied:

> We have always lived in slums and holes in the wall. We will know how to accommodate ourselves for a time. For you must not forget that we can also build. It is we who built these palaces and cities, here in Spain and America and everywhere. We, the workers. We can build others to take their place. And better ones. We are not in the least afraid of ruins. We are going to inherit the earth. There is not the slightest doubt about that. The bourgeoisie might blast and ruin its own world before it leaves the stage of history. We carry a new world, here, in our hearts. That world is growing in this minute.[7]

Further Reading

The more ambitious reader can check footnotes to discover what books and articles they might be interested in checking out. But for convenience's sake, I've compiled a few short and medium-length lists of books and articles I think are good things to follow up with after you've read this book.

Many of the articles and books by Marx, Engels, Lenin, Luxemburg, Trotsky and others referenced in this book are available at www.marxists.org. I highly recommend visiting that site: it is chock full of articles and books from the Marxist tradition. Many books mentioned below are available on order from Haymarket books (www.haymarketbooks.org). If there's a book I refer to and you can't find it in either of the above two places, I recommend searching for it on two web sites: www.fetchbook.info or www.bookfinder.org.

The *Sociailst Worker* and *International Socialist Review* web sites (www.socialistworker.org and www.isreview.org) are also places to get both contemporary and historical Marxist analysis and commentary.

I. Ten to get you started

If I were to suggest ten books to follow up this one with that would help round out your understanding of Marxism and its application to different questions, from the role of the working class to imperialism, and from national to women's liberation, this is what they would be:

***The Communist Manifesto: A Road Map to History's Most Important Political Document*, edited and annotated by Phil Gasper** This edition not only offers a paragraph by paragraph notation that explains and illuminates Marx and Engel's seminal statement of their politics, but it includes an essay about the relevance of Marx today and key excerpts from Marx's and Engel's other works.

Peter Binns, Ahmed Shawki, and others, ***Russia: From Worker's State to State Capitalism*** For many people considering Marxism, the key question is: What happened in Russia? This short series of essays takes you through the Russian Revolution, both its rise and decline, and offers a Marxist analysis of why it failed.

Tony Cliff, Duncan Hallas, Chris Harman, ***Party and Class*** The question of organization is perhaps the most contentious one on the left. These series of essays explain how Marxists view the question—and clarifies Lenin's ideas about the party, which the critics have completely distorted.

Duncan Hallas, ***Trotsky's Marxism*** The best introduction to the ideas of one of the great Marxists of the twentieth century

Duncan Hallas, ***The Comintern*** In its early years, the Third International, or Comintern, was a school of revolutionary strategy and tactics. Hallas' brief history takes us through this period, as well as its tragic decline under Stalin's tutelage.

Colin Barker, ed., ***Revolutionary Rehearsals*** In the late twentieth century, a series of working-class upheavals and revolutions challenged and even overthrew hated regimes, from Chile in 1973 to Poland in 1980. Yet in each case they failed to seize control of society and build a new world on the ruins of capitalism. This book reviews several of these struggles and draws the lessons.

Sharon Smith, ***Subterranean Fire: A History of Working-Class Radicalism in the United States*** There is a rich and turbulent history of working class struggle in the United States, and often radicals and socialists were at the center of them. This book takes us through the history of the socialist left and the working class in the United States, revealing a hidden history that holds important lessons for activists today who are fighting to revitalize an ailing labor movement.

Ahmed Shawki, ***Black Liberation and Socialism*** A concise primer on the history and future of the struggle against racism in the United States, this book takes us from the struggle against slavery, through the Civil Rights and Black Power movements, to the retreats of recent decades. It reveals the connection between capitalism and slavery, and race and class, and makes the case for linking the struggle for Black liberation with the fight for a socialist world.

Sharon Smith, ***Women and Socialism: Essays on Women's Liberation*** This book takes up the question of women's oppression and women's liberation from many different angles. There is an essay on Engels and the origins of women's oppression, and it also takes up the question of women in the Russian Revolution and the struggle for women's rights in the United States.

Sidney Lens, ***The Forging of the American Empire*** Every socialist must be able to cut through the lies about how the United States in its history of overseas intervention has always been about spreading freedom and democracy. Lens provides us with a lively, detailed history that completely destroys this dangerous myth.

Bonus readings:

On Oppression:

There are a couple of other articles on the question of oppression that are worth reading, which are available on line: "The Roots of Gay Oppression" by Sherry Wolf (www.isreview.org/issues/37/gay_oppression.shtml), and Sharon Smith, "Mistaken Identity: Or Can Identity Politics Liberate the Oppressed?" (http://pubs.socialistreview-index.org.uk/isj62/smith.htm).

On Imperialism:

Lens' book stops at Vietnam. There are a series of articles on imperialism available at the *International Socialist Review* Web site that take the reader further. Joe Allen's three part series on Vietnam (www.isreview.org/issues/40/vietnamIII.shtml); "From Cold War to Kosovo," by Lance Selfa (www.isreview.org/issues/08/cold_war_to_kosovo.shtml); "Imperialism and the State" by Paul D'Amato (www.isreview.org/issues/17/state_and_imperialism.shtml); "A New Colonial Age of Empire?" by Lance Selfa (www.isreview.org/issues/23/age_of_empire.shtml); and "The Bush Doctrine Since September 11" by Lance Selfa (www.isreview.org/issues/40/bushdoctrine.shtml).

II. Delving into the classics

Here is a by no means exhaustive list of books by the classic Marxist writers, as well as some good secondary sources:

Marx and Engels

The Communist Manifesto: A Road Map to History's Most Important Political Document, edited and annotated by Phil Gasper

Socialism: Utopian and Scientific This is a great follow-up to the *Manifesto.* Written by Engels (culled from a much longer polemical work), it is one of the most complete statements of Marx and Engels' materialist conception of history, of class struggle, and of socialism.

The Eighteenth Brumaire of Louis Napoleon This is one of the finest examples of Marx's incisive contemporary analysis frm a materialist perspective. From this work comes the famous statement, "Men make their own history, but they do not make it as they please; they do not make it under self-selected circumstances, but under circumstances existing already, given and transmitted from the past."

The Civil War in France Marx delivered a series of addresses about the Paris Commune of 1871 where he argued that the Commune showed, for the first time, what the "dictatorship of the proletariat" would look like in practice.

Origin of the Family, Private Property and the State Though some of the research on which he based his theories is now outdated, this remains a convincing explanation of the rise not only of class society, but of the oppression of women that accompanied it.

About Marx and Marxism:

Hal Draper's series of volumes, ***Karl Marx's Theory of Revolution,*** in particular volumes 1 (*State and Bureaucracy*), 2 (*The Politics of Social Classes*), and 4 (*Critique of Other Socialisms*), are an excellent way to delve more deeply into the politics of Marx and Engels. The first part of Volume 1 has a particularly good explanation of how Marx became a Marxist, and Volume 2 has one of the best expositions of Marx's conception of the working class and of working class power. John Molyneux's *What is the Real Marxist Tradition* answers the vexing question, how, given all the conflicting ideas claiming the mantle of socialism and Marxism, do we identify the genuine article?

Lenin

The best way to get beyond the absurd myths about Lenin is to read Lenin.

State and Revolution Here Lenin rescues Marx's argument that workers cannot take over the existing capitalist state, but must erect a new, directly-democratic, workers' state on its ruins.

Left Wing Communism: An Infantile Disorder After the founding of the Communist International in 1919, Lenin started a debate with "ultra-left" socialists in Europe who argued that revolutionaries should turn their backs on elections and trade unions. Lenin argued that until a majority of workers' were won to the task of overthrowing capitalism, socialists must work inside parliaments and trade unions in order to influence and lead wider layers of workers. But the relevance of Lenin's arguments go far beyond the immediate context of the debate.

Imperialism: The Highest Stage of Capitalism Lenin explains, in the midst of world war, that capitalism has entered the phase of imperialism, when the world is being carved up between a handful of great powers. For readers who want to delve further into this topic, I recommend Nikolai Bukharin's (one of the Bolshevik's chief theoreticians) *Imperialism and World Economy.*

Lenin on national self-determination Lenin developed, in many articles, the best and most consistent Marxist position on the right of oppressed nations to self-determination. Among them are *The Right of Nations to Self Determination* and *The Discussion on Self-Determination Summed up*. They are excellent places to start in this question.

Lenin on the question of organization

This, of course, is the most controversial and maligned aspect of Lenin's politics.

Lenin's ***What Is to Be Done*** is very much worth reading, but it is not the final statement on his ideas of party organization. The ideas he developed on the question are scattered in many different articles and developed over a period of years. Here are the best places to start: Chris Harman, *Party and Class*; John Molyneaux, *Marxism and the Party*; Paul LeBlanc, *Lenin and the Revolutionary Party*; and finally, Tony Cliff, *Lenin: Building the Party* and *All Power to the Soviets.* These are great volumes that place Lenin's ideas and life in a broader historical context. Alexander Rabinowitch's *The Bolsheviks Come to Power* In glorious detail, Rabinowitch completely debunks the myth that the Bolsheviks were a band of conspirators that "imposed" its power over the working class.

In addition to the few I've just mentioned, I'd also recommend Leon Trotsky's *The Young Lenin* and Marcel Leibman's *Leninism under Lenin. Lenin* by George Lukacs is a good short assessment of Lenin's contribution to Marxism.

Trotsky

Trotsky was a prolific writer, but here are a few of his classic works:

The Permanent Revolution **and** ***Results and Prospects*** This book outlines his classic theory that workers' could come to power in a backward country before an advanced one.

My Life Reading like a great novel, this summary of his life also works as a great political introduction to many ideas and events in the history of the socialist movement in the early twentieth century.

History of the Russian Revolution Still the best history of any revolution written in any language. Don't be intimidated by its length—over a thousand pages.

The Struggle Against Fascism in Germany In the early 1930s, Trotsky penned a series of articles analyzing the rise of Hitler and outlining to the German Communists the united front policy necessary to defeat him. These are perhaps the finest writings by a Marxist on current events ever written.

The Revolution Betrayed Trotsky may have never made a complete break from his belief that, however distorted, Russia's nationalized property made it somehow still a "workers' state." Nevertheless, this remains a masterful analysis of the degeneration of the Russian revolution, a fierce indictment of the rise of the Stalinist bureaucracy and a ringing defense of genuine Marxism.

Their Morals and Ours Trotsky takes up the question "do the ends justify the means" and in the process writes a tightly-argued polemic on the question of Marxism and morality.

Duncan Hallas' *Trotsky's Marxism* is the best short introduction to Trotsky's politics.

The Prophet Armed, The Prophet Unarmed, and *The Prophet Outcast,* Isaac Deustcher's trilogy on the life of Trotsky, is unsurpassed in the field of political biography. However, as a political corrective (in the last volume Deustcher comes perilously close to apologizing for Stalin's rule), *The Darker the Night, the Brighter the Star* Tony Cliff's four-volume biography of Trotsky, in particular this final volume, is essential reading.

Rosa Luxemburg

Reform or Revolution The most definitive statement on the need for revolution and the limits of reform as a means for transforming society.

The Mass Strike, the Political Party and the Trade Union Rosa's masterful analysis of the most important weapon in the arsenal of the working class: the mass strike.

Tony Cliff's *Rosa Luxemburg* is a good short introduction. Paul Frölich, a contemporary of Luxemburg's, also wrote a biography of her by the same title.

Pierre Broué's *The German Revolution* describes in detail the years of revolutionary upheaval in Germany between 1918 and 1923.

State Capitalism

Tony Cliff's *State Capitalism in Russia* is a seminal work that offers a Marxist analysis of how the Russian Revolution's isolation and defeat produced a regime socialist in name only, but which in reality had been transformed into a new type of bureaucratic capitalism.

To some on the left, Cuba remains the last beacon of socialism. Yet it is a one-party state in which a small privileged elite at the top makes all the decision, and in which blatantly capitalist relations flourish in Cuba's most important industries, for example tourism. While Cuba's sovereignty needs to be defended against U.S. intervention, we should not on those grounds offer political support for Castro's regime. For a better understanding of this dynamic, read Cuba: Crisis of State Capitalism" by Hector Reyes, available at www.isreview.org/issues/11/cuba_crisis.shtml and "Castro's Cuba in Perspective" by Sam Farber available at www.isreview.org/issues/36/farber_ext.shtml.

III. The essential classics

Here is the short list of the five classic texts (all of them fairly short) that a reader might start with (assuming you've already read the *Communist Manifesto)*:

Socialism: Utopian and Scientific by Engels
Reform or Revolution by Rosa Luxemburg
State and Revolution By Lenin
Left-Wing Communism, an Infantile Disorder by Lenin
Imperialism: Highest Stage of Capitalism by Lenin

Notes

Introduction: The Relevance of Marxism

1. Daniel Singer, *Prelude to Revolution: France in May 1968*, 2nd ed. (Boston: South End Press, 2002), xxvi.
2. Sombart quoted in Daniel Bell, *The End of Ideology* (New York: Collier Books, 1962), 277.
3. Bell, *The End of Ideology*, 16.
4. Marcuse quoted in Paul Mattick, *Critique of Marcuse: One-Dimensional Man in Class Society* (London: Merlin Press, 1972).
5. Some examples of this line of argument, in various permutations, can be found, for example, in: "Marcuse Defines His New Left Line," interview with Marcuse in *The New Left of the 1960s: The Collected Papers of Herbert Marcuse,* ed. Douglass Kellner (New York: Routledge, 2005); Ernest Laclau and Chantalle Mouffe, *Hegemony and Socialist Strategy* (London: Verso, 1985); and André Gorz, *Farewell to the Working Class* (London: Pluto Press, 1982). Many other examples could be cited. The most rabidly anti-Marxist tract against the central role of the working class in achieving a new society is Murray Bookchin's nasty little essay, "Listen, Marxist!," in *Post-Scarcity Anarchism* (Buffalo, N.Y.: Black Rose Books, 1986), 193–242.
6. Francis Fukuyama, "By Way of an Introduction," in *The End of History and the Last Man* (London: Penguin, 1992).
7. *UN Human Development Report 1999: Globalization with a Human Face* (New York: Oxford University Press, 1999), 3.
8. Jane Chapman, "Forbes Report: Billionaires' Wealth Grew by 36 Percent in Last Year," March 9, 2004, World Socialist Web site.
9. *United Nations Human Development Report 2003: Millennium Development Goals* (New York: Oxford University Press, 2003), 5.
10. Sara Anderson et al., *Executive Excess 2005: Defense Contractors Get More Bucks for the Bang,* 12th Annual CEO Compensation Survey for the Institute for Policy Studies, August 30, 2005, 13. Available at http://www.faireconomy.org/press/2005/EE2005.pdf (accessed August 1, 2006).
11. Ibid., 14–15.

12. Americans for Democratic Action, "Income and Inequality: Millions Left Behind," report, February 2004, 5. Available at http://www.adaction.org/Income2004.htm (accessed August 1, 2006).
13. Ibid.
14. *Human Development Report 2003*, 155.
15. Frederick Engels, "Karl Marx's Funeral," in Karl Marx and Frederick Engels, *Collected Works* (hereafter *MECW*), vol. 24 (New York: International Publishers, 1989), 468. Note: Many of the Marxist works cited in this book can be found at the Marx-Engels Internet archive at http://www.marxists.org.
16. Frances Moore Lappé et al., *World Hunger: Twelve Myths* (New York: Grove Press, 1998), 8. *The State of Food Insecurity in the World 2005* (Rome: United Nations Food and Agricultural Organization, 2005), 20.
17. Karl Marx and Frederick Engels, *Manifesto of the Communist Party*, in *The Communist Manifesto: A Road Map to History's Most Important Political Document*, ed. Phil Gasper (Chicago: Haymarket Books, 2005), 72. (Hereafter, *Communist Manifesto*.)
18. Karl Marx, *Civil War in France: The Paris Commune* (New York: International Publishers, 1989); Frederick Engels, *Socialism: Utopian and Scientific* (New York: International Publishers, 1989); Rosa Luxemburg, *Reform or Revolution*, in *Rosa Luxemburg Speaks* (New York: Pathfinder Press, 1970); Leon Trotsky, *The Lessons of October* (London: Bookmarks, 1987); V. I. Lenin, *State and Revolution* (New York: International Publishers, 1994).
19. Lenin, *State and Revolution*.

Chapter One: From Millenarianism to Marx

1. Quoted in Karl Kautsky, *Foundations of Christianity* (New York: Monthly Review Press, 1972), 332.
2. Jean Froissairt, quoted in Norman Cohn, *The Pursuit of the Millennium* (London: Oxford University Press, 1970), 199.
3. Quoted in ibid., 199.
4. Quoted in R. B. Rose, *Gracchus Babeuf: The First Revolutionary Communist* (Stanford, CA: Stanford University Press, 1978), 195.
5. Quoted in Lillian Symes and Travers Clement, *Rebel America: The Story of Social Revolt in the United States* (New York: Harper Brothers, 1934), 40.
6. Quoted in Karl Marx, *Capital: A Critique of Political Economy*, vol. 1, trans. Ben Fowkes (New York: Vintage, 1977), 801. All references hereafter will be to this version of *Capital*, unless otherwise noted.
7. Engels, *Socialism: Utopian and Scientific*, 36.
8. Luxemburg, *Reform or Revolution*.
9. Karl Marx and Frederick Engels, *The German Ideology*, in *MECW*, vol. 5 (New York: International Publishers, 1976), 49.
10. Ibid., 36.
11. Ibid., 38.
12. My line of argument here is developed in detail in Michael Löwy, *The Theory of Revolution in the Young Marx* (Chicago: Haymarket Books, 2005), chapter 1.
13. Quoted in Georgi Plekhanov, "Initial Phases of the Class Struggle Theory," in *Selected Works*, vol. 2 (Moscow: Progress Publishers, 1976), 433–34.
14. Karl Marx, "Theses on Feuerbach," in *MECW*, vol. 5, 7.

Chapter Two: Marx's Materialist Method

1. Ibid.
2. Bob Dylan, "Subterranean Homesick Blues," from the album *Bringing It All Back Home*, Columbia Records, 1965.
3. Carl Sagan, *Cosmos* (New York: Ballantine Books, 1985), 32.
4. Marx and Engels, *The German Ideology*, 59.
5. Ibid.
6. Mike Marqusee, "Attacking the Outside Agitators," *Red Pepper* (September 2005).
7. Marx, "Postface to the Second Edition," in *Capital*, vol. 1, 97.
8. V. I. Lenin, "Three Sources and Three Component Parts of Marxism," in *Collected Works* (hereafter *CW*), vol. 19 (Moscow: Progress Publishers, 1977), 23.
9. Marx, "Postface to the Second Edition," 98.
10. Marx, "Theses on Feuerbach," 6.
11. Plekhanov, "Socialism and the Political Struggle," in *Selected Works*, vol. 1, 90.
12. Leon Trotsky, "Revolution and War in China," in *Leon Trotsky on China* (New York: Monad Press, 1976), 579.
13. Marx and Engels, *The German Ideology*, 37.
14. Peter Dreier, "Reagan's Legacy: Homelessness in America," *Shelterforce*, Issue #135 (May/June 2004).
15. Ibid.
16. Marx and Engels, *The German Ideology*, 24.
17. Karl Marx, "Preface," in *Contribution to a Critique of Political Economy* (Moscow: Progress Publishers, 1977), 21.
18. Frederick Engels, *Anti-Duhring*, in *MECW*, vol. 25 (New York: Progress Publishers, 1987), 87.
19. Ibid.
20. Marx and Engels, *The German Ideology*, 30.
21. Ibid., 45.
22. For an excellent account of the history of social Darwinism, see Allan Chase, *The Legacy of Malthus: The Social Costs of the New Scientific Racism* (Urbana, IL: University of Illinois Press, 1980).
23. Richard J. Herrnstein and Charles Murray, *The Bell Curve* (New York: The Free Press, 1994).
24. Stephen Jay Gould, *The Mismeasure of Man* (New York: W. W. Norton, 1996), 28.
25. Quoted in R. C. Lewontin, *Biology as Ideology* (New York: Harper Perennial, 1992), 93.
26. Ibid., 89.
27. Stephen Rose, "Escaping Evolutionary Psychology," in *Alas Poor Darwin: Arguments Against Evolutionary Psychology*, ed. Hilary Rose and Steven Rose (New York: Harmony Books, 2000), 306.
28. Theodosius Dobzhansky, *Mankind Evolving: The Evolution of the Human Species* (New Haven, CT: Yale University Press, 1971), 8.
29. Quoted in Eleanor Burke Leacock, *Myths of Male Dominance* (New York: Monthly Review Press, 1981), 35.
30. Ibid, 57–58.
31. Ibid, 50.
32. Frederick Engels, "Ludwig Feuerbach and the End of Classical German Philosophy," in *MECW*, vol. 26 (New York: International Publishers, 1990), 383.
33. Quoted in George Novak, *The Origins of Materialism* (New York: Pathfinder Press,

1971), 97–100.

34. Karl Marx to his father, November 10, 1837, in *MECW*, vol. 1 (New York: International Publishers, 1975), 18.
35. G. W. F. Hegel, "Preface," in *The Phenomenology of Spirit* (New York: Oxford University Press, 1977), 2.
36. Marx, *Capital*, vol. 1, 103.
37. Engels, "Ludwig Feuerbach," 359.
38. Leon Trotsky, *In Defense of Marxism* (New York: Pioneer Publishers, 1942), 53–54.

Chapter Three: The Marxist View of History

1. Marx, *Capital*, vol. 1, 286.
2. Ibid.
3. Marx and Engels, *The German Ideology*, 31.
4. Karl Marx, *Contribution to the Critique of Political Economy*, in *MECW*, vol. 29 (New York: International Publishers, 1987), 263.
5. Ibid.
6. Ibid.
7. Marx and Engels, *Communist Manifesto*, 39–40.
8. Karl Marx, *The Eighteenth Brumaire of Louis Napoleon*, in *MECW*, vol. 11 (New York: International Publishers, 1979), 103.
9. Karl Marx, "Letter to *Otechestvenniye Zapiski*," in *MECW* 24, 200.
10. See Engels, "Ludwig Feuerbach," 387–88.
11. Frederick Engels to J. Bloch, September 21, 1890, in *Historical Materialism* (Moscow: Progress Publishers, 1972), 294–96.
12. Frederick Engels, "Introduction to the English Edition (1892) of *Socialism: Utopian and Scientific*," in *MECW*, vol. 27 (New York: International Publishers, 1990), 289.
13. Marx and Engels, *Communist Manifesto*, 39.
14. Frederick Engels, *The Origins of the Family, Private Property and the State*, in *MECW*, vol. 26, 202.
15. Quoted in Paul Lafargue, "Idealism and Materialism in the Conception of History," lecture to the Group of Collectivist Students of Paris, 1895, *Socialist Standard*, May 1915. Available at http://www.marxists.org/archive/lafargue/1895/xx/idealism.htm#f1 (accessed August 1, 2006).
16. Engels, *Origins of the Family*, 203.
17. Quoted in ibid., 158.
18. Irven De Vore at al., *Man the Hunter* (New York: Aldine de Gruyter, 1968), 5–6.
19. Richard B. Lee, "What Hunters Do for a Living, or, How to Make Out on Scarce Resources," in ibid., 37l.
20. See, for example, Ernest Brandewie, "The Place of the Big Man in Traditional Hagen Society in the Central Highlands of New Guinea," in *Anthropological Approaches to Political Behavior*, ed. Frank McGlynn and Arthur Tuden (Pittsburgh: University of Pittsburgh Press, 1991), 62.
21. Marvin Harris, *Cannibals and Kings: The Origins of Cultures* (New York: Vintage, 1977), 113.
22. Engels, *Anti-Duhring, 167.*
23. Ibid., 166–68.
24. Engels, *Socialism: Utopian and Scientific*, 70.

25. Engels, *Origins of the Family,* 204.
26. Ibid., 221.
27. Ibid., 269.
28. Thomas Hobbes, *Leviathan* (New York: Touchstone Books, 1997), 100.
29. Engels, *Origins of the Family,* 270–71.
30. Marx, *Capital,* vol. 1, 874.
31. Ibid., 344.
32. Ibid., 325.
33. Ibid., 874.
34. Ibid., 914.
35. Karl Marx, *Value, Price and Profit,* in *MECW,* vol. 20 (New York: International Publishers, 1985), 129; *Capital,* vol. 1, 876.
36. Ibid., 898.
37. Ibid., 899.
38. Ibid., 925.
39. Marx and Engels, *Communist Manifesto,* 41.
40. Ibid., 875.
41. Ibid., 915.
42. Ibid., 43.
43. Marx, *Capital,* vol. 1, 926.
44. Marx and Engels, *Communist Manifesto,* 44.
45. Frederick Engels, "The Housing Question," in *MECW,* vol. 23 (New York: International Publishers, 1988), 324–25.
46. Engels, *Anti-Duhring,* 169.

Chapter Four: Marxist Economics—How Capitalism Works, and How It Doesn't

1. Karl Marx, *Capital: A Critique of Political Economy,* vol. 1, trans. Samuel Moore and Edward Aveling (London: Lawrence and Wishart, 1974), 43. I cite this edition, because the Vintage edition uses the less poetic phrase, "immense collection of commodities."
2. Karl Marx, *A Contribution to the Critique of Political Economy,* in *MECW* , vol. 29, 270.
3. David Ricardo, *Principles of Political Economy* (New York: E. P. Dutton & Co., 1926), 5.
4. Marx, *Value, Price and Profit,* 118.
5. Marx, *Capital,* vol. 1, 165.
6. Ibid., 165.
7. William Shakespeare, *Timon of Athens,* act 4, scene 3, lines 26–29, http://www.williamshakespeare.info/act4-script-text-timon-of-athens.htm (accessed August 1, 2006).
8. Marx, *Critique of Political Economy,* 276.
9. Marx, *Capital,* vol. 1, 182.
10. Ibid., 159.
11. Marx, *Capital,* vol. 1, 187.
12. Ibid., 291–92.
13. Adam Smith, *The Wealth of Nations* (New York: Modern Library, 1937), 13.
14. Paul A. Samuelson and William D. Nordhaus, *Economics,* (Boston: Irwin/McGraw Hill, 1998).
15. A. Smith, *Wealth of Nations,* xxxiv.
16. Marx, *Capital,* vol. 1, 254.

17. Marx, *Capital*, vol. 1, Lawrence and Wishart edition, 152.
18. Karl Marx, *Theories of Surplus Value, Part II* (Moscow: Progress Publishers, 1968), 495.
19. Shakespeare, *King Lear*, act 1, scene 1, line 92, http://www.enotes.com/shakespeare-quotes/nothing-can-come-nothing (accessed August 1, 2006).
20. Marx, *Capital*, vol. 1, 280.
21. Marx, *Value, Price and Profit*, 118.
22. Marx, *Capital*, vol. 1, 301.
23. John Stuart Mill, *Principles of Political Economy*, vol. 1 (New York: D. Appleton and Company, 1883), 495.
24. Ibid., 509.
25. Marx and Engels, *Communist Manifesto*, 44.
26. Marx, *Capital*, vol. 1, 254.
27. *Ibid.*, 742.
28. See Harry Braverman, *Labor and Monopoly Capital: The Degredation of Work in the Twentieth Century* (New York: Monthly Review Press, 1974), chapters 4–8.
29. Dan Labotz, *Rank and File Rebellion* (New York: Verso Press, 1990), 213.
30. Michel Beaud, *A History of Capitalism, 1500–2000*, trans. Tom Dickman and Anny Lefebvre (New York: Monthly Review Press, 2001), 131.
31. Jan Fagerberg, "Specialization and Growth: World Manufacturing Productivity 1973–1990," paper prepared for "Technology, Employment and European Cohesion" project, April 1999, available at http://meritbbs.unimaas.nl/tser/tser.html (accessed August 1, 2006).
32. Bureau of Labor Statistics, U.S. Department of Labor, "Steel Manufacturing," *Career Guide to Industries, 2006-07 Edition*, available at http://www.bls.gov/oco/cg/cgs014.htm (accessed August 02, 2006).
33. Karl Marx, *Capital: A Critique of Political Economy*, vol. 1, in *MECW*, vol. 35, trans. Samuel Moore and Edward Aveling (New York: Progress Publishers, 1996), 750. The phrase reads better in this Moscow translation than in the Vintage version.
34. Michael Zweig, *The Working Class Majority* (Ithaca, NY: Cornell University Press, 2000), 18.
35. Anthony P. D'Costa, *The Global Restructuring of the Steel Industry: Innovations, Institutions, and Industrial Change* (New York: Routledge, 1999), 31.
36. A contraction of a statement by Marx and Engels in the *Communist Manifesto*: "The bourgeoisie, wherever it has got the upper hand, has put an end to all feudal, patriarchal, idyllic relations. It has pitilessly torn asunder the motley feudal ties that bound man to his "natural superiors," and has left remaining no other nexus between man and man than naked self-interest, than callous 'cash payment'" (Marx and Engels, *Communist Manifesto*, 43).
37. Marx, *Capital*, vol. 1, 568–69.
38. Lewis Mumford, *The Story of Utopias* (New York: Boni and Liveright, 1922), 115–16.
39. Marx and Engels, *Communist Manifesto*, 47–48.
40. Ibid., 48.
41. Frances Moore Lappé, "The Myth—Scarcity: The Reality—There IS Enough Food," *Institute for Food and Development Policy Backgrounder* 5, no. 1 (Spring 1998).
42. Karl Marx, *Capital: A Critique of Political Economy*, vol. 3, trans. David Fernbach (London: Penguin, 1991), 367.
43. Karl Marx, *Theories of Surplus Value, Part II* (Moscow: Progress Publishers, 1968), 527.
44. Ibid., 522.
45. Lewis Corey, *The Decline of American Capitalism* (New York: Covici-Friede, 1934), 20.
46. Quoted in Joel Geier and Ahmed Shawki, "Contradictions of the 'Miracle Economy,'"

International Socialist Review 2 (Fall 1997), available at http://www.isreview.org/issues/02/miracle_economy.shtml (accessed August 2, 2006).

47. Martin Wolf, "Flows and Blows," *Financial Times,* March 3, 1998.
48. Anthony Arnove, "Indonesia: Crisis and Revolt," *International Socialist Review* 5 (Fall 1998).
49. Joel Geier, "U.S. Economy: A New Boom?" *International Socialist Review* 33 (January–February 2004).
50. Paul Krugman, "Will Asia Bounce Back?" speech delivered for Credit Suisse First Boston, Hong Kong, March 1998, available at http://web.mit.edu/krugman/www/suisse.html (accessed August 2, 2006).
51. See, for example, the New School for Social Research's biography of Say at http://cepa.newschool.edu/het/profiles/say.htm, and of James Mill at http://cepa.newschool.edu/het/profiles/jamesmill.htm.
52. Karl Marx, *Capital,* vol. 1, in *MECW,* vol. 36 (New York: International Publishers,1996), 123.
53. Marx, *Capital,* vol. 3, 616.
54. Luxemburg, *Reform or Revolution*, 41–42.
55. Ibid., 42.
56. Marx introduces these terms in *Capital: A Critique of Political Economy,* vol. 2, trans. David Fernbach (New York: Penguin Classics, 1993), 471.
57. Marx, *Capital,* vol. 3, 362.
58. Bureau of Labor Statistics, "Steel Manufacturing," http://www.bls.gov/oco/cg/cgs014.htm (accessed August 2, 2006).
59. For an explanation of the "permanent arms economy" theory, see Michael Kidron, *Capitalism and Theory* (London: Pluto Press, 1974), 19–23. See also Michael Kidron, "A Permanent Arms Economy," *International Socialism* 1:28 (Spring 1967), available at http://www.marxists.org/archive/kidron/works/1967/xx/permarms.htm (accessed August 2, 2006).
60. Leon Trotsky, *The First Five Years of the Communist International* (New York: Pioneer Publishers, 1945), 62.

Chapter Five: No Power Greater—the Working Class

1. Engels, *Anti-Duhring*, 145.
2. Mary Parsons, "Deir el-Medina," Tour Egypt Web site, available at http://www.touregypt.net/featurestories/medina.htm (accessed August 2, 2006).
3. W. W. Tarn, *Hellenistic Civilization* (New York: Meridian, 1975), 199.
4. Little was actually written about Spartacus, whose story Roman historians weren't keen on playing up. See the chapter on Crassus in Plutarch, *The Fall of the Roman Republic: Six Lives*, trans. Rex Warner (Hammondsworth, UK: Penguin, 1972), 122–27.
5. A. L. Morton, *A People's History of England* (London: Lawrence and Wishart, 1996), 102.
6. Frederick Engels, "Principles of Communism," in Marx and Engels, *Communist Manifesto,* 128.
7. Marx, *Capital,* vol. 1, 799.
8. Karl Marx, *Economic and Philosophical Manuscripts,* in *MECW*, vol. 3 (New York: International Publishers, 1975), 274.
9. Engels, "Principles of Communism," 135.
10. Eugene Debs, "Class Unionism," in *Debs: His Life, Writings and Speeches* (Girard, KS: Appeal to Reason, 1908), 419.

11. Ralph Chapin, "Solidarity Forever." Lyrics can be found in *The IWW Songbook*, available at http://www.sacredchao.net/iww/index.shtml (accessed August 2, 2006).
12. V. I. Lenin, "On Strikes," in *CW*, vol. 4 (Moscow: Progress Publishers, 1977), 315.
13. Ibid.
14. Marx and Engels, *Communist Manifesto*, 56.
15. Raya Dunayevskaya, *Marxism and Freedom* (London: Pluto Press, 1971), 81.
16. Marx and Engels, *Communist Manifesto*, 68.
17. Karl Marx, *The Civil War in France*, in *MECW*, vol. 22 (New York: International Publishers, 1986), 328.
18. Ibid., 329.
19. Ibid., 334.
20. Ibid., 333.
21. Quoted in Edith Thomas, *The Women Incendiaries* (New York: George Braziller, 1966), x.
22. Marx, *Civil War in France*, 331.
23. Frederick Engels, "Introduction to Karl Marx's *Civil War in France*," in *MECW*, vol. 27, 191.
24. Ibid., 189
25. Ibid., 190.
26. Eugene Debs, "Unionism and Socialism," in *Debs: His Life, Writings and Speeches*, 127.
27. Marx, *Value, Price and Profit*, 149.
28. Rosa Luxemburg, *The Mass Strike, The Political Party, and the Trade Unions*, in *Rosa Luxemburg Speaks*, 214–15.
29. Debs, "Unionism and Socialism," 129.
30. Leon Trotsky, *1905*, trans. Anya Bostock (New York: Random House, 1971), 224.
31. John Reed, "Soviets in Action," *What Next?*, Issue 8 (October 1918), available at http://www.marxists.org/history/etol/revhist/otherdox/whatnext/reedsovs.html (accessed August 2, 2006).
32. Sharon Smith, *Subterranean Fire: A History of Working Class Radicalism in the United States* (Chicago: Haymarket Books, 2006), 141.
33. Quoted in Harvey O'Connor, *Revolution in Seattle* (New York: Monthly Review Press, 1964), 133.
34. "General Rules and Administrative Regulations of the International Workingmen's Association," in *MECW*, vol. 23, 3.
35. Eugène Pottier, "The Internationale" (English version), June 1871, lyrics available at http://www.marxists.org/history/ussr/sounds/lyrics/international.htm (accessed August 2, 2006).
36. Eugene Debs, "Craft Unionism," in *Debs: His Life, Writings and Speeches*, 392–93.
37. Frederick Engels, "Program of the Blanquist Commune Refugees," in *MECW*, vol. 24, 13.
38. Mikhail Bakunin, *Selected Writings*, ed. Arthur Lehning (New York: Grove Press, 1973), 180, 172.
39. Engels, "Program of the Blanquist Commune Refugees," 17.
40. Leon Trotsky, "On Terrorism," in *Marxism and Terrorism* (New York: Pathfinder Press, 1997), 10.
41. Michel De Montaigne, "On the Cannibals," in *The Complete Essays* (London: Penguin, 1991), 240–41.
42. George Orwell, *1984* (New York: Signet Classics, 1984), 60.
43. Ibid., 61–62.
44. Ibid., 61.

45. Voltaire, *Candide* (New York: Modern Library, 1918), 2.
46. Leon Trotsky, *History of the Russian Revolution* (Ann Arbor: University of Michigan Press, 1974), xviii.
47. Antonio Gramsci, *Selections from the Prison Notebooks* (New York: International Publishers, 1980), 333.
48. Marx and Engels, *The German Ideology*, 75.
49. Hal Draper, *Karl Marx's Theory of Revolution*, vol. 2 (New York: Monthly Review Press, 1978), 42.
50. Lenin, "On Strikes," 317.
51. V. I. Lenin, "Lecture on the 1905 Revolution," in *CW*, vol. 23 (Moscow: Progress Publishers, 1981), 243.
52. Karl Marx to W. Bracke, May 5, 1875, in *MECW*, vol. 45 (New York: International Publishers, 1991), 70.
53. Trotsky, *History of the Russian Revolution*, xviii.
54. Quoted in Maryam Poya, "Iran 1979: Long Live Revolution!... Long Live Islam?" ed. Colin Barker, *Revolutionary Rehearsals* (Chicago: Haymarket Books, 2002), 147–48.
55. Farrell Dobbs, *Teamster Rebellion* (New York: Pathfinder Press, 1981), 50.

Chapter Six: Democracy, Reform, and Revolution

1. Quoted in Henry S. Kariel, *Frontiers of Democratic Theory* (New York: Random House, 1970), 257.
2. Paul Foot, *The Politics of Harold Wilson* (London: Penguin Books, 1968), 338.
3. Chuck Collins, Chris Hartman, and Holly Sklar, "Divided Decade: Economic Disparity at the Century's Turn," United for a Fair Economy report, December 15, 1999, available at http://www.faireconomy.org/press/archive/1999/Divided_Decade/divided_decade.html (accessed August 6, 2006).
4. David Cay Johnston, "Corporate Wealth Share Rises for Top-income Americans," *New York Times*, January 29, 2006.
5. Marx and Engels, *Communist Manifesto*, 43.
6. Michael Parenti, *Democracy for the Few* (New York: St. Martins, 1988), 11.
7. Quoted in Leon Trotsky, *Terrorism and Communism* (Ann Arbor: Ann Arbor Paperbacks, 1972), 41.
8. Parenti, *Democracy for the Few*, 302.
9. Karl Marx, *The Eighteenth Brumaire of Louis Napoleon*, in *MECW*, vol. 11, 115.
10. Quoted in Stephen M. Kohn, *American Political Prisoners: Prosecutions under the Espionage and Sedition Acts* (Westport, CT: Praeger, 1994), 8.
11. Quoted in ibid., 9.
12. See James P. Cannon, *Socialism on Trial* (New York: Pathfinder Press, 1986).
13. Jim Robbins, "Pardons Granted 88 Years After Crimes of Sedition," *New York Times*, May 3, 2006.
14. Quoted in Kohn, *American Political Prisoners*, 114.
15. Quoted in ibid., 77.
16. Anatole France, *The Red Lily*, available as an e-book at http://www.gutenberg.org/files/3922/3922.txt (accessed August 2, 2006).
17. Eugene Debs, "The Role of the Courts," in *Eugene V. Debs Speaks* (New York: Pathfinder Press, 1980), 52.
18. Quoted in Philip S. Foner, *The Great Labor Uprising of 1877* (New York: Pathfinder Press, 1977), 167.

19. "FAMM Facts: Crack vs. Cocaine Sentencing," report, Families Against Mandatory Minimums Web site, 2002, available at http://www.famm.org/si_crack_powder_sentencing_fact_sheet.htm (accessed August 2, 2006).
20. Ted Nace, *Gangs of America: The Rise of Corporate Power and the Disabling of Democracy* (San Francisco: Berrett-Koehler, 2003), 8. Available for free at http://www.gangsofamerica.com/read.html (accessed August 7, 2006).
21. Kevin Phillips, *The Politics of Rich and Poor* (New York: Random House, 1990), 32.
22. Frederick Engels to Friedrich Adolph Sorge, December 2, 1893, in *Marx and Engels on the United States* (Moscow: Progress Publishers, 1979), 333.
23. Frederick Engels, "Introduction to Karl Marx's *The Civil War in France,*" in *MECW*, vol. 27, 189.
24. Eugene Debs, "Outlook for Socialism in the United States," in *Debs: His Life, Writings and Speeches*, 90–91.
25. Richard A. Harris and Sidney M. Milkis, *Remaking American Politics* (Boulder, CO: Westview Press, 1989), 185n.
26. Quoted in C. Vann Woodward, *Tom Watson: Agrarian Radical* (New York: Oxford University Press, 1963), 328.
27. Ibid., 311.
28. Joe Allen, "Vietnam: The War the U.S. Lost: Part II," *International Socialist Review* 33 (January–February 2004).
29. Frederick Engels to Friedrich Adolph Sorge, November 29, 1886, in *Collected Works*, vol. 47 (New York: Progress Publishers, 1995), 532.
30. Karl Marx and Frederick Engels, "Address of the Central Authority to the League," in *MECW*, vol. 10 (New York: International Publishers, 1978), 284.
31. Quoted in Paul D'Amato, "Kucinich: Kerry's Bagman," *International Socialist Review* 37 (September–October 2004).
32. Hal Draper, "Who Is Going to Be the Lesser Evil in 1968?" in *The New Left of the Sixties*, ed. Michael Friedman (Berkeley: Independent Socialist Press, 1972), 57. Available at http://www.isreview.org/issues/32/draper.shtml (accessed August 7, 2006).
33. Herbert Haines, *Against Capital Punishment: the Anti-Death Penalty Movement in America, 1972–1994* (New York: Oxford University Press, 1999), 133.
34. "The Sleeping Giant," *New York Times* editorial, April 29, 2006.
35. Martin Luther King Jr., "Letter from a Birmingham Jail," in *Let Freedom Ring: A Documentary History of the Modern Civil Rights Movement* (Westport, CT: Praeger, 1992), 111.
36. Leon Trotsky, "Mr. Baldwin and … Gradualness," in *Trotsky's Writings on Britain*, vol. 2 (London: New Park Publications, 1974), 20.
37. Engels, *Anti-Duhring*, 171.
38. Eduard Bernstein, *Evolutionary Socialism* (New York: Schocken, 1961), 202.
39. Quoted in John Riddell, ed., *Lenin's Struggle for a Revolutionary International: Documents, 1907–1916* (New York: Monad Press, 1984), 10.
40. Albert Rhys Williams, *Through the Russian Revolution* (New York: Boni and Liveright, 1921), 174.
41. Quoted in James Hinton, *Labour and Socialism: A History of the British Labour Movement, 1867–1974* (Amherst, MA: University of Massachusetts Press, 1983), 149.
42. Luxemburg, *Reform or Revolution*, 56.
43. See Tom Lewis, "Chile: The State and Revolution," *International Socialist Review* 6 (Spring 1999).
44. Quoted in Paul Ginsborg, *A History of Comtemporary Italy: Society and Politics 1943–1988* (London: Penguin Books, 1990), 355.

45. Leon Trotsky, "Whither France?" in *Leon Trotsky on France* (New York: Monad Press, 1979), 45. The original quote (without the ellipsis points) is "do not balk," which must be a mistake either by Trotsky or his translator, since balk means to stop short. If the working class balks (i.e., stops short) then the ruling class is not obliged to stop them.
46. See, for example, Marx, "*The Eighteenth Brumaire*," in *MECW*, vol. 11, 161.
47. Karl Marx and Frederick Engels, "Circular Letter to Bebel, Liebknecht, Bracke and Others," in *MECW*, vol. 24, 266.
48. Karl Marx, "Address to the Central Committee of the Communist League," in *On Revolution*, ed. Saul K. Padover (New York: McGraw-Hill, 1971), 117.
49. Ibid., 269.
50. Rosa Luxemburg, "Opportunism and the Art of the Possible," *Sachsische Arbeiter Zeitung*, September 30, 1898. Available at the Rosa Luxemburg Internet archive, http://www.marxists.org/archive/luxemburg/1898/09/30.htm (accessed August 7, 2006).
51. It was a phrase coined by Wilhelm Leibknecht in 1871, quoted in Gary P. Steensen, *Not One Man! Not One Penny! German Social Democracy, 1863–1914* (Pittsburgh: University of Pittsburgh Press, 1981), xi.
52. Quoted in Rosa Luxemburg, "Rebuilding the International," *Die Internationale*, no. 1, 1915. Available at the Rosa Luxemburg Internet archive, http://www.marxists.org/archive/luxemburg/1915/rebuild-int.htm (accessed August 7, 2006).
53. Ibid.
54. See, for example, Daniel Singer, *Is Socialism Doomed? The Meaning of Mitterand* (New York: Oxford University Press, 1988), and Daniel Singer, *Whose Millenium? Theirs or Ours?* (New York: Monthly Review Press, 1999), 129–49.
55. Daniel Singer, *Is Socialism Doomed?*, 265.
56. Ibid., 267.
57. Ibid., 267.
58. The term "third way" was popularized by Bill Clinton and Tony Blair in the 1990s. Its theorist is Anthony Giddens. See his book, *The Third Way: The Renewal of Social Democracy* (London: Polity Press, 2000).
59. Luxemburg, *Reform or Revolution*, 77–78.
60. Marx and Engels, *The German Ideology*, 52–53.
61. Trotsky, *History of the Russian Revolution*, xvii.
62. V. I. Lenin, "The Collapse of the Second International," in *CW*, vol. 21 (Moscow: Progress Publishers, 1980), 213–14.
63. Trotsky, *1905*, 102.
64. Trotsky, *History of the Russian Revolution*, 105.
65. From Foner, *The Great Labor Uprising of 1877*, 72.
66. Tony Cliff, *Portugal at the Crossroads*, in *Selected Writings*, vol. 1, 238.
67. Leon Trotsky, *The Intelligentsia and Socialism* (London: New Park, 1974), 10–11.
68. Ibid., 8.
69. Marx and Engels, *Communist Manifesto*, 78.
70. Draper, *Karl Marx's Theory of Revolution*, vol. 2, 297.
71. Tom Lewis, "Throwing Out a President," *International Socialist Review* 32 (November–December 2003).
72. Quoted in Alex Callinicos, *South Africa Between Reform and Revolution* (London: Bookmarks, 1988), 64–65.
73. Quoted in Ashwin Desai, "Mandela's Legacy," *International Socialist Review* 35 (May-June 2004).
74. V. I. Lenin, *Two Tactics of Social Democracy in the Democratic Revolution*, in *CW*, vol. 9

(Moscow: Progress Publishers, 1972), 19.
75. Sam Webb, "Keynote to the 28th National Convention of the Communist Party, USA," address, July 3, 2005, available at http://www.cpusa.org/article/articleprint/649/ (accessed August 7, 2006).
76. Quoted in Julius Jacobson, "The Soviet Union Is Dead: The 'Russian Question' Remains, Part I," *New Politics* 5, no. 2 (Winter 1995).
77. Quoted in S. Smith, *Subterranean Fire*, 160.
78. Marx and Engels, "Address of the Central Authority to the League," 280.
79. Ibid., 281.

Chapter Seven: The Need for Socialist Organization

1. Duncan Hallas, "Toward a Revolutionary Socialist Party," in *Party and Class* (Chicago: Haymarket Books, 2003), 52.
2. Marx and Engels, *Communist Manifesto,* 58–59.
3. Karl Schorske, *German Social Democracy, 1905–1917: The Development of the Great Schism* (Boston: Harvard University Press, 1983), 7.
4. R. N. Carew Hunt, *The Theory and Practice of Communism* (Baltimore, MD: Penguin Books, 1966), 187.
5. David Shub, *Lenin* (London: Penguin Books, 1967), 9.
6. Ibid.
7. V. I. Lenin, "The Social Democrats and the Elections in St. Petersburg," in *CW,* vol. 11 (Moscow: Progress Publishers, 1972), 434.
8. Ibid., 434–35.
9. V. I. Lenin, *One Step Forward, Two Steps Back,* in *CW*, vol. 7 (Moscow: Progress Publishers, 1977), 258–59.
10. Marx and Engels, *Communist Manifesto,* 87.
11. Hallas, "Toward a Revolutionary Socialist Party," 38.
12. Colin Barker, "Solidarnosc: From Gdansk to Military Repression," *International Socialism* 15 (Winter 1982), 93.
13. Colin Barker, *Festival of the Oppressed: Solidarity, Reform and Revolution in Poland 1980–81* (London: Bookmarks, 1986), 150.
14. Quoted in Mike Gonzalez, "The Coup and the Left in Chile," *International Socialism* 22 (Winter 1984), 66.
15. Trotsky, *History of the Russian Revolution,*

Chapter Eight: Russia: The God That Failed?

1. Eugene Debs, "The Day of the People," *Eugene V. Debs Speaks,* 293.
2. Ibid.
3. For an excellent account of the party's growth, its debates, and its overall conduct in the months before October, read Alexander Rabinowitch, *The Bolsheviks Come to Power* (Chicago: Haymarket Books, 2004).
4. Morgan Phillips Price, *Dispatches from the Revolution: Russia 1916–1918* (Durham, NC: Duke University Press, 1998), 81.
5. Russia was still using the Julian calendar.
6. Trotsky, *History of the Russian Revolution*, 378.
7. Ibid., 468.
8. The irony is that the French Revolution was actually led by the radical petty bour-

geoisie, pushed on from below by the sansculottes, even though the bourgeoisie was the main beneficiary of the revolution. Neil Davidson's recent articles in *Historical Materialism* are good on this question: "How Revolutionary Were the Bourgeois Revolutions?" *Historical Materialism* 13, numbers 3 and 4 (2005). In fact there may never have been a bourgeois revolution actually led by the bourgeoisie.

9. V. I. Lenin, "The Democratic Tasks of the Revolutionary Proletariat," in *CW*, vol. 8 (Progress Publishers, 1962), 511–12.
10. Quoted in Marcel Leibman, *The Russian Revolution* (New York: Random House, 1970), 112.
11. See Leon Trotsky, "Results and Prospects," in *The Permanent Revolution and Results and Prospects* (New York: Pathfinder Press, 1969).
12. Trotsky, *History of the Russian Revolution,* 59.
13. Ibid., 57.
14. See Trotsky, "Dual Power" chapter in *History of the Russian Revolution,* 206–15.
15. Trotsky, *History of the Russian Revolution,* 159.
16. Ibid., 167.
17. Ibid., 173.
18. V. I. Lenin, "The Tasks of the Proletariat in the Present Revolution," in *CW*, vol. 24 (Moscow: Progress Publishers, 1980), 22.
19. V. I. Lenin, "Letters from Afar," in *CW,* vol. 23, 304–05.
20. John Reed, *Ten Days that Shook the World* (New York: International Publishers, 1982), 292.
21. Lenin quoted in Tony Cliff, *State Capitalism in Russia* (London: Pluto Press, 1974), 144–45. The quote was stricken, according to Cliff, from the fourth edition of Volume 25 of Lenin's *Collected Works.*
22. Leon Trotsky, "Three Concepts of the Russian Revolution," appendix, *Stalin* (New York: Harper and Brothers Publishing, 1941), 432. I used this version of the quote because I think it reads better than the Pathfinder translation of Trotsky's 1906 work, *Results and Prospects,* from which it comes,
23. Tony Cliff, *State Capitalism in Russia*, 148.
24. Marx and Engels, *The German Ideology*, 49.
25. Frederick Engels, *The Peasant War in Germany*, in *MECW*, vol. 10, 469–70.
26. See Pierre Broué's masterful history, *The German Revolution* (Chicago: Haymarket Books, 2006).
27. Victor Serge, *Year One of the Russian Revolution* (New York: Holt, Rinehart and Winston, 1972), 79, 89.
28. E. H. Carr, *The Bolshevik Revolution: 1917–1923*, vol. 2 (London: Pelican Books, 1972), 197–98.
29. Hallas, "Toward a Revolutionary Socialist Party," 43.
30. V. I. Lenin, "Political Report to the Central Committee of the RCP(B)," in *CW*, vol. 33 (Moscow: Progress Publishers, 1980), 288.
31. Leon Trotsky, *The Revolution Betrayed* (New York: Pathfinder Press, 2002), 86.
32. Hallas, "Toward a Revolutionary Socialist Party."
33. Quoted in Alex Nove, *An Economic History of the USSR* (London: Pelican Books, 1982), 189.
34. Rosa Luxemburg, "The Russian Revolution," in *Rosa Luxemburg Speaks*, 394–95.
35. Frederick Engels, *Socialism: Utopian and Scientific,* in *MECW*, vol. 24, 318n.
36. Ibid., 319.
37. Leon Trotsky, "Trade Unions in the Epoch of Imperialist Decay," in *Marxism and the Trade Unions* (New York: Labor Publications, 1973), 17.

38. Quoted in Barker, *Festival of the Oppressed*, 93.
39. Engels, *Socialism: Utopian and Scientific*, in *MECW*, vol. 24, 319.
40. For an analysis of the Cuban Revolution and its aftermath, see Sam Farber, *The Origins of the Cuban Revolution Reconsidered* (Chapel Hill, NC: University of North Carolina Press, 2006).
41. Quoted in Carmelo Mesa-Lago, *Cuba in the 1970s: Pragmatism and Institutionalization* (Albuquerque: University of Arizona Press, 1974), 80.
42. Ibid., 81.
43. Engels, *Socialism: Utopian and Scientific*, in MECW, vol. 24, 325.

Chapter Nine: Imperialism, Nationalism, and War

1. Eric Hobsbawn, "War and Peace in the 20th Century," *London Review of Books* 24, no. 4 (February 2002), available at http://www.lrb.co.uk/v24/n04/hobs01_.html (accessed August 7, 2006).
2. R. Brian Ferguson, "The Birth of War," *Natural History* (July/August 2003).
3. Robert H. Lowie, *Indians of the Plains* (Garden City, NY: The Natural History Press, 1963), 117–18.
4. Quoted in Francis Jennings, *The Invasion of America: Indians, Colonialism and the Cant of Conquest* (New York: Norton, 1976), 150.
5. Quoted in ibid.
6. Ashley Montagu, *Man in Process* (Cleveland, OH: World Publishing Company, 1961), 92.
7. Marx, *Capital*, vol. 1, 915–16.
8. Lance Selfa, "A New Colonial 'Age of Empire'?" *International Socialist Review* 23 (May–June 2002).
9. Stefan Kanfer, *The Last Empire: De Beers, Diamonds, and the World* (New York: Noonday Press, 1993), 116–25.
10. Ibid., 124.
11. Adam Hochschild, *King Leopold's Ghost* (New York, Houghton Mifflin, 1998), 66.
12. Ibid., 160.
13. Mike Davis, *Late Victorian Holocausts* (New York: Verso, 2001), 32.
14. Ibid., 311.
15. Sidney Lens, *The Forging of the American Empire* (Chicago: Haymarket Books, 2004), 2.
16. William McKinley, "Remarks to Methodist Delegation," in *The Philippines Reader*, ed. Daniel B. Schirmer and Stephen R. Shalom (Boston: South End Press, 1987), 22.
17. Luzviminda Francisco, "The Philippine-American War," in *The Phillipines Reader*, ed. Daniel B. Schirmer and Stephen R. Shalom, 17.
18. Ibid., 18–19.
19. Quoted in Helen Scott, "The Mark Twain They Didn't Teach Us in School," *International Socialist Review* 10 (Winter 2000).
20. Scott Nearing and Joseph Freeman, *Dollar Diplomacy* (New York: Modern Reader, 1969), 133, 151; Hans Schmidt, *The United States Occupation of Haiti, 1915–1934* (New Brunswick, NJ: Rutgers University Press, 1995).
21. Quoted in Lens, *Forging of the American Empire*, 195.
22. V. I. Lenin, *Imperialism: The Highest Stage of Capitalism*, in *CW*, vol. 22, 298, 300.
23. See Massimo Salvadori, *Karl Kautsky and the Socialist Revolution, 1880–1938* (London: New Left Books, 1980), 181–203. Kautsky's 1914 article, "Ultra-Imperialism," can be found online at the Marxist Internet Archive, at http://www.marxists.org/archive/kaut-

sky/1914/09/ultra-imp.htm (accessed August 7, 2006).

24. V. I. Lenin, "Critical Remarks on the National Question," *Questions of National Policy and Proletarian Internationalism* (Moscow: Progress Publishers, 1970), 20.
25. Nikolai Bukharin, *Imperialism and World Economy* (New York: Monthly Review Press, 1973), 106–7.
26. Leon Trotsky, *The Bolsheviki and World Peace* (New York: Boni & Liveright, Inc., 1918), 20–22.
27. Ibid.
28. For a rundown of U.S. Cold War interventions, see William Blum, *Rogue State: A Guide to the World's Only Superpower* (Monroe, ME: Common Courage Press, 2000); and William Blum, *The CIA: A Forgotten History* (London: Zed Books, 1986).
29. Peter Starck, "World Military Spending Topped $1 Trillion in 2004," Reuters, June 7, 2005.
30. Chalmers Johnson, *The Sorrows of Empire: Militarism, Secrecy, and the End of the Republic* (New York: Metropolitan Books, 2004), 4.
31. Condoleezza Rice, address at the Paul H. Nitze School of Advanced International Studies, Johns Hopkins University, Washington, D.C., April 29, 2002.
32. "The President's Real Goal in Iraq," *Atlanta Journal-Constitution,* September 29, 2002.
33. George W. Bush, "President Outlines Priorities," press conference, November 7, 2002. Available at http://www.whitehouse.gov/news/releases/2002/11/20021107-2.html (accessed August 7, 2006).
34. William Christie MacLeod, *The American Indian Frontier* (New York: Alfred A. Knopf, 1928), 76.
35. Quoted in "This Isn't Liberation, This Is Conquest," *Socialist Worker* editorial, April 18, 2003.
36. See Lance Selfa, "Eight Years of Clinton-Gore: The Price of Lesser-Evilism," *International Socialist Review* 13 (August–September 2000); Sami Farsoun, "Roots of the American Anti-terrorism crusade," in *Civil Rights in Peril: The Targeting of Arabs and Muslims,* ed. Elaine C. Hagopian (Chicago and London: Haymarket Books/Pluto Press, 2004), 133–146.
37. Johnson, *Sorrows of Empire,* 151–52.
38. Quoted in ibid., 67.
39. Benedict Anderson, "Indonesian Nationalism Today and In the Future," *New Left Review* 235 (May/June 1999).
40. V. I. Lenin, "Who Stands to Gain?" in *CW*, vol. 19, 53.
41. Eugene Debs, "The Canton Speech," in *Eugene V. Debs Speaks*, 260.
42. Lee Sustar, "Globalization: Myths and Realities," *International Socialist Review* 12 (June–July 2000).
43. Ibid.
44. William I. Robinson, *A Theory of Global Capitalism: Production, Class, and State in a Transnational World* (Baltimore, MD: The Johns Hopkins University Press, 2004), 16.
45. Ibid., 25, 28.
46. United Nations Conference on Trade and Development, "World Investment Report," 2000, available at http://www.unctad.org/wir (accessed August 7, 2006).
47. Robinson, *A Theory of Global Capitalism,* 28.
48. Michael Hardt and Antonio Negri, *Empire* (Boston: Harvard University Press, 2000), xiii–xiv.
49. Quoted in J. Patrice McSherry, "Preserving Hegemony: National Security Doctrine in the Post-Cold War Era," *NACLA Report on the Americas* 24, no. 3 (November/December 2000), 10.
50. Philip Mattera and Anna Purinton, "Shopping for Subsidies: How Wal-Mart Uses Tax-

payer Money to Finance Its Never-Ending Growth," Good Jobs First report, May 2004, available at http://www.goodjobsfirst.org/pdf/wmtstudy.pdf (accessed August 7, 2006).
51. Charles M. Sennott, "The $150 Billion 'Welfare' Recipients: U.S. Corporations," *Boston Globe*, July 7, 1996.
52. Kevin Danaher and Jason Mark, *Insurrection: Citizen Challenge to Corporate Power* (New York: Routledge, 2003), 7.
53. See Keith Rosenthal, "What do Socialists Say About World Hunger?" *International Socialist Review* 45, (January–February 2006).
54. Ibid.
55. Michael Skapinker, "Worlds Apart: Despite a Wave of Mergers and Acquisitions, the Long-Predicted Global Corporation Remains a Distant Ideal," *Financial Times*, March 1, 2001.
56. Thomas Friedman, "What the World Needs Now," *New York Times*, March 28, 1999.
57. Bukharin, *Imperialism and World Economy*, 61–62.
58. John Keegan, *A History of Warfare* (New York: Vintage, 1993), 391.
59. Carl von Clausewitz, *On War* (London: Penguin, 1986), 119.
60. Quoted in Phyllis Bennis, *Calling the Shots: How Washington Dominates Today's UN*, dated ed. (New York: Olive Branch Press, 2000), xxiii.
61. Leon Trotsky, *Terrorism and Communism* (Ann Arbor, MI: Anne Arbor Paperbacks, 1972), 63.
62. See Stanley Weintraub, *Silent Night: The Story of the World War I Christmas Truce* (New York: Plume Books, 2001).
63. Quoted in Ahmed Shawki, "80 Years Since the Russian Revolution," *International Socialist Review* 3 (Winter 1997).
64. Victor Serge, *Year One of the Russian Revolution*, 325.
65. Engels, "Principles of Communism," in *Communist Manifesto*, 141.

Chapter Ten: Marxism and Oppression

1. See, for example, George W. Bush, "President Addresses the Nation," Washington, D.C., September 7, 2003, available at https://www.whitehouse.gov/news/releases/2003/09/20030907-1.html (accessed August 7, 2006).
2. Quoted in Robert Middlekauff, *The Glorious Cause: The American Revolution, 1763–1789* (New York: Oxford University Press, 1982), 372.
3. Ibid., 372.
4. Quoted in V. I. Lenin, "The National Program of the RSDLP," in *Questions of National Policy and Proletarian Internationalism* (Moscow: Progress Publishers, 1970), 10.
5. Karl Marx, "The General Council to the Federal Council of Romance Switzerland," in *MECW*, vol. 21, 89.
6. Marx, *Capital*, vol. 1, 414.
7. V. I. Lenin, *The Right of Nations to Self-Determination*, in *CW*, vol. 20, 410.
8. Woodrow Wilson, "Speech on the Fourteen Points," *Congressional Record*, 65th Cong., 2nd sess., 1918, 680,681. Available at http://www.fordham.edu/halsall/mod/1918wilson.html (accessed August 7, 2006).
9. In pre-revolutionary Russia, women did not have the right to divorce their husbands. This was granted during the Russian Revolution, on the understanding that it was key to women achieving equality with men.
10. Lenin, *The Right of Nations to Self Determination*, 410.
11. Jane Degras, ed., *The Communist International, 1919–1943, Documents*, vol. 1 (Lon-

don: F. Cass, 1971), 143–44.
12. Bronislav Malinowski, *The Sexual Life of Savages* (New York: Harvest Books, 1929), 3.
13. Ibid., 53.
14. Ibid., 59.
15. Engels, *Origins of the Family*, 165.
16. Ibid.
17. Sharon Smith, *Women and Socialism: Essays on Women's Liberation* (Chicago: Haymarket Books, 2005), 85–86.
18. Ibid., 55.
19. Arlene Skolnick, *Embattled Paradise: The American Family in an Age of Uncertainty* (New York: Basic Books, 1991), 10.
20. Ibid, 9.
21. S. Smith, *Women and Socialism*, 56.
22. Alix Holt, ed. and trans., *Selected Writings of Alexandra Kollontai*, (London: Alison and Busby, 1977), 59.
23. August Bebel, *Women Under Socialism* (New York: Schocken Books, 1971), 5.
24. V. I. Lenin, "A Great Beginning," in *Not By Politics Alone: The Other Lenin*, ed. Tamara Deutscher (Westport, CT: Lawrence Hill & Co., 1983), 215.
25. Leon Trotsky, *The Revolution Betrayed* (New York: Pathfinder Press, 1972), 145.
26. Richard J. Herrnstein and Charles Murray, *The Bell Curve: Intelligence and Class Structure in American Life* (New York: Free Press, 1996).
27. Dobzhansky, *Mankind Evolving*, 21.
28. Ashley Montagu, *Race & IQ* (New York: Galaxy Books, 1975), 3.
29. Eric Williams, *Capitalism and Slavery* (New York: Perigee Books, 1980), 7.
30. Quoted in Ahmed Shawki, *Black Liberation and Socialism* (Chicago: Haymarket Books, 2006), 34.
31. Lance Selfa, "Slavery and the Origins of Racism," *International Socialist Review* 26 (November–December 2002).
32. Karl Marx, "Confidential Communication," in *MECW*, vol. 25, 120.
33. Quoted in Shawki, *Black Liberation and Socialism*, 66.
34. Quoted in ibid., 72.
35. Ibid., 74.
36. Ibid., 75.
37. Jack Bloom, *Class, Race & the Civil Rights Movement* (Bloomington, IN: Indiana University Press, 1987), 49.
38. Quoted in Shawki, *Black Liberation and Socialism*, 81.
39. Quoted in Jacqueline Jones, *American Work: Four Centuries of Black and White Labor* (New York: W. W. Norton & Company, 1998), 311.
40. Philip S. Foner, *Organized Labor and the Black Worker* (New York: Progress Publishers, 1981), 116, 117.
41. Ibid., 227.
42. Shawki, *Black Liberation and Socialism*, 247–48.
43. Selfa, "Slavery and the Origins of Racism."
44. Engels, *Anti-Duhring*, MECW 25, 87.
45. Michael Albert, "Marxism: Virtues and Problems," *Z* magazine, available at http://www.zmag.org/marxismdebate.htm (accessed August 7, 2006).
46. Quoted in V. I. Lenin, "The Question of Peace," in *CW*, vol. 21, 293.
47. Bebel, *Women Under Socialism*, 6.
48. V. I. Lenin, *What Is to Be Done?* (New York: Progress Publishers, 1992), 69.

49. Lenin, "Two Tactics of Social Democracy in the Democratic Revolution," 113.
50. James Connolly, *The Reconquest of Ireland* (Dublin: New Books, 1972), Chapter 6, available at http://www.marxists.org/archive/connolly/1915/rcoi/index.htm

Chapter Eleven: Capitalism and the Environment

1. Thomas Robert Malthus, *An Essay on the Principle of Population* (New York: W. W. Norton & Company, 1976), 20.
2. Frederick Engels, *Outlines of a Critique of Political Economy*, in *MECW*, vol. 3 (New York: International Publishers, 1975), 437.
3. Paul R. Erlich and Anne H. Erlich, *The Population Explosion* (London: Hutchinson, 1990), 9.
4. Ibid., 224.
5. Ibid., 226–28.
6. Garrett Hardin, *Living Within Limits: Ecology, Economics and Population Taboos* (New York: Oxford University Press, 1993), 294.
7. Garrett Hardin, "The Tragedy of the Commons," in *Valuing the Earth: Economics, Ecology, Ethics,* ed. Herman E. Daly and Kenneth N. Townsend (Cambridge, MA: MIT Press, 1994), 135.
8. See Lester Brown, *Building a Sustainable Society* (Washington, D.C.: Worldwatch Institute, 1981).
9. UN Food and Agricultural Organization, Thirty-third Session, "Review of the State of Food and Agriculture," (Rome, November 19–26, 2005). Text available at http://www.fao.org/docrep/meeting/010/j6091e/j6091e.htm (accessed August 7, 2006).
10. Lappé, "The Myth—Scarcity: The Reality—There IS Enough Food."
11. See ibid.; and figures from Jean Ziegler, the UN's Special Rapporteur on the Right to Food, cited in Eulàlia Iglesias, "UN Food Expert Condemns U.S. Tactics in Iraq," *Inter-Press Service,* November 12, 2005.
12. Engels, *Outlines of a Critique of Political Economy*, in *MECW*, vol. 3, 438.
13. Ibid.
14. "World Population Growth Slows Down," *The Age,* March 24, 2004.
15. "Incredible Shrinking Countries," *Economist,* January 5, 2006.
16. "AIDS, Few Births Slowing Population Growth," Associated Press, March 23, 2004.
17. Ibid., 438.
18. Frederick Engels, *The Part Played By Labor in the Transition from Ape to Man*, in *MECW*, vol. 25, 461.
19. Ibid., 460–461.
20. Ibid., 463.
21. Ibid., 461.
22. Ibid., 462.
23. Engels, *Outlines of a Critique of Political Economy*, 439.
24. "Scorched Earth: Global Climate Change Impacts on Public Lands and Waters" Bluewater Network special report, June 2002, available at http://www.bluewaternetwork.org/reports/rep_ca_global_scorched.pdf (accessed August 7, 2006).
25. World Wildlife Fund, "Why is the West Burning?" *Common Dreams* Progressive Newswire, June 26, 2002, available at http://www.commondreams.org/news2002/0626-08.htm (accessed August 7, 2006).
26. Jack Weatherford, *Native Roots: How the Indians Enriched America* (New York: Crown Publishers, 1991), 45.

27. World Wildlife Fund, "Why is the West Burning?"
28. *United Nations Human Development Report 2005*: *International Cooperation at the Crossroads*, 4. Available at http://hdr.undp.org/reports/global/2005/ (accessed August 7, 2006).
29. U.S. Bureau of the Census, "Poverty" report, 2004, available at http://www.census.gov/hhes/www/poverty/overview.html (accessed August 7, 2006).
30. The Census Bureau's poverty threshold for a family of four is a pitiful $18,850 per year, an amount that two people would have difficulty living on.
31. William Morris, "How We Live and How We Might Live," lecture delivered to the Hammersmith Branch of the Socialist Democratic Federation, Hammersmith, UK, November 30, 1884, available at http://www.marxists.org/archive/morris/works/1884/hwl/hwl.htm.

Chapter Twelve: But What about...? Arguments against Socialism

1. David U. Himmelstein et al., "The Cost to the Nation, the States and the District of Columbia, with State-Specific Estimates of Potential Savings," *Public Citizen*, available at http://www.citizen.org/publications/release.cfm?ID=7271 (accessed August 7, 2006).
2. Victoria Colliver, "Excessive Medical Expenses: Study Finds That Half of Health Care Dollars are Wasted," *San Francisco Chronicle*, February 7, 2005.
3. Fourier quoted in Engels, *Anti-Duhring*, 317.
4. James P. Cannon, "What Will Socialism in American Look Like?" in *Speeches for Socialism* (New York: Pathfinder Press, 1971), 405–06.
5. Ibid., 406.
6. Marx and Engels, *Communist Manifesto,* 63.
7. Quoted in Jamie Court and Francis Smith, *Making a Killling: HMOs and the Threat to Your Health* (Monroe, ME: Common Courage Press, 1999), chapter 3, available at http://www.makingakilling.org/chapter3.html (accessed August 7, 2006).
8. Madeline Albright, interview by Leslie Stahl, *60 Minutes,* CBS, May 12, 1996.
9. Leon Trotsky, *Their Morals and Ours* (New York: Pathfinder Press, 1992), 20–21.
10. Ibid., 14.
11. Clayborne Carson, *In Struggle: SNCC and the Black Awakening of the 1960s* (Cambridge, MA: Harvard University Press, 1981), 164.
12. Charles R. Sims, Deacons of Defense leader from Bogalusa, Louisiana, in Howell Raines, *My Soul Is Rested: The Story of the Civil Rights Movement in the Deep South* (London: Penguin Books, 1987), 416–23.
13. Trotsky, *Their Morals and Ours*, 48.
14. Ibid., 49.
15. James W. Loewen, *Lies My Teacher Told Me: Everything Your American History Textbook Got Wrong* (New York: The New Press, 1995), 196.
16. Frederick R. Strobel and Wallace C. Peterson, *The Coming Class War and How to Avoid It: Rebuilding the American Middle Class* (Armonk, NY: M. E. Sharpe, 1999), xii.
17. Zweig, *Working Class Majority,* 19.
18. Barbara Ehrenriech's 1979 study put the figure higher, but she included teachers and social workers in her estimation of the size of what she calls the "professional managerial class." But teachers and social workers are part of the working class by any reasonable assessment. See Pat Walker, ed., *Between Labor and Capital* (Boston: South End Press, 1979).
19. André Gorz, *Farewell to the Working Class: An Essay on Post-Industrial Socialism* (Boston: South End Press,1980), 28.
20. Barry Bluestone, "Economic Inequality and the Macrostructuralist Debate," in *Political*

Economy for the 21st Century: Contemporary Views on the Trend of Economics, ed. Charles J. Whalen (Armonk, NY: M. E. Sharpe, 1995), 177.

21. Cited in Barry Bluestone and Bennett Harrison, *The Great U-Turn: Corporate Restructuring and the Polarizing of America* (New York: Basic Books, 1988), 37.
22. "Total Employment by Economic Activity, Republic of South Korea," International Labor Organization Web site, http://laborsta.ilo.org (accessed August 7, 2006).
23. Ahmed Shawki, "Between Things Ended and Things Begun," *International Socialist Review* 18 (June–July 2001).
24. "The Productivity Surge," *Washington Times*, November 3, 2002.
25. Zweig, *Working Class Majority*, 29.
26. George W. Bush, interview by *NBC Nightly News*, NBC, December 12, 2005.
27. Elisabeth Bumiller and Larry Rohter, "Bush's Vision for Latin America: He Calls for Strong Democracies in Response to Leftists," *San Francisco Chronicle*, November 7, 2005.
28. Paul Foot, *Why You Should Be a Socialist* (London: Socialist Workers Party, 1977), chapter 3. The text is available at http://www.marxists.org/archive/foot-paul/1977/wysbas/index.htm (accessed August 7, 2006).
29. Frederick Engels, "Social Classes: Necessary and Superfluous," in *MECW*, vol. 24, 417.
30. Ibid., 416.
31. Clifford D. Conner, *A People's History of Science* (New York: Nation Books, 2005), 2.
32. Paul Foot, *Why You Should Be a Socialist*, chapter 3.
33. Quoted in Robert C. Tucker, *Stalin in Power: The Revolution from Above, 1929–1941* (New York: Norton, 1990), 282.
34. Quoted in Ygael Gluckstein, *Mao's China* (Boston: Beacon Press, 1957), 379.
35. John Keats, *The Crack in the Picture Window* (New York: Houghton Mifflin, 1957), xi.
36. Leon Trotsky, *The Revolution Betrayed*, 180.

Chapter Thirteen: Can It Happen Here?

1. "Class Matters" series, *New York Times*, April–May 2005, available at http://www.nytimes.com/pages/national/class/index.html (accessed August 7, 2006).
2. Frederick Engels, "Appendix to the American edition of *The Condition of the Working Class in England*," in *MECW*, vol. 26, 403.
3. U.S. Small Business Administration, "Employer Firms, Establishments, Employment, and Annual Payroll Small Firm Size Classes, 2003" table, available at http://www.sba.gov/advo/research/us_03ss.pdf (accessed August 7, 2006).
4. U.S. Small Business Administration, "Frequently Asked Questions," available at http://app1.sba.gov/faqs/faqindex.cfm?areaID=24 (accessed August 7, 2006). These statistics are misleading because they consider a small business any firm that employs fewer than five hundred workers. The businesses that have the most difficulty surviving, however, are the small "mom and pop" stores, and businesses run by individuals out of their homes.
5. Quoted in Janny Scott and Danny Leonhardt, "Shadowy Lines That Still Divide" in the "Class Matters" series, *New York Times*, May 15, 2005.
6. S. Smith, *Subterreanean Fire*, 300.
7. Lee Sustar, "Autopsy of the American Dream," *Socialist Worker*, September 17, 2004.
8. Frederick Engels to Herman Schluter, in *Marx and Engels on the United States*, 328.
9. Ibid., 328.
10. Foner, *Organized Labor and the Black Worker*, 82–84.
11. William Haywood, *The Autobiography of Big Bill Haywood* (New York: International Publishers, 1929), 252.

12. Philip S. Foner, *History of the Labor Movement in the United States*, vol. 4 (New York: International Publishers, 1997), 318.
13. Leon Trotsky, "American Problems," *Writings of Leon Trotsky, 1939–1940* (New York: Pathfinder Press, 1973), 335.
14. Quoted in Dick Cluster, *They Should Have Served That Cup of Coffee* (Boston: South End Press, 1979), 44.
15. Quoted in Philip S. Foner, *History of the Labor Movement in the United States*, vol. 3 (New York: International Publishers, 1981), 254.
16. Facts and quotes in this section, unless otherwise cited, come from Sharon Smith, "Depression Decade: The Turning Point," in *Subterranean Fire*, 102–52.
17. Paul D'Amato, "The Communist Party and Black Liberation in the 1930s," *International Socialist Review* 1, Summer 1997.
18. Bert Cochran, *Labor and Communism: The Conflict That Shaped American Unions* (Princeton: Princeton University Press, 1977), 138.
19. See S. Smith, *Subterranean Fire*, 219–223.
20. Shawki, "Between Things Ended and Things Begun."
21. Ibid.
22. Ibid.
23. S. Smith, *Subterranean Fire*, 298.
24. "Income Gap Widens," Associated Press, August 26, 2004.
25. Shawki, "Between Things Ended and Things Begun."
26. Ibid.

Chapter Fourteen: Imagine... The Future Socialist Society

1. Debs, "Unionism and Socialism," 154–55.
2. Karl Marx, "Critique of the Goth Program," in *MECW*, vol. 24, 85–86.
3. Ibid., 95.
4. Engels, "Socialism: Utopian and Scientific," in *MECW*, vol. 24, 325.
5. Marx and Engels, *Communist Manifesto*, 69–70.
6. Marx, "Critique of the Goth Program," 87.

Conclusion: The Point Is to Change It

1. *UN Human Development Report 1994: New Dimensions of Human Security*, 50. Available at http://hdr.undp.org/reports/global/1994/en/ (accessed August 7, 2006).
2. *UN Human Development Report 1999: Globalization with a Human Face*, 29. Available at http://hdr.undp.org/reports/global/1999/en/ (accessed August 7, 2006).
3. Marx and Engels, *Communist Manifesto*, 56–57.
4. Debs, *Eugene V. Debs Speaks*, 47.
5. Larry Bradshaw and Lorrie Beth Slonsky, "The Real Heroes and Sheroes of New Orleans," *Socialist Worker*, September 9, 2005.
6. Ibid.
7. Quoted in Abel Paz, *Durruti: The People Armed* (New York: Black Rose Books, 1977), 229.

Index